TWAYNE'S WORLD AUTHORS SERIES

A Survey of the World's Literature

Sylvia E. Bowman, Indiana University

GENERAL EDITOR

SWEDEN

Leif Sjöberg, State University of New York, Stony Brook

EDITOR

Pär Lagerkvist

(TWAS 267)

TWAYNE'S WORLD AUTHORS SERIES (TWAS)

The purpose of TWAS is to survey the major writers
—novelists, dramatists, historians, poets, philosophers,
and critics—of the nations of the world. Among the
national literatures covered are those of Australia,
Canada, China, Eastern Europe, France, Germany,
Greece, India, Italy, Japan, Latin America, the Nether-
lands, New Zealand, Poland, Russia, Scandinavia, Spain,
and the African nations, as well as Hebrew, Yiddish,
and Latin Classical literatures. This survey is comple-
mented by Twayne's United States Authors Series and
English Authors Series.

The intent of each volume in these series is to present a
critical-analytical study of the works of the writer; to
include biographical and historical material that may be
necessary for understanding, appreciation, and critical
appraisal of the writer; and to present all material in
clear, concise English—but not to vitiate the scholarly
content of the work by doing so.

Pär Lagerkvist

By ROBERT DONALD SPECTOR

ABOUT THE AUTHOR

Professor of English and Comparative Literature and chairman of the department at Long Island University, Robert Donald Spector is the author of three books and editor of nine others. He has published more than 300 articles and reviews in scholarly and commercial journals. His work on Lagerkvist has appeared in *Scandinavian Studies,* the *American-Scandinavian Review, Modern Language Notes,* and *Western Humanities Review.* He has read papers on Lagerkvist's poetry and drama at conferences held in such universities as Columbia, Chicago, Kentucky, and Nebraska. For more than ten years he has served as a member of the Committee on Publications of the American-Scandinavian Foundation. In 1966 the Swedish government awarded him a travel grant to work on Lagerkvist in Stockholm and Växjö.

His study of the English novelist Tobias Smollett in the TEAS was described as "an excellent critical introduction" (*Studies in English Literature*) , "which should be on the reading list of all serious modern students" (*Johnsonian News Letter*). His analysis of *English Literary Periodicals* was acclaimed as "the most uniquely useful scholarly study of 1966" (*Studies in English Literature*).

ew York

Preface

Pär Lagerkvist, Swedish winner of the Nobel Prize for Literature, has had his work translated into at least 34 languages. Almost all of his important fiction, a majority of his plays, and a selection of his poetry are available in English. Until now, however, no full-length book written in English has attempted to give a general account of his achievement.

As even my Selected Bibliography indicates, however, Lagerkvist has not wanted for Scandinavian critics, who have indeed produced important volumes on his work. I have profited from them, but in presenting my book I have emphasized particularly the English criticism that has appeared in periodicals and pamphlets easily available to the majority of my readers. I have covered Lagerkvist's own work in the original as well as in translation, but again I have concentrated on what my audience will be able to read at first hand. In my choice of Swedish texts, too, I have selected those most accessible in this country, although at times that creates the oddity of my referring to Swedish editions published after the English translations had appeared.

As a volume in the Twayne World Authors Series, my study naturally is directed primarily at an English-language audience. I hope, however, that it offers new insights and observations even to those familiar with Lagerkvist's works in their originals. As a critic of his fiction, especially, I have sought to examine structure, point-of-view, and symbolism in ways that they have not been studied previously. My argument for a fundamental unity in Lagerkvist's prose, drama, and poetry is, I believe, the first time that idea has been fully developed.

The organization of my book reflects both my estimate of Lagerkvist's achievement as an artist and my own qualifications, as a non-Swedish critic, to deal with it in a volume of limited space. Unquestionably, Lagerkvist's fiction deserves primary consideration and emphasis, and that has determined both the order of my presentation and the extent of my discussions. In

the opening chapter, while offering some idea of his development as a writer of short fiction, I am more concerned with
describing Lagerkvist's literary techniques, his remarkable ability
to provide a sense of variety in his fictive world despite what
I regard as the binding unity in all his work. My study of
Lagerkvist's novels follows the chronology of their publication—
individual chapters devoted to *The Dwarf, Barabbas,* and *The
Sibyl,* one to the trilogy of "pilgrim novels" which Lagerkvist
himself joined together in a single volume following their original
publication, and one to *Herod and Mariamne.*

By placing discussion of Lagerkvist's poetry and drama at
the end of my study, I have suggested that they are less important
than his fiction—a judgment with which few critics would
quarrel. Yet that is not the sole reason it appears last. For
several reasons, poetry and drama will be less meaningful to
the general audience of this book. The poetry, in particular,
will be less accessible than the fiction to English-language
readers. Reading that poetry in translation is to lose the major
effect of Lagerkvist's particular contribution to Swedish verse,
and what remains, while essential to an understanding of his
attitudes and ideas, is something different from the true nature
of poetry. As an American critic who has written extensively
on English poetry, I am too aware of the subtleties of verse
to pretend to having the kind of linguistic knowledge crucial
to grasping the nuances of Swedish poetry.

Although Lagerkvist's drama in translation poses a less for-
midable barrier, a full appreciation of it requires a familiarity
with Swedish stage history, a subject that can be touched upon
only peripherally within the limits of this book. Moreover, to
do full justice to the drama, as to the poetry, would demand
more than a chapter for each, since Lagerkvist has published
fifteen plays and nine volumes of poems. What I have sought
to present in my criticism of Lagerkvist's drama and poetry is
a sense of the fundamental unity in his work, a unity that has
too often been overlooked by critics tracing his development
through the many periods of his long and gratifyingly produc-
tive life.

R.D.S.

Acknowledgments

My work on Lagerkvist would not have been possible without the help of many people and institutions. In particular, I am indebted to Professor Leif Sjöberg, who read, corrected, and improved my manuscript; Dr. Jöran Mjöberg, who kindly provided me with an unpublished translation of his earlier study of Lagerkvist; and Mr. Erik J. Friis, who prepared my text for the press. Professor George Schoolfield and Mr. Kai Henmark contributed information and encouragement. Ambassador Tore Tallroth and his government enabled me to visit Sweden and to meet the following persons who kindly shared their knowledge with me and made otherwise inaccessible material available to me: Dr. Erik Hörnström, Professor Gustaf Fredén, Dr. Alf Sjöberg, Dr. Olof Lagerkrantz, Mr. Claes Hoogland, Professor Gösta Bergman, Dr. Bengt Larsson, Dr. Lars Gustafsson, Mrs. Eva Skavén, and the late Erik Lindegren. To Mr. Jan Rudbeck and the Swedish Information Service, I owe innumerable favors, and to Long Island University I owe the precious gift of time to allow me to complete my work.

Although I have noted by an asterisk the most significant foreign works listed in my bibliography, I would like to express here my particular obligation to the books by Sven Linnér, Kai Henmark, Jöran Mjöberg, Otto Oberholzer, Erik Hjalmar Linder (bibliography by Eric and Ingrid Lilliehöök), Gunnel Malmström, and Gunnar Tideström.

I am grateful to the Society for the Advancement of Scandinavian Study for allowing me to reprint parts of my articles that have appeared in *Scandinavian Studies*. I thank The American-Scandinavian Foundation for permitting me to use material contributed by me to *Scandinavian Studies: Essays Presented to Dr. Henry Goddard Leach, Five Modern Scandinavian Plays*, and *The American-Scandinavian Review*.

Albert Bonniers Förlag has kindly granted me permission to quote from all of Lagerkvist's works. For translations I am indebted to The American-Scandinavian Foundation for "The

Grieving North" (tr. by C. W. Stork), "The Salvation Army" (tr. by M. S. Allwood and E. Wahlgren), "Thought Has Nowhere a Goal" (tr. by M. S. Allwood), "I Shall Die and You Will Live On" (tr. by T. Heywood), all in *The American-Scandinavian Review,* and *The Man Without a Soul* (tr. by Alrik Gustafson) in *Scandinavian Plays of the Twentieth Century. First Series,* and *Let Man Live* (tr. by H. Alexander and L. Jones) in *Scandinavian Plays of the Twentieth Century. Third Series.* I thank Chatto and Windus Ltd. and Random House, Inc. for allowing me to quote from translations by Naomi Walford of *The Sibyl, The Death of Ahasuerus, Pilgrim at Sea, The Holy Land, Herod and Mariamne,* and Alan Blair's translation of *Barabbas.* Chatto and Windus and Hill and Wang, a division of Farrar, Straus & Giroux, have granted permission to quote from translations of *The Dwarf* and *The Eternal Smile.* Quotations from Thomas Buckman's edition of *Modern Theatre: Seven Plays and an Essay* are with the permission of the University of Nebraska Press. *The Norseman* has allowed me to use quotations from translations of two poems and from "The Strange Country" by Alan Blair; *The Times Literary Supplement,* and Leif Sjöberg and W. H. Auden have granted permission to quote from two translations from *Aftonland.* For Frederic Fleisher's translations in *Seven Swedish Poets,* I am grateful to Bo Cavefors Förlag and for those in *Twentieth-Century Scandinavian Poetry* to Martin S. Allwood. *Western Humanities Review* has allowed me to quote from Grace Hunter's translation of "Fisherman's Burial" and Augustana Book Concern from Kenneth Laycock's translation of "Beauty Is Most at Twilight's Close" from *Modern Swedish Poems.*

Contents

Preface

Acknowledgments

Chronology

1. The Fabulist in Short Fiction   15

2. The First Novel: *Dvärgen*   45

3. *Barabbas*: The Bible as Modern Literature   64

4. *Sibyllan*: A Dialogue on God   82

5. Tobias's Pilgrimage: Lagerkvist's Trilogy   99

6. *Mariamne*: The Dialogue Continues   127

7. Poetic Landscape of the Soul   137

8. Dramatist of the New Wave   153

Notes and References   175

Selected Bibliography   187

Index   193

Chronology

1891   Born on May 23 in the cathedral town of Växjö in province of Småland. Youngest of seven children of Anders Johan Lagerkvist and Johanna (Blad) Lagerkvist. Father employed at railway station. Family lives in small apartment above the station's restaurant. Strictly orthodox paternal grandparents live on farm outside the city.

c. 1900   Registered in Växjö school once attended by Linnaeus.

1908-
1909   Despite a certain interest in the Salvation Army and membership in a conventionally patriotic literary group, joins small student group known for their "anarchistic" and "radical" views.

1909   Publishes imitations of Heidenstam and other Swedish poets in provincial newspapers.

1910   Graduates from Växjö *gymnasium*. Graduation essay on "The Swedish Hymn-Book." Passes matriculation examination. Leaves home and lives with brother Gunnar, a schoolteacher in western Sweden.

1910-
1911   Publishes poems in *Fram,* a monthly journal.

1911   Begins short stay—fall term—at Uppsala for humanistic studies.

1912   Writes idealistic and revolutionary poetry for *Stormklockan,* a socialist journal. Publishes *Människor (People),* a novella,

1913   Spends a few months in Paris and displays interest in fauvist, cubist, and naïvist art. Writes reviews of modern fiction—praises Dostoevsky. Publishes *Ordkonst och bildkonst (Word Art and Picture Art),* first critical work. Publishes *Två sagor om livet (Two Tales about Life).*

1914   Publishes *Motiv (Motifs).*

c. 1915   Settles in Copenhagen and begins serious study of drama. Publishes *Järn och människor (Iron and Men).*

1916   Publishes *Ångest (Anguish),* first volume of poems.

1917   Publishes *Sista mänskan (The Last Man),* first published drama, although an earlier play, *Livet (Life),* 1911, exists in manuscript. *The Last Man* is the only published Lagerkvist drama that has never been produced. Begins writing reviews of drama.

1918   Marries Karen Dagmar Johanne Sörensen, a Dane. Becomes drama critic for *Svenska Dagbladet*. Publishes the essay *Teater* (*Modern Theater*) and the drama *Den svåra stunden* (*The Difficult Hour*). Latter is produced in Düsseldorf.

1919   In June publishes last review in *Svenska Dagbladet*. Publishes *Kaos* (*Chaos*), a volume of poems that also includes the play *Himlens hemlighet* (*The Secret of Heaven*).

1920   Travels through the Mediterranean countries: Italy, France, North Africa. Publishes *Det eviga leendet* (*The Eternal Smile*) and "Morgonen" ("The Morning").

1921   In spring, *The Secret of Heaven,* the first Lagerkvist play produced in Sweden, appears at Collijn's Intima Theater in Stockholm. Publishes *Den lyckliges väg* (*The Way of the Happy One*).

1923   Publishes *Den Osynlige* (*The Invisible One*).

1924   *The Invisible One* is staged at the Royal Dramatic Theater in Stockholm, directed by Olof Molander. Publishes *Onda sagor* (*Evil Tales*).

1925   Divorces first wife and marries Elaine Luella Hallberg, widow of Swedish painter Gösta Sandels. Publishes first selection from his poetry and prose. Publishes *Gäst hos verkligheten* (*Guest of Reality*).

1926   Publishes *Hjärtats sånger* (*Songs of the Heart*).

1927   Publishes *Det besegrade livet* (*The Conquered Life*).

1928   Receives prestigious award from Samfundet De Nio. Publishes *Han som fick leva om sitt liv* (*The Man Who Lived His Life Over*), which Per Lindberg directs at the Royal Dramatic Theater.

1930   Settles in Lidingö, Stockholm suburb, but travels frequently to Europe and Near East. Publishes *Kämpande ande* (*The Struggling Spirit*).

1932   First collected edition of his work appears in three volumes. Publishes *Konungen* (*The King*), not produced until 1950. Publishes *Vid lägereld* (*Beside the Campfire*).

1933   Publishes novella *Bödeln* (*The Hangman*).

1933-   Journeys to Palestine and Greece.
1934

1934   Publishes *Den Knutna näven* (*The Clenched Fist*), essays based on his travels. Dramatized version of *The Hangman,* directed by Per Lindberg, enjoys great success at Den Nationale Scene in Bergen, Norway, and then at the Vasa Theater in Stockholm.

1935   Publishes *I den tiden* (*In That Time*).

1936   Publishes *Mannen utan själ* (*The Man Without a Soul*).

Chronology

1937   Publishes *Genius* (*Genius*).

1938   *The Man Without a Soul*, directed by Alf Sjöberg, appears at the Royal Dramatic Theater.

1939   Publishes *Den befriade människan* (*The Liberated Man*). Publishes *Seger i mörker* (*Victory in the Dark*).

1940   Alf Sjöberg directs *Victory in the Dark* at the Royal Dramatic Theater. Publishes *Sång och strid* (*Song and Battle*). On being elected one of the "Eighteen Immortals" of the Swedish Academy of Literature, gives an inaugural address on Verner von Heidenstam.

1941   Receives honorary doctorate from the University of Gothenburg. Publishes *Midsommardröm i fattighuset* (*Midsummer Dream in the Workhouse*), which Alf Sjöberg directs at the Royal Dramatic Theater.

1942   Publishes *Hemmet och stjärnan* (*Heaven and Stars*).

1944   Publishes *Dvärgen* (*The Dwarf*).

1945   Receives the Bellman Prize.

1946   Dramatic version of *The Hangman* first published in *Pär Lagerkvist, Dramatik*.

1947   Publishes *De vises sten* (tr. as *The Philosopher's Stone*).

1948   Directed by Alf Sjöberg at the Royal Dramatic Theater, *The Philosopher's Stone* becomes Lagerkvist's greatest success in the Swedish theater.

1949   Publishes *Låt människan leva* (*Let Man Live*), which Olof Widgren directs at the Royal Dramatic Theater.

1950   First production of *The King* at Malmö City Theater. Publishes *Barabbas*. "The Tunnel," the first part of *The Difficult Hour*, becomes the first of seven Lagerkvist plays to be broadcast by the Swedish radio.

1951   Receives the Nobel Prize for Literature.

1953   Publishes *Aftonland* (*The Evening Land*). Publishes dramatic version of *Barabbas*, which Olof Molander directs at the Royal Dramatic Theater.

1956   Publishes *Sibyllan* (*The Sibyl*).

1958   In letter to *Dagens Nyheter* denies authenticity of an interview with him reported in *Dansk Kirketidende*.

1960   Publishes *Ahasverus död* (*Death of Ahasuerus*).

1962   Publishes *Pilgrim på havet* (*Pilgrim at Sea*).

1964   Publishes *Det heliga landet* (*The Holy Land*).

1966   Publishes *Pilgrimen* (*Pilgrims*), a one-volume collection of the "Tobias novels," thus emphasizing their unity.

1967   Publishes *Mariamne* (*Herod and Mariamne*). Death of Elaine Lagerkvist, his second wife.

CHAPTER 1

The Fabulist in Short Fiction

I Background

U NABLE to accept the conservative values of the town in which he was born or the household in which he was raised, young Pär Lagerkvist openly rebelled against them. He joined the radical youths of the Växjö *gymnasium,* the "Socialists of the Sixth Form," who held anarchistic meetings when the "good people" of the town were filling the churches on Sunday mornings. He espoused the Darwinian theories that outraged the Lutheran establishment that governed the existence of the vast majority of his fellow citizens. In literature he shared the excitement of those who championed the cause of Strindberg against the Church.[1]

Young Lagerkvist must surely have felt that he had left the past behind him when he departed from Växjö to study literature and art history at Uppsala University in 1912. In 1913, absorbing the avant-garde theories of art in a Paris alive with the cubist activities of Picasso and Braque, Lagerkvist must have believed himself light years removed from his birthplace. The poet and fiction writer, experimenting with cubist theories in *Motiv* (1914) and *Järn och människor* (1915), and the essayist programing a revolutionary esthetic change in *Ordkonst och bildkonst* (1913) did indeed appear to be a stranger to his origins.

And yet, and with the paradoxical Lagerkvist there seems always to be an "and yet," Lagerkvist never severed the umbilical cord to his youth. The further he seemed to progress, the more he found himself tied to his past. The quiet cathedral town of Växjö that stubbornly refused to yield its faith to the onslaught of *fin de siècle* forces, the pietistic religion of his parents' and grandparents' households—these nagged at his conscience, beckoned to him in his insecurities, and lured him with their sim-

15

plicity. He had rejected the orthodoxy of his grandfather, who, when "he heard the thunder rolling," could proclaim, "It is good to know that the Lord reigns."[2] He had turned away from the farmhouse that rested secure in its faith of the single star that shined eternally overhead, and he had gone forth to wander beneath a maze of stars that attracted his intellect, but could not satisfy his soul.[3] The past has remained a part of Lagerkvist throughout his adult life, shaping his personality and his work.

Lagerkvist's mode of living suggests how much he longs for the quiet simplicity of an earlier age, for a Växjö removed from the pressures and demands of the modern world. His home in Lidingö, outside of Stockholm, is a sanctuary from the activity of a lively and cosmopolitan city of the twentieth century. Despite his countrymen's admiration and affection for this member of the Swedish Academy (1940) and Nobel laureate for literature (1951), he refuses to become a literary celebrity or play the role of a showman. He scoffs at promotional ventures in connection with such things as cinematic adaptations of his novels and rejects offers to write articles "to order" on special occasions. Warm and at ease with friends, he nevertheless speaks enviously of those medieval monks who were left entirely to the pursuit of their labors. In the modern literary climate that radiates activity, he has remained a simple child bound to the country life of his peasant and working-class ancestors settled in southeastern Sweden's quiet provinciality.

Forty volumes of work attest to the continuous effect of Lagerkvist's past upon his writing. His major theme is a quest for a god who will replace the deity of his youth. He seeks answers to the mystery of existence with the same passion that his grandfather pronounced his faith in the Lord who controlled the thunder. Having turned his back on his parents' faith, he has been obsessed with a longing to find the security it gave them. His writing, regardless of genre, is characterized by the ambiguities and tensions that derive from a conflict between an intellect developed in the twentieth century and a soul or emotions that belong to the Växjö of his youth.

Everywhere in Lagerkvist's writing, the tug-of-war between the intellect and emotions goes on. The duality of his own personality, the ambiguities in his own nature have been turned into the material of literature. Writing in 1933, his friend Erik

Blomberg recognized the burning contradictions in Lagerkvist the man that deeply influenced the artist.[4] Irene Scobbie has remarked on "the strange hold which religion has had over him ever since childhood," and although she believed that its influence had ended with *Ahasverus död*,[5] both *Det heliga landet* and *Mariamne* suggest that it will continue to affect his work until he ceases to write. The past has never slackened its influence on his writing.

At the same time, that past constantly conflicts with those values of modernism that so attracted Lagerkvist to cubist and expressionistic art. In *Ordkonst och bildkonst* (*Word Art and Picture Art*, 1913)—an essay showing his awareness of the relationship between the arts—he combines these contrasting elements in such a way that they forge what amounts to a revolutionary esthetic for Swedish literature in his time and a kind of literary manifesto for Lagerkvist himself.[6]

The essay, indeed, became a guide for Lagerkvist's development in both prose and poetry, and Johannes Edfelt properly remarks, "The ideas set down in this book have guided his later life as a writer to a greater extent than could have been expected from so youthful a work."[7] Drawing a parallel between painting and literature, the essay attacks the very standards upon which Swedish poetry had depended up until that time. Lagerkvist's manifesto resembles those of the abstract painters; its sense of prophecy and anti-nationalism links it to such artists and writers as Courbet, Apollinaire, Cézanne, Poe, and Baudelaire.[8] Like the English Romantic poets who spurned their eighteenth-century predecessors and turned for inspiration to the Middle Ages and to folk values, Lagerkvist eschewed the realistic and didactic tradition of the nineteenth century and reached into the past for his models and into contemporary anti-rationalistic painting for his techniques.

In a brief but sweeping survey of the past, Lagerkvist in *Word Art and Picture Art* praises Aztec hymns for their monumental grandeur, African elegies for their simple but passionate lamentation of death. In the Egyptian *Book of the Dead*, he discovers an admirable mixture of controlled form and wild fantasy. He acclaims the "miracle of the human spirit" set forth in Babylonian prayers and hymns;[9] he praises the literature of India, the masterpiece of the Bible, the Avesta, and the Koran.

Clarity of expression, as found in primitive poetry, enhances the grand passions of subject matter. Lagerkvist urges modern writers to return to the poetic world of primitive literature, which brought man to a direct confrontation with universal life forces. For models, Lagerkvist suggests the Icelandic sagas and medieval Swedish ballads and folk epics.

At the same time, to "renew the style of Swedish poetry . . . ," to achieve both a "monumental [yet] simplified form," Lagerkvist argues for a poetry that, like expressionism and cubism in painting, directs itself toward the proper function of creativity, a study of the truth that goes beyond surface realism.[10] Looking at the developments in sculpture and architecture, as well as in painting, Lagerkvist concludes that the intense search for mathematical principles, the simple lines and clear geometrical forms, would lead to a purification of art, would release literature from the encumbrances of particular social or political tendencies, allowing it to achieve a universal significance, permitting it to capture abstract ideals beyond the narrow limits of reality.

The continuing relationship between *Word Art and Picture Art* and Lagerkvist's poetry and prose throughout his career suggests the unity of the entire corpus of his work and the way in which, although it has gone through various stages, it provides a single fictive world of techniques and values characteristically his own. Arthur Flodstrom's comments on *Anguish* apply equally well to what goes on within each of Lagerkvist's books and to how those books relate to one another:

[His technique] is an analytic study of an object which the spectator then reassembles in his mind. . . . [The work becomes] an organic entity which transforms the raw data of poetic experience into some higher, more significant reality, in which each individual poem, and each element within the poem, explores, develops, or emphasizes one aspect of or fragment of the totality.[11]

Accurate as a description of *Anguish*, the statement describes as well the methods of Lagerkvist's poetry through *Aftonland* and the techniques of point of view, structure, and characterization in all of Lagerkvist's prose works of fiction.

While it is possible to examine that unity running throughout Lagerkvist's works in any of the genres he has used, pride of place properly belongs to his fiction. Not only does his fiction represent his finest achievement and the basis of his international reputation; it is that genre that Lagerkvist himself regards as the most sacred form of writing.

II *General Characteristics*

Like the large body of his poetry, drama, and novels, Lagerkvist's short fiction, published between 1912 and 1935, presents an odd combination of limited range in subject matter or areas of interest and a remarkable variety of literary techniques even within a particular form. To be sure, over the years, Lagerkvist's short fiction, like his work in other genres, has shifted its emphasis and adjusted its moods according to changing conditions in the world and in his personal life, and there has been a deepening philosophical understanding as he has developed as a writer. Nevertheless, the focus has remained essentially unchanged.

Undeniable stylistic differences separate his earlier stories from those beginning with the novella *Det eviga leendet* (*The Eternal Smile*, 1920). In *Människor* (*People*, 1912), *Två sagor om livet* (*Two Tales about Life*, 1913), and *Järn och människor* (*Iron and Man*, 1915) the esthetic ideas expressed in *Word Art and Picture Art* are most clearly in play. The darkly pessimistic mood is conveyed in a style—although by no means identical in all three works, as *Iron and Man* certainly indicates—characterized by the "raucous symbolistic experiments" resembling Edvard Munch's paintings and the works of cubist and German expressionistic artists.[12] The more mature fiction of *Onda sagor* (*Evil Tales*, 1924), *Kämpande ande* (*Struggling Spirit*, 1930), *I den tiden* (*In That Time*, 1935), as well as such novellas as *The Eternal Smile*, *Gäst hos verkligheten* (*Guest of Reality*, 1925), and *Bödeln* (*The Hangman*, 1933), display Lagerkvist's control of his technique, his ability to range through a greater emotional scale by use of "subtle undertones and irony" in a style that has, at least superficially, become greatly simplified.[13]

Nevertheless, neither this stylistic development nor the clearer emergence of "the warm humanitarianism of his message" should obscure the sense of continuity and the feeling of unity that mark Lagerkvist's short fiction as much as they do the entire body of his writing.[14] Even in style, this sense of continuity and unity remain. Kai Henmark correctly points to the relationship between Lagerkvist's stylistic concerns and his awareness of his audience;[15] H. O. Granlid accurately notes the drive to achieve a literary primitivism that will precisely express the balance of antithetical ideas that characteristically mark Lagerkvist's fiction.[16] Both points only suggest what it is that holds together Lagerkvist's work from the point of view of style. The ideas expressed in *Word Art and Picture Art* have their effect not only upon his earliest writing; the influence, better controlled and handled more maturely, extends to the later short stories and novellas and even to the final novels. Who, after reading *The Hangman,* could truly argue that the early expressionism has disappeared from Lagerkvist's work?

In his prose fiction from the outset Lagerkvist opposed the sociological and psychological conventions that governed the work of contemporary realists.[17] Throughout his writing Lagerkvist has expressed his interest in the themes of man's problems with identity and the individual's struggle to maintain or discover his essence in face of the social and metaphysical forces that impress upon him his insignificance or indeed nonexistence in their overwhelming vastness and seemingly total disregard for any particular man's physical and psychic needs. Otto Oberholzer's discussion of Lagerkvist's work, although making the author seem a kind of twentieth-century Thomas Carlyle who plays between saying "yes" and "no" to life, demonstrates the continual weighing and balancing of varied attitudes that mark his fiction early and late.[18] It is a weighing and balancing concerned with the mysteries of existence, the investigation of the dualities of life, and the constant probing into the nature and relationship of good and evil. Like the rest of his work, the short fiction provides no ultimate and simple answers, moving instead from one point of view to another and playing out a debate that in its entirety may very well be called an unending dialogue of the soul.

The range of subject matter in Lagerkvist's short fiction, inescapably, is narrow, but the varied literary treatment—although Lagerkvist maintains a fundamentally fabulist role throughout—has made its fictional possibilities appear unlimited. That literary treatment has kept critics searching for an appropriate nomenclature to describe some of its forms. Richard B.

Vowles, who has difficulty even in labeling Lagerkvist as "a writer of fiction," describes his work as "the creation of a mystic and a seer,"[19] a description that hardly does justice to a good part of Lagerkvist's political and social comment. Vowles hesitates in naming what he calls Lagerkvist's "most common prose vehicle" as either "parable or fable, for it lacks the moral tag of the one and the utter brevity of the other."[20] Individual short works by Lagerkvist have been called choral fiction, antiphonal poems, and cosmic fantasy—names that suggest the impossibility of ordinary classification. Writing about the last three collections of Lagerkvist's short fiction, Alrik Gustafson emphasizes their great diversity in forms and types: "symbolical episode and the fable, ... moralizing fairy tales and grimly satiric sketches, ... realistic tales and lurid episodic sequences...."[21]

From the point of view of general form, however, and for the sake of examining Lagerkvist's ingenious technical variety, it is possible to group his short fiction into three rather distinct categories: the fable, the short story, and the novella. The first stresses a particular moral point; the second, a sudden insight or a character assessment; the third devotes itself to an explication of a way of life, a philosophical or social problem, or a question about the relationship of illusion and reality. Within these groupings, Lagerkvist's infinite variety of treatment is striking.

III   *The Fables*

Even in the fable, where it would seem that the fictional possibilities are most limited, Lagerkvist proves inventive. "Paradiset" ("Paradise"), a brief narrative, does have the pronounced qualities of a parable, concluding with man's exile from Eden and God's luxuriating beneath his best-loved tree of knowledge after man's ouster. Yet the form itself combines parable and parody, in some ways foreshadowing Lagerkvist's technique in his later biblical-historical novels: appearing to retell a biblical or historical episode while altering its meaning as well as its details. For Lagerkvist, God is not omnipotent. Even as in *The Eternal Smile*, the novella, God announces his own limitations in such phrases as "as best I can"; "I hope you will like it"; and "the best I could do" (P. 135-36; E. 167-68).[22]

Lagerkvist's God does not prohibit man from eating the fruit
of the tree; indeed, He urges it as the means for man's becoming
sensible, and what enrages Him is man's inability to use his
knowledge constructively. The message is hardly derived from
the Bible, but instead is consistent with Lagerkvist's own philosophy that fixes upon man the responsibility for the way he lives
his life.

Parables like "Äventyret" ("The Adventure") and "Experimentvärlden" ("The Experimental World") do not have a moral
tag, but briefly outline Lagerkvist's vision of man's failures as
being no more than attempts at finding the right way to exist,
holding out the prospect of further opportunities despite the
errors. These are not developed narratives, but rather abstract
comments or aphorisms on the nature of mankind. Their tone is
straightforward, but the details are vague, their characters abstractions, maintaining the qualities necessary for the effect of
a vision.

In "På Osiris' våg" ("The Scales of Osiris"),[23] an Egyptian
king rises in his tomb, looks with bewilderment at those worldly
possessions that once meant so much to him, turns to a mysterious
statue of a woman which stirs something within him, and then
goes in to the throne of Osiris. It is a simple fable, concrete
enough in its detail, but—as in "The Adventure" and "The Experimental World"—Lagerkvist speaks indirectly, and without a
moral tag, about the nature of mankind and the needs of man.
Vowles finds this fable a statement of Lagerkvist's belief in
"the regeneration of man through love," and he sees in it an
example of the author's preference for Egyptian gods rather than
the Christian deity.[24]

However, Lagerkvist's brief fable is naturally more complicated than Vowles suggests. The image must be identified with
the Madonna, and the treatment by Lagerkvist, as Mjöberg
proposes, links the theme of final judgment and resurrection
with the ancient Egyptian Book of the Dead, a way of renewing
Christian doctrine by linking it to ancient Egyptian beliefs.[25]
In its paradox and final deliberate ambiguity, Lagerkvist's fable
prefigures his treatment of the same theme in Sibyllan, where
the ambiguity between the two traditions is not resolved, but
instead in combination suggests the author's willingness to accept
the necessity of love in man's nature as that which is knowable

when there are no metaphysical answers to the mystery of existence.

But Lagerkvist's little fables are also capable of richly ironic tone. In "Kärleken och döden" ("Love and Death"), a single paragraph, Lagerkvist introduces a Cupid who is "a large man, heavy and muscular, with hair all over his body" (S. II, 216; E. 102),[26] and the arrow that strikes the lover does not unite him with his sweetheart, but leaves him lying pathetically behind her, his life's blood oozing, as she walks on. In the same way, in "Den onda ängeln" ("The Evil Angel"), an angel, fettered for centuries in a village church, escapes and warns the town's inhabitants that they are to die, but the warning is to no avail, no more than an anticlimax, since it is something they have always known.

Only occasionally does Lagerkvist pursue the traditional form of the fable, using the formulaic "Once upon a time" and pointing his moral. In "Prinsessan och hela riket" ("The Princess and the Kingdom"), he clearly points the moral that power demands the assumption of responsibilities not bargained for in the quest to achieve it. Lagerkvist's Prince, who has fought for and won the beautiful Princess, is informed by an aged Chancellor that he now has the responsibility of the kingdom. As a prince, he had believed that courage and his own happiness were all that was involved. In the irony of his moral, Lagerkvist shows the pleasures and pains of kingship: "When the young ruler felt [the crown] on his brow he stood silent and moved, more erect than before. And gravely, with his head crowned for power on earth, he went in to his beloved to share her bed" (S. II, 234; E. 116).

In "Myten om människorna" ("The Myth of Mankind"), too, Lagerkvist uses the formulaic "Once upon a time," this time to recreate the story of Genesis in his own terms. His unnamed characters visit a strange world, intending to remain briefly. The strange world attracts them because it makes something special of their love for each other. They have children and remain in the world; the children, not aware of any other home, are disturbed when they are finally told about it, and the death of a young child serves only to underscore the difference between the two worlds. When the parents grow old and die, the older sons go forth, feeling free of the ties to their parents' other world.

Although here Lagerkvist never makes his moral explicit, it seems quite clear that he is rewriting orthodox religious expression in his own idiom and from his own point of view. As Vowles observes, for Lagerkvist, "The earth is man's home; human happiness lies in the acceptance of this world and our life in it."[27] Perhaps Lagerkvist's attitude is less optimistic than this statement suggests, but there can be little question that the willingness to accept life for what it is as Lagerkvist expresses it in his fable is central to his writing going back as far as his unpublished 1911 play, *Life*. The fact that "The Myth of Mankind" was written in 1922 but not published until after Lagerkvist read it in 1951 at his Nobel Prize banquet indicates how fundamental its point of view is to Lagerkvist's lifetime philosophy.[28]

In "The Myth of Mankind," as in all his work, Lagerkvist clearly seeks a form that will best express what, despite differences in changing circumstances, remains his basic attitude toward man and his experiences. Yet the possibilities for him even within a particular form may be observed in Lagerkvist's use of the fable for purposes that are less concerned with man's metaphysical problems and more intent upon dealing with social matters. Lagerkvist writes fables that have nothing to do with this vague fairy-tale world about men in some bizarre locale or princes and princesses or biblical settings. These are tales firmly rooted in contemporary events, concerned with modern materialistic greed, ludicrous patriotism, and inane warfare.

Despite the modernity of their material, the fabulist's voice and the expressionistic influence are apparent in two early stories, "Skärvorna" ("The Fragments") and "Maurice Fleury." *Iron and Man*, in which they appear, is an intense demonstration of the horrors of war and the hatred it breeds. Written during World War I, "The Fragments" is a grim fairy tale not only of the war's horrors, but of the effect upon the decency of mankind. No dialogue, no truly developed dramatic incidents, but the quiet, almost unnatural, voice of a narrator characterizes Lagerkvist's method of presenting the ugly detail. For Lagerkvist, life, even without the war, is no idyl, but rather the quiet, hardwork, and routine existence that ordinary survival demands. Arnold and his sons labor in factories without complaining, finding their happiness in tending their small vegetable gardens or enjoying their families.

Even their modest demands on life, however, are altogether denied with the outbreak of war. Arnold's five sons go off to battle, and the pregnant wives of his two eldest come to live with him. First his twins, having gone into the navy, are killed at sea. Then his youngest, hardly mature, falls in the fighting. Finally, the report of the deaths of his remaining sons leaves Arnold a shattered man. Actually, that is not quite the end; the sons' wives, broken by their experiences, die.

Lagerkvist relates this tale in measured tones. He describes calmly Arnold's responses to the deaths of his children—responses of increasingly desperate efforts to produce munitions more deadly than those already in use, munitions that will avenge his sons' deaths by tearing asunder his enemies. When the mines, filled with fragments by Arnold and his co-workers, destroy an enemy submarine, and the bodies of its sailors, not yet dead, are washed ashore, Arnold pulls the fragments from the wounds of the dead and dying. With quiet reportorial understatement, Lagerkvist emphasizes the brutalizing effects of war as he describes Arnold's treasuring the shell fragments and hoping to use them again. Lagerkvist's journalistic prose conveys the full horror of Arnold's bearing the bloody mess home to the young children.

Lagerkvist uses nature itself to comment ironically on what man makes of man. He surrounds Arnold with nature's fresh beauty: a benign morning sun and sweetly scented flowers. Arnold places the fragments with torn flesh before the children and explains his triumph. As they return to their beds, they have lost their innocence—the odor of man's inhumanity clings to the sensitive membranes of their nostrils.

"Maurice Fleury," equally grisly in its content, displays Lagerkvist's narrative virtuosity and his characteristic balancing of attitudes toward the same subject even between stories contained in a single volume. For all its bitterness and anguish, "Maurice Fleury" clearly expresses his ultimate faith in mankind and the human spirit, a faith that sees beyond the superficial meanness of the moment. Lagerkvist, in a style that combines the traditional narrative mode with a symbolism that compresses the material of a novel into a few pages, relates the anguished experience of a soldier so mutilated that his wife and children cannot recognize him.

After he faints on his doorstep and is taken into his home, Maurice is shocked to learn that his wife and children do not know him. Angry, hurt, and now without identity, he plays the role of a soldier who had known Maurice and had witnessed his death. By relating the story of Maurice's slow death through the spread of poison in his blood, he allegorizes his own anguish at what he regards as his family's betrayal of him. He deliberately hurts them by telling them that Maurice had renounced his family and friends and yielded willingly to death.

After their shock and out of kindness, Maurice's wife and children ask the stranger to remain. He wins their trust and affection and feels a warmth growing within his wife, who somehow seems not to notice his awesome disfigurement. Ultimately, Maurice makes love to her, comes to experience gentle sensitivity, to see her feelings as a spiritual purity far superior to any simple physical response. The experience shatters Maurice and drives him out into the night to confront his own identity. He returns prepared to reveal himself to his family.

Lagerkvist's story, like "The Fragments," savagely assails warfare and what this age of iron does to men. Yet in this tale of Maurice, he has also shown how humanity can reach beyond the artificialities that mask genuine emotion and how love can probe deeply beneath the surface to get to what is the genuine relationship of souls, that bond of humanity that binds mankind.

"Den fordringsfulla gästen" ("The Demanding Guest"), another early story, is also a fable of modern times. It combines a bizarre setting, fairy-tale atmosphere, and expressionistic style to produce a portrait of modern man in his anguish. Lagerkvist's hotel for tourists, a contemporary Pandemonium, reflects the chaos and disorder of the modern world, turbulent in its insecurities. The guest enters upon a wild scene of workmen, building and demolishing in a crazy frenzy. His room itself is a nightmare of decay and terror in which he ages rapidly and becomes conscious of impending death. In despair and madness, he questions the purpose of life, only to discover that for the individual, at least, there can be no answer. His departure into the darkness from which he had come goes unnoticed by an indifferent, self-concerned world. In Kafkaesque terms of nightmare and horror, Lagerkvist presents in his fable an object lesson in twentieth-century alienation.

"En hjältes död" ("A Hero's Death"), a later story, is another modern fable. Failing to name either the place or the hero who has been hired to dive to his death as a public entertainment, it shows the same vagueness in detail as a fairy tale, a vagueness that allows Lagerkvist to raise his tale out of the particular and into a more universal comment. Lagerkvist maintains the simple expression characteristic of the fable, but plays it off against the harsh reality of a public that assents to the spectacle until it has ended, then questions responsibility, and finally seeks shelter behind its condemnation of public officials. Lagerkvist, here in fable form, strikes at the values of twentieth-century society, and even the fundamental motivation for the willing suicide is offered in the commonest modern cliché. Asked by sensation-seeking journalists why he is willing to perform his act, the hero replies, "But one does anything for money" (S. II, 184; E. 77), a response that for contemporary society requires no further explanation.

In "De vördade benen" ("The Venerated Bones"), too, Lagerkvist maintains the fabulist's technique of generalizing his material by refusing to specify places or persons. Yet once again he grounds his fantasy in the reality of the modern world. Here the groundwork is the senseless emotionalism of a patriotism disturbed by rumors of fraternizing among the dead of the two nations. Even Lagerkvist's concluding irony—the satisfied relief when the living learn that all that has been going on is the exchange of bones between the two sides—depends for its effect on the actual stupidity that characterizes chauvinism.

"Det lilla fälttåget" ("The Children's Campaign") and "Det märkvärdiga landet" ("The Strange Country") exemplify Lagerkvist's most sustained use of the fable in his short fiction. In "The Children's Campaign," his Swiftian irony about a children's army that gains national prominence as it successfully wages the country's war requires no moral tag. Instead, Lagerkvist achieves his moral through the device of irony and through the rhythmic repetition of phrases. Scaling down the sizes and ages of his warriors, Lagerkvist has no need to make a direct statement about their symbolic representation of real soldiers involved in real warfare. When he remarks on how children are naturally suited to the pursuit of war, it becomes a comment on the nature of war itself. His report on the battle casualties on both sides, setting the figure precisely at "12,924" for each (P. 150-51; E. 179), ridicules the statistical game that converts human lives into abstract figures. Lagerkvist derides the rhetoric of war by calling his infants "men" and turning the cliché "armed to the teeth" into "armed to the very milk teeth" (P. 154; E. 181).

Beyond the fantasy of Lagerkvist's story stands the actuality of the youth movements in Mussolini's Italy and Hitler's Germany. The allusion itself acts as a moral comment. The love of spectacle in the parades of those totalitarian nations becomes the object of ridicule in Lagerkvist's repeated use of "unforgettable" to describe the horrifying spectacle of children in arms, children at war, children mutilated and returning to march before an enthusiastically applauding nation (P. 143, 145, 157; E. 173, 175, 183).

Like "The Children's Campaign," with which it appeared in the same volume, "The Strange Country" takes a great part of its effect from contemporary events. The totalitarian world that was threatening in the 1930's becomes in Lagerkvist's terrifying fable the entire world, or at least so dominant that the enclaves of freedom exist only as the oddity of a tourist attraction. In his fabulist voice, Lagerkvist presents his narrative using the inhabitants of the world of the new order as his narrative point of view.

Lagerkvist describes a visit by a tourist steamer to a strange country in which the novelty of the natives' apparently undisciplined lives provides a curious attraction to the visitors of the greater world. In this peculiar land of Liberania, people do not look alike, talk alike, or think alike. Lagerkvist himself is not unmindful of the inconveniences that such freedom brings, of the contradictions it presents, and of the confusion it sometimes creates. But, as he points out in his innocent narrative voice, this is the condition natural to man, representing man's "real inner need," for "human life [has] its own values, apart from its value in the society to which it belong[s], and . . . this value [is] of a higher and more primary nature" (P. 175).[29]

Of course, his "good-soldier" tourists, "a very correct group of people, all extraordinarily like each other" (P. 161; 189-90), willingly obeying orders even to go to sleep, do not regard this natural way of life as being at all natural. The people in the strange country are interesting oddities, appropriate to the investigation of scientists and the researches of historians, but "In the modern shaping of the world, far-off Liberania was of no importance whatsoever," a relic "from a forgotten, long-departed age..." (P. 161; 189). When the tourists return home to their wonderfully ordered land and those who had spoken or acted incautiously are carried off for special treatment, while the rest are "settled down comfortably in one's corner" in "the coaches reserved by the travel bureau," they indeed feel it is "nice to be home again after all" (P. 179; 197-98).

Lagerkvist's irony in "The Strange Country," as in "The Children's Campaign," is scathingly Swiftian. However, even more significant is his attitude toward evil as it emerges from these stories. Lagerkvist never seems appalled by sin, for that he regards as a necessary part of the human condition. Like William Blake, however, he cannot abide what for him is the true evil, that which denies man's humanity, that which stifles the human spirit. In the totalitarian threat to Europe and indeed the world, Lagerkvist found the real evil, and in his fiction he was one of the first major writers to oppose it.

IV The Short Stories

Lagerkvist's fables are clearly the work of a moralist, whether they are cast in the forms of visions, parodies, or satires, but just as his moral code is no mere copy of orthodoxy, neither is literary technique bound to the conventional. What is true of the fables is equally true of his short stories, which retain his fabulist's mannerisms, eschewing modern naturalism and psychologizing, while refusing to fall into traditional patterns. What, for example, is an appropriate label for "Frälsar-Johan" ("Saviour John"), a kind of dramatic monologue or a soliloquy dealing with the messianic impulses that end in a sort of crucifixion or self-immolation? Ordinarily such material would be used for a psychological probing of the character, but Lagerkvist, who does show the vacillations between faith and despair in this modern Christ, concerns himself less with the character than with the confusion in modern religious and social attitudes.

The point of "Saviour John" is an attack on modern professions of religious faith. Were Christ Himself to return to earth, could He expect anything other than the treatment accorded to

Saviour John? John, who "must believe" for others because they
clearly do not believe (S. II, 188; E. 83), suffers the ridicule and
torment of adults and children. Even the word "crucified" is
used to mock him. He suffers the anguish of doubt and despair,
and his final gesture—an attempt to rescue victims from a fire
in an empty workhouse—symbolizes the futility even of his
martyrdom in a scoffing and unbelieving world.

In "Hissen som gick ner i helvete" ("The Lift That Went
Down into Hell"), Lagerkvist again displays the complexity of
his technique. The story combines harsh reality with fantasy in
sending adulterous lovers down into Hell, confronting them in
their sordid surroundings with the bizarre figure of the woman's
husband, who has just committed suicide. Another modern writer
might have concluded his narrative at that point, depending on
the epiphany for his shocking effect. Lagerkvist, however, pro-
ceeds to a deliberate anticlimax, allowing the illicit lovers to
return to their customary behavior as they ascend to their own
world. It is the fabulist's rather than the modern short-story
writer's technique, but again Lagerkvist creates his own form,
for, instead of adding the moral tag himself, he allows the
action to become the comment on their conduct. Indeed, throughout the work, he has combined the simple narrative development
of the fable with a subtle set of ironic contrasts in detail and a
continual word-play on their visit to Hell, both devices natural
to the short-story form.

This odd combination of the realistic short story and the
illusion of fable characterizes two more ambitious works by
Lagerkvist—"Bröllopsfesten" ("The Marriage Feast") and "Guds
lille handelsresande" ("God's Little Traveling Salesman"). Both
are well-developed, full-length stories, allowing for considerably
more detail than a fable offers. In "The Marriage Feast" Lagerkvist uses this detail to achieve verisimilitude in a story about
two unlikely lovers, two outsiders for whom marriage seemed
the remotest possibility. Their oddity sets them off from the
others, makes their romance a movingly pathetic experience.
Inherent in their tale, however, is an emotionalism dangerously
open to sentimentality. By surrounding them with townspeople
crudely realistic and by relying on wit and irony in his narrative,
Lagerkvist manages to maintain the balance. The realism belongs
to the realm of the short story, but Lagerkvist manages to point

his fable element toward an unforced conclusion, the very language of which combines the disparate qualities of his story:

They lay there together in the darkness, near each other, with burning cheeks and their mouths half open for a kiss. And like a heavenly song of praise, like a hosanna of light around the only living thing, the stars rose around their bed in mighty hosts, their numbers increasing with the darkness. (E. 280)[30]

Despite its use of such techniques as inner monologue and flashbacks, "God's Little Traveling Salesman," too, contains many elements of the fable in its study of religious faith in our times. Despite, too, the particularities of his circumstances, the salesman of religious tracts serves as a kind of modern Everyman as he wavers between devotion and doubt. Emanuel Olsson, an unsuccessful preacher, fails dismally in his attempt to sell religious tracts until he resorts to lies, distortion, and deception. Even then, he finally fails and must turn to the Salvation Army for help. His position at the end of the story, as he returns to his religious beliefs a more honest man, though no saint, represents Lagerkvist's attitude toward man's possibilities.

In a kind of moral tag, Lagerkvist concludes: "With him, as with so many others, it was just that he had a slovenly soul" (E. 300).[31] Even the manner of statement, while having an appropriateness to the fable, suggests Lagerkvist's ability to combine two forms—the sense of an epiphany, the ironic tone (which characterizes, as well, the manner throughout a story heavy with criticism of social and religious hypocrisy), these belong less to the fable form than to the technique of the modern short story.

With both "Far och jag" ("Father and I") and "Källarvåningen" ("The Basement"), Lagerkvist demonstrates his ability to write what has come to be regarded as the modern short story. At the same time, in both works he concerns himself with material that is familiar throughout his writing: the mystery of existence, the dualities of life, and the nature of good and evil. Both employ the balances and contrasts which are his technical devices in all his fiction, and the sense of moral commitment in the two stories is the persistent tone throughout his created fictional world.

"Father and I," together with *Gäst hos verkligheten* an unusual example of Lagerkvist's seemingly direct use of autobiography,[32] belongs to a genre of revelation that includes James Joyce's stories about a child's maturation in *The Dubliners*. Like Joyce's famous story "Araby," "Father and I" uses a narrator who tries to capture the experience of youth although maintaining the point of view of an adult. Lagerkvist's narrative line is thin, no more than a young boy out for a walk with his father and suddenly confronted by the terror of night. Narrowly escaping from the tracks as an unscheduled train hurtles by, the boy identifies the experience as a foreshadowing of life, a portent of "anguish to come, the unknown, all that Father knew nothing about, that he wouldn't be able to protect me against" (S. II, 180; E. 73).

But the richness of Lagerkvist's story does not come from its epiphany. The revelation is meaningful because it emerges from the contrasts that Lagerkvist has previously developed: a contrast between the warm, live world of day and the dreadful fear of dark and abyss in the night; a contrast between generations, the father's confidence and security in God and the boy's skepticism and insecurity in his rejection of his ancestors' faith.

"The Basement," too, depends for its effect on the contrasts that provide the structure of the story. While the narrator appears to be recounting the story of Lindgren, a beggar with withered legs, whom he accompanies home, the major concern is with the character of the narrator himself. The deformed beggar has adjusted to life; the seemingly healthy narrator suffers from spiritual malaise. Walking behind Lindgren, the narrator mentally notes his movements, and while apparently praising the cripple, uses language that patronizes and makes metaphorical comparisons in animal imagery. And yet, Lindgren is more a man than the narrator.

Lagerkvist employs an epiphany to drive home the point of his story. Leaving Lindgren's apartment, the narrator observes that only the cripple's light burns, and rather despairingly he remarks, "it lighted me nearly all the way home" (S. II, 228; E. 111), indicating still the despair within himself. Coming as it does after a series of descriptions in which the cripple's determination to give balance and meaning to his life hints continually of the narrator's own inadequacies, the epiphany underscores Lagerkvist's intention. The epiphany here, as in "Father and I," serves instead of a moral tag, but Lagerkvist remains the fabulist even though the form masks the allegorical character of his preaching.

V   *The Novellas*: *General Characteristics*

Add to these varied stories and fables, the complexity of Lagerkvist's forms in the novella, which are equally the work of a fabulist and moralist, and the technical virtuosity that he achieves in treating similar materials is truly remarkable. For Lagerkvist, in fact, the genre of the novella seems a particularly appropriate form. He is not generally concerned with providing the kind of sudden illumination characteristic of the short story. What happens along the way in his fiction is as important to him as his conclusion; and, indeed, the endings of his narratives, often as not, do not provide resolutions so much as they do harmonizings of the ambiguities that make up the substance of his content. His major themes in his longer fiction do not vary greatly from those in his short stories and fables; they are, to repeat, a concern for the mysteries of existence, an investigation of the dualities of life, and a constant probing into the nature of good and evil. These require a careful and detailed examination: exposition, analysis, and illustration. The process is far more natural to the novella than it is to the short story, and even Lagerkvist's familiar fabulist technique—his authorial voice offering moral comment—seems more suited to the longer fictional form.

Most readers might be inclined to describe even what are called his novels—the fiction from *Dvärgen* to *Mariamne*—as novellas, and at least superficially they are. Yet on closer examination, those works, compared to the four examined here, prove more complex in their structures and effects than at first appears— complex in their depth of characterization, in their philosophical ramifications, and in their use of rhythm to provide unity and develop extended meaning. Not that any of the four novellas studied here is simple or lacking in development; it is rather a matter of comparative complexity.

These novellas are not only complex themselves, but show— as even his short stories do—Lagerkvist's surprising variety in treating a relatively limited range of subject matter. Whatever form he uses, Lagerkvist manages to maintain the unity of his

own fictional world, with its own value system and its particular
preoccupations, and yet he offers a variety of literary treatment
that makes each work distinct from the others. Here, within
four novellas so obviously a part of that fictional world and so
clearly concerned with the moralizing characteristic of the fabulist, he offers four very different uses of the form: the autobiographical probing of *Gäst hos verkligheten* (*Guest of Reality*); the philosophical quest of *Det eviga leendet* (*The Eternal
Smile*); the idyllic romance of *Själarnas maskerad* (*Masquerade
of Souls*); and the social commentary of *Bödeln* (*The Hangman*).

VI Gäst hos verkligheten

Critical interest in *Guest of Reality* runs high, for the autobiographical suggestiveness of the novella offers something unusual in Lagerkvist's work. Although Granlid's warning about
using the novella as any reliable source for Lagerkvist's life is
well taken,[33] it is clear that the author has turned fact to useful
fictional advantage, and critics have made the most of their
opportunities. The hero, Anders, has been described as Lagerkvist's "alter ego"; the character's "struggle to come to terms
with life" and his "almost pathological fear of death" have been
equated with those of the author.[34] Several critics have pointed
out, accurately enough, the detailed relationship between points
in the narrative and those in Lagerkvist's life. Sven Linnér,
who knows as much as any scholar about Lagerkvist's youth,
has pointed out the serious conflict in values between Lagerkvist's home environment and that of the larger world, as well
as the clash of opposing forces within Lagerkvist himself.[35]
The conflicts obviously go into the composition of the novella,
which uses the setting of Lagerkvist's childhood, the atmosphere
of a small cathedral town that is making its way from nineteenth-
century orthodoxy to twentieth-century religious and social
skepticism.[36]

Yet ultimately the value of *Guest of Reality*, like that of all
important literature, is greater than its autobiographical revelation. What truly matters is what Lagerkvist has done with the
facts of his life, how he has rendered them in fictional form.
Nothing better demonstrates his literary skill—his ability to make
the most appropriate use of a genre in his quest for the most

expressive form—than a comparison between the novella and the similarly autobiographical short story "Father and I."

As described earlier, in "Father and I" Lagerkvist focuses upon a single event in a single day of its narrator, a boy of ten, who is out for a walk with his father, and, late in returning, is frightened by an unexpected encounter with an unscheduled freight train in the darkness of the night. Suddenly, for the boy, the uncertainties of his future, life without the security of his father's faith, the threat of the abyss, all become clear in a sudden illumination, an epiphany. In *Guest of Reality*, there is a similar concluding statement, a comment upon life and the nature of experience. For Anders, the narrator says, "So ended his early youth, in nothing but dissolution, falsity, confusion" (S. II, 343; E. 260).

Yet the effect is nothing like the revelation of "Father and I," for it has not come out of the same suddenness, the thrust of a single insight played off against the values earlier described in the story. What is involved in *Guest of Reality* is apparent in the specific terms of its final epiphany, an illumination that takes its meaning from a series of epiphanies that have preceded it. The focus is not upon a particular event, but rather on a way of life that has characterized his "early youth." The enlightenment is not nearly so specific; it is the inclusiveness that is suggested by experience necessary to account for "dissolution, falsity, confusion." What is implied in "Father and I" is spelled out specifically, explored, examined, and evaluated in *Guest of Reality*.

Guest of Reality is a novella, and Lagerkvist needs the form to cover a sufficient time span, to include a variety of experiences, and to take some philosophical by-paths in covering his material. It would be possible, for example, to think of the first major portion of the novella as the material for a short story. The fear and confusion of the hero—a little boy awaking to the terrors of death—culminate quite naturally in the scene in which he lies alongside his grandparents, uncertain whether they are sleeping or dead. Lagerkvist clearly regards it as a unit, for the next scene skips to the boy's twelfth year. Yet, if it were a short story, what would have to be done with the earlier material? Instead of the very first scene, devoted to expository details of the boy's home, parents, and their values, the fourth scene—

Anders's visit to his grandparents' farm—could have provided
the starting point. All that emerges from the scene itself, however, is the sense of the boy's "confusion," only one element in
the culminating epiphany.

The epiphanies in *Guest of Reality* do not exist for themselves,
but contribute rhythmically to the overall conclusion in the
final line. The scene in his grandparents' bed anticipates the
actual death of his grandmother in the seventh scene. In between,
Lagerkvist describes the boy's own terror of death, his taking
to relieving his anguish at a "prayer stone" during a rainfall.
That material, in turn, provides a counterpart to Anders's looking
through the window and watching his grandfather pray after
the death of his wife. And so it goes, each epiphany tying in
with the others to inform the whole.

Guest of Reality requires the slow development through time
of Anders's character: from childhood to earlier manhood. But
Lagerkvist's concern is with the emotional and spiritual changes,
which particularly require fictional time to develop. To cover
that time, Lagerkvist uses summary, expressions to convey a
mode of life, rather than the details of every event. He makes
explicit the values of home and society that Anders rejects at
the conclusion. To convey the duality of Anders's experience,
Lagerkvist needs considerable expository material. All of these
are characteristic of a novella—a form that borrows some of the
qualities of a novel, some of the short story, and combines them
for its own purposes.

Contrasts between the values of two generations, between
faith and skepticism, between the security of childhood and the
freedom of maturation, these are Lagerkvist's main concerns.
At the heart of these is the relationship of illusion and reality.
Although it is particularly apparent in the boy's inability to
distinguish between his grandparents' sleeping and their being
dead, it is more fundamental than that in the novella. It makes
up the very structure: whether Lagerkvist is describing the
household, that is, the physical circumstances of Anders's family
(peasants who have moved to town, an apartment over the rail-
road restaurant, never quite the right size for their needs); or
he is contrasting the outward calm and inner turmoil of Anders's
life; or he is comparing the sense of security in the one-armed
Jonas with the insecurity of the physically sound Anders. None

of these stands apart from the rest, and the combination requires the development of a novella, a form which also permits Lager- kvist to offer moral comment in his characteristically fabulist manner.

VII   Det eviga leendet

Lagerkvist's *The Eternal Smile* is a remarkably different kind of novella. A kind of frame story, it uses a bizarre narrative quest of souls in limbo—seeking the answer to the mystery of existence in a journey to God—to present a variety of examples of the human condition. Despite critics' suggestions that the work concludes with a philosophy that willingly accepts life as it is,[37] Lagerkvist's technique of presenting a multiplicity of enigmatic revelations allows for no such easy solution. His artis- tic principles in the novella develop his earlier ideas in *Word Art and Picture Art* and show the continuing influence of cubist painting on his literary experimentation, an influence that extends to even his latest novels.[38] While the simplicity of his prose style follows the primitivistic works he had admired in his essay, his deliberately ambiguous meaning results from a literary cubism that offers a variety of perspectives to the reader without ever fixing upon a single point of view.

The conclusion of *The Eternal Smile*, apart from Lagerkvist's final fabulist knot-tying, comes in the words of an aged man, "I acknowledge you, dear life, as the one thing conceivable among all that is inconceivable" (S. I, 297; E. 65). The state- ment appears to have the force of an epiphany, and yet it does not differ in kind from the earlier discovery that God is no remote deity, no great master, but simply a workman, who "when he didn't have his work it was as if he didn't know what to do with his hands" (S. I, 285; E. 56). God's explanation of the creation, quite naturally, itself has the qualities of revela- tion; to the pilgrims' insistent demands that he explain the meaning of life, he responds:

I have worked untiringly. I have stood by my work day after day for as long as I know. I have demanded nothing. Neither joy nor sorrow, neither faith nor doubt, nothing. I only intended that you need never be content with nothing. (S. I, 288; E. 58)

As each of the souls in Lagerkvist's limbo recalls his experience, it reveals a particular insight. Some suggest how they have allowed their individual deformities to become so all-consuming that it is their total meaning of life. Yet these small epiphanies merge into a larger as one character remarks: "It is a fact that a hunchback is born into the world every minute. It seems, therefore, that there exists in the race a definite need to be in part hunchbacked" (S. I, 296; E. 64). That revelation, too, becomes part of the concluding epiphany of life's being "the one thing conceivable among all that is inconceivable." Life, in all its elements and divergencies, makes up the nature of human existence. The anguish of deformity is no more than another part of the human condition.

Nor do these epiphanies that evolve from deformity exhaust the minor revelations in *The Eternal Smile*. Each character provides a revelation of some part of the human condition; and compositely these develop into the concluding idea. The lovers who insist upon the importance of *their* love, even while each is "alone with what was theirs" (S. I, 233; E. 19), illustrate another part of the central idea; this time as it applies to the role of physical love in this existence. Even the little keeper of the subterranean lavatory provides a small epiphany as he looks at the other souls:

They had all experienced something great or rich; in them something had flowered and borne fruit. Perhaps they didn't always feel it themselves as anything so great; but he felt it, knew that it was so. . . . Those who spoke ill of life, he didn't believe those. But even in them there was such passion, such depth in their pain; he understood what their meaning had been. . . . he had not experienced anything great himself, nor felt anything rich and powerful within him. He had only lived with quiet gladness. (S. I, 227; E. 14)

His existence, too, contributes to the larger epiphany that controls the story, while his comment offers meaning to the revelations provided by others.

Like *Guest of Reality*, then, *The Eternal Smile* seeks its effect through all of its parts and not through its ending. His story's structure is gradual: building up the separate speakers and their individual voices and revelations in choral fashion, each voice insisting on its apartness, its own note. To what might be called the thesis of their individual concerns, however, he ultimately juxtaposes the scene in which the multitude loses all sense of its individuality and merges into one to become the human condition itself:

But now at last when all that lived had been gathered together, and had mingled with itself, like waves that mingle with each other when a struggling sea grows quiet and motionless . . . they were seized with the sense of being one, not more than one. They felt that they belonged together, one thing fitted to the other, everything fitted together, it was a whole. (S. I, 275-76; E. 49)

This is Lagerkvist's antithesis to all that has gone before. In itself it is no resolution, but together the parts are like the two voices in Hebrew antiphonal poetry in which the meaning comes out of the harmony of the whole.

Although the form of *The Eternal Smile* has been labeled in many different ways, it is surely a novella, one which demonstrates by comparison with his other works in the genre, the great variety in his technical achievement. Here he has used it for the philosophical probing of the mysteries of existence. The form seems ideally suited to his needs as a moralist, and it allows him to maintain a narrative voice of a fabulist, a voice that persists throughout much of his work.

VIII Själarnas maskerad

Through long stretches of summary, punctuated by informing scenes, the novella form in *Masquerade of Souls* allows Lagerkvist to cover a way of life over months and even years. He needs the genre to enable him to move at an easy pace, to create an idyllic mood, against which the force of reality can provide a crushing contrast. His contrasts between illusion and reality, the latter coming in brief denuding comments, cannot be wrought swiftly for Lagerkvist would then seem to be describing a momentary oddity rather than his theme: the difference between the illusory desires of humanity and the actuality of human experience.

Individual episodes in Lagerkvist's story build to present this theme. No part of his narrative about a couple whose souls bring them together and cause them to seek a life apart from society, a happiness in their merging existence, is intended to stand on its own. The opening and closing episodes, in themselves the material of short stories, illustrate Lagerkvist's process. In the first scene, the hero and heroine meet, talk, and find the union of their souls amid the usual occurrences of a fashionable dinner party. It concludes with their going together toward the door, "she in front and he a few steps behind her." He pauses for a moment, his attention "drawn to something," and then he observes: "She was lame" (Sm. 13; E. 306).[39] It could be the epiphany of a short story, although not a particularly striking one. In fact, its very conventionality serves Lagerkvist's purpose: pricking the illusions of romanticism. More importantly, it sets the stage for Lagerkvist's mode of handling his material throughout the novella.

By the time Lagerkvist reaches his concluding scene, he has built to the expectancy of his denuding the grand and heroic. The accrual of individual experiences builds to a final force as his hero, tragically useless without his soul-mate and unable to continue without her, writes a letter trying unsuccessfully to express his deepest feelings to his brother. Having taken poison to insure his death, he goes out into the Paris streets, "his gaze turned to the somewhat misty sky," his eyes shining "with a deep and secret fire...." All gloriously romantic, and yet, with his death, the heroic becomes paltry and insignificant, for Lagerkvist concludes, "A passing dog nosed his sock, lifted his leg and peed on him" (Sm. 127; E. 380).

Like the first scene, the last is functional, not an end in itself. Lagerkvist, unconcerned with providing a witty comment on life or seeking a small sensationalistic shock, focuses on the relationship between illusion and reality. Everything in the novella reinforces the duality. His hero's desire for complete absorption in his love conflicts with the need to carry on the ordinary business activities of the world. When the couple seem most at ease with each other, the outside world does not, after all, dissolve. It enters their consciousness with the woman's desire to have a child. The incompleteness of that world of illusion is expressed by her physical need. When her anguish at not being able to conceive is finally resolved in her pregnancy, Lagerkvist punctures the idyllic with reminders of her physical condition, a warning of threatening reality. Her physical deformity, overlooked when the husband has been absorbed in her soul, cannot be dismissed after the child has died and reality has so entered their lives that her handicap becomes spiritual decadence. With disintegration of her spiritual strength, Lagerkvist says, she becomes "more of a woman who was lame" (Sm. 99; E. 361).

Contrasts between illusion and reality are reflected, as well, in Lagerkvist's descriptive passages. Going for a crucial meeting with his beloved, his mind confused between how he feels about her and what his intelligence tells him about her, the hero is placed in a setting that conveys the dualism of nature itself:

The sun was shining, trying to thaw the ice on the road, but in the shade the hoarfrost lay untouched and white. Not at all a bad day. Lovely and bracing. One felt reborn coming out into this. The trees were like strange, dualistic beings in black and white. They seemed in a kind of cheerful mourning—it was beautiful anyway. (Sm. 25; E. 314)

But as he walks, whatever was good in the weather seems to change, whatever was threatening becomes more manifest and depressing; the transience of nature suggests that of life, a reminder of man's mortality.

The choice of the novella form for *Masquerade of Souls* provides another example of Lagerkvist's concern for the expressive ideal in his work. To be sure, it would be possible to condense the novella so that several opening episodes would become one, or the scenes about the stillborn birth would not afford the same detail, or the concluding portions on the coarseness of Parisian life could be narrowed in its summary; but effectiveness in probing character, exploring theme, and creating tone would suffer. Even Lagerkvist's use of a fabulist's frame serves in its philosophical comment to underscore his theme. It seems a proper part of the mood of the novella when he twice declares that the soul has its own land, "And in that land there is always festival. There it is always masquerade" (Sm. 5, 128; E. 301, 380).

IX Bödeln

The novella form in *The Hangman* is unlike any that Lagerkvist uses in his other stories.[40] To be sure, the fabulist narrator is present, but his function is extremely restricted, providing atmosphere and symbolic detail for what is essentially a two-part drama. He sets the medieval scene in part one, placing the hangman apart from society even when functioning as part of it. Within the tavern, the hangman sits at a "dimly-lit table," separate from the others, marked off by his "blood-red uniform" (P. 9; ER. 153), and inspiring terror in the girl who waits upon him. Throughout the medieval scene, the silent hangman remains a presence by the authorial comments on the manner in which he evokes the anecdotes of the others.

Again in the second scene, the narrator provides the setting through what amounts to stage directions in the details of a night-club in Nazi Germany—the "people in the night-club, milling around in the half-light among the sounds of voices, laughter, and the clinking of glasses; in the middle of the room couples ... dancing slowly to soft music under the dim greenish and violet light cast by the slowly revolving globe in the ceiling." Once more, the hangman—at least until the final moments—remains silent, but his presence emerges from the consciousness of others and the relevance of their horrible actions to his being there.

Lagerkvist's technique, limiting the fabulist's voice and choosing a dramatic device to cover a time span of centuries, results from his awareness that the story is formidably didactic and from his desire to turn particular social commentary into larger observations of the role of evil in mankind's experience. On one hand, *The Hangman* stands as the most didactic of his novellas, as the first attack by a major Swedish author against Nazi totalitarianism—a forerunner of Eyvind Johnson's *Night Training* (1938), *The Soldier's Return* (1940), the "so-called Krilon novels" (1941-43), and Vilhelm Moberg's *Ride This Night!*[41] Yet the first scene and the hangman's concluding speech indicate the meaning beyond contemporary comment.

No more than the major action of the second scene—*sans* the hangman himself—would have provided the attack on Nazi evil. The specific attack stands clear in its brutal action. The true believers of Hitler's Germany are intent upon making the world acquiesce or on wiping out the doubters. A man whose face has been destroyed by shrapnel celebrates the virtues of war. The hired killers, bored by their celebrity and mechanical in their destruction, shoot a man unwilling to dig up bodies of early opponents of the regime and drop them in a swamp. His death disturbs no one and appears commonplace as the dancing continues around him. Then, in a wild scene, the Negro musicians, who have taken time out from entertaining the patrons, become the object of a vicious attack designed to demonstrate their inferiority according to the new Nazi chain of being.

But Lagerkvist's purpose, as his first scene indicates, goes beyond this. As the hangman sits in a medieval tavern, surrounded by, though apart from, the ordinary customers, his presence evokes speculation about a forthcoming execution and various superstitions connected with the executioner. Individual anecdotes suggest the hangman's important role in society and show the close relationship of good and evil in man's experience. One particularly stresses the tie between good and evil as the speaker describes a childhood experience in which, by touching the executioner's sword, he had been forewarned of his evil destiny and could only be saved by the executioner's ritualistic purging of his fate. Another argues the persistency of evil through a story of a hangman whose love for his victim temporarily gains her pardon, but who eventually must bury her alive for having strangled her child born with the gallows' mark that had been burnt into the mother's forehead. And finally, Gallow's Lasse, who boasts of having bound himself to evil by digging up the mandrake root under the gallows, serves to argue the unending role of evil in society, an episode which ties together the two parts of the novella.

Lagerkvist's larger theme is made explicit in the hangman's final speech. A spectator to centuries of man's evil and a character in Lagerkvist's story, he can speak dramatically in protest and explanation without seeming didactic. He recounts the scapegoat role he has played in mankind's history, serving to carry the burden of evil, removing the guilt from mankind and allowing that evil to lead to man's more positive achievements. Mankind's guilt becomes his burden, and while he suffers its "lust for blood," man is permitted to enjoy, as he cannot, "the beautiful meadows with their flowers and trees in the magnificent, peaceful stillness of the evening. . . ." Life itself, as he notes, "can be so beautiful" (P. 68; ER. 199).

For the executioner, bound to man's evil, Christ's crucifixion and death are his own experience; Christ is no son of God, but "just an ordinary man" (P. 75, ER. 204), no savior, but a victim. The executioner is that part of mankind not to be released from the evils of this world, a part of man's experience that will continue for as long as man exists.

And yet, Lagerkvist does not see this evil as the whole of man's experience. If for the executioner, there is Good Friday, for mankind there is also Easter Sunday. Even here, as in all Lagerkvist's work, the obverse side of man's evil is love, a saving grace in the human experience. Describing the woe of the executioner, Lagerkvist presents the woman who awaits his return, who is there for him to rest his head in her lap, to kiss his "burning forehead and wash the flood from [him]" (P. 77; ER. 206).

The Hangman, like all Lagerkvist's work whatever its immediate purpose, does not offer a one-sided argument. Damning the evils of totalitarianism, it does not despair of humankind. Its dramatic structure successfully links the evils in the long history of man, but its ultimate didacticism insists that evil is not the only role in that history.

CHAPTER 2

The First Novel: Dvärgen

I Background

WITH the publication of *Dvärgen* (*The Dwarf*) in 1944,
Lagerkvist managed two achievements in a combination
rather remarkable in literature—the creation of a best seller which
was, at the same time, a masterpiece of its kind. *The Dwarf*
brought him a popularity far beyond the reputation slowly
wrought by his poems, plays, and short fiction, but more importantly, it demonstrated his ability to shape longer works of
fiction according to the principles he had outlined in *Word Art
and Picture Art* and principles he had envisioned in his earliest
experiments with applying cubist techniques to literature.

In many respects, his short novel clearly reflects the larger
fictional world he has created: its techniques, values, and tone.[1]
Here again is Lagerkvist's "search for the most expressive overall structural form" to explore the relationship of good and
evil, the dualities of man's existence.[2] His use of the persona of
the Dwarf characteristically attempts to restrain the author's
natural emotions even while it reveals a "partially-concealed
exhilaration" in "scenes of destruction."[3] The influence of Swift,
although more pronounced than ever in the novel, is of a piece
with that in much of his work.[4] His setting—Renaissance court life
and society, with obvious allusions to the Borgias and Da Vinci—
shows Lagerkvist's customary concern for the truth of historical
detail. Even the central character of the Dwarf—with its symbolic use of deformity—is foreshadowed in both *The Secret of
Heaven* (an early drama) and *The Eternal Smile*. The minor
character in Lagerkvist's short play reflects the crucial vices of
the Dwarf, and in Lagerkvist's novella, the symbolism of the
dwarf, hunchbacked and seemingly outside the pale of mankind,
is, like the Dwarf, given its universal meaning: "It is a fact that
a hunchback is born into the world every minute. It seems,

therefore, that there exists in the race a definite need to be in part hunchbacked" (S. I, 296; E. 64).

II Plot

Even the plot of *The Dwarf*, when summarized, suggests the simplicity of narrative outline, the fabulist's concern for storytelling, customary in Lagerkvist's fiction. Stripped of its complexities of point of view, its symbolic and allegorical intentions, kept at the superficial level of its narrative, *The Dwarf* presents a simple enough story.

Despite its concern for storytelling, the plot is a vehicle for exposition, particularly the opening sections, in which the Dwarf depicts characters in such a way as to stress man's stupid, hypocritical, designing, and base nature. Having described how he had strangled Jehoshaphat to become the only dwarf at court, he then recounts the lesser evils of the Renaissance court as though they were the most grievous sins: the Princess Teodora's illicit romance with Don Riccardo; the Prince's vanity; the young Princess Angelica's innocent assumption that because of his size he is a proper playmate. With great disdain, the Dwarf disparages the self-seeking conduct of courtiers, clerics, scholars, artists, philosophers, and astrologers. Distrustful of what he does not understand, the Dwarf judges others by his own limitations.

With the arrival at court of Don Bernardo, a Da Vinci-type Renaissance man, the narrative pace picks up, but remains fundamentally expository. The Dwarf is puzzled by Bernardo, but mocks his comments on the miracles of nature, his curiosity about all things, his absorption in the mysteries of existence. Finally, when Bernardo seeks to study him, to examine him while he is naked, the Dwarf explodes in outrage, damning Bernardo along with the entire human race.

With a sudden burst of court activity—the departure of Boccarossa, the mercenary, and the in-and-out movements of important visitors—the Dwarf accurately concludes that war is at hand, a battle against the hated Montanzas and their leader, Il Toro. The Dwarf is overjoyed, proud of his master who has launched a treacherous attack, puzzled by Bernardo's ability to turn from art and science to creating war machines. Most excit-

ing to the Dwarf is the fact that he will accompany the Prince
to battle.

The opening skirmishes are all successful, and the Dwarf
revels in their descriptions. For him, Boccarossa, the condottiere,
is the epitome of manhood. The Dwarf condemns his Prince's
reluctance to take advantage of the enemy's lack of preparedness,
but his happiness revives with a great military victory. The
rains, however, put an end to the fighting, and a dull wait
begins.

During the interim, the Dwarf reflects on his own emotions,
his desire to kill. He assesses the others, particularly Don Riccardo, of whom he is evidently jealous because of Teodora, and
Boccarossa, a cold-blooded killer. He is critical of the Prince,
whom he can admire only when he is devious and ruthless. The
only sinful conduct the Dwarf cannot condone is sexual sport,
and when the Prince and Don Riccardo take some strumpets
during the lull in battle, the Dwarf, with Swiftian invective,
condemns man's animality, the odors and defects of the human
body.

Reflecting on the previous day's battle, the Dwarf reports
the rumors that the Prince had deliberately sent Don Riccardo
into a death trap, but, when he appeared doomed, the Prince
had come to his rescue. The Dwarf cannot believe the reports,
rejecting Don Riccardo's bravery and the Prince's desire to
save him. The Dwarf cannot comprehend man's dualistic nature.

With the end of the rain, a fierce battle rages, but at its conclusion, the Prince must withdraw and return home. He has
run out of funds and must reorganize his troops and come to
satisfactory terms with Boccarossa. The Dwarf is most puzzled
by Boccarossa's mercenary demands. Angry, as well, that his own
exploits are scoffed at, the Dwarf wishes he could tell his detrac-
tors of his own role in battle. He had ruthlessly slain an unarmed
dwarf, just as he had earlier killed Jehoshaphat.

Time passes without the Prince's being able to raise money,
and, instead, he arranges for a pact with Montanza. The idea
of lasting peace infuriates the Dwarf, who seethes at the prepara-
tions for a feast to celebrate the signing of a treaty. When the
Prince and Il Toro get on well together and a romance develops between Montanza's son Giovanni and Angelica, the
Dwarf is disgusted.

At the height of the festivities, the Dwarf—sensing, he be-
lieves, the Prince's desires—serves poisoned wine that kills Il
Toro and his bodyguards as well as the Dwarf's rival, Don
Riccardo. Fighting ensues, and those of Il Toro's men, including
Giovanni, who were not poisoned, escape only because rein-
forcements have arrived.

Suspicions about the Prince's involvement do not prevent him
from attending Don Riccardo's funeral and expressing his
grief. Whatever the public's sentiment about Riccardo's death,
they evidently are pleased with the destruction of the enemy,
although some fear the outcome. Despite the Dwarf's initial
depreciation of the rumors that Montanza's men, led by Giovanni's uncle, are planning revenge, the army begins to pour
into the country. Boccarossa and his mercenaries lead them.
They lay siege to the town, and public sentiment turns against
the Prince.

The greatest physical suffering, of course, is by the townspeople. Within the court, Bernardo works with the Prince on
plans for lifting the siege. Angelica pines for her lover; but the
greatest change is in Teodora, who has delivered herself up for
judgment by God. The Dwarf, who years before had enacted
the role of bishop in a mock ceremony, becomes her confessor.
He stands judgment over her, assuming the powers of Christ—
with whom he has earlier identified himself—and chastises her
for her misconduct with Riccardo, indicating the depth of his
jealousy.

As the siege continues, the Dwarf discovers Angelica's secret
meetings with Giovanni. The Dwarf seeks out the Prince, who is
making love to Fiametta, his mistress. Told by the Dwarf that
Angelica is being raped by Giovanni, the Prince rushes to her
room, and with a sudden burst of morality, beheads Giovanni.
Angelica, after a brief illness, drowns herself.

The plague, which has broken out in town, now infects the
court. Fiametta, whose evil the Dwarf has admired as he did
Boccarossa's, dies. Martyred by the cruel treatment of the Dwarf,
Teodora, too, dies—the Dwarf refusing to believe stories about
the resemblance she bore in death to the Madonna. As a result
of the plague, however, the siege is lifted, and the two devas-
tated countries end their war.

Cast into prison, the Dwarf refuses to reveal what his hold

had been over Teodora. He is accused of having served the poisoned wine and of having caused the deaths of Angelica and the Princess Teodora, both of whom the public now reveres. However, he is firm in his belief that the Prince, in need of his Dwarf's evil genius, will ultimately set him free.

Simple though it seems in summary, even the plot suggests some of the complexity of *The Dwarf.* How many stories, after all, is Lagerkvist conveying under a single heading? One entire narrative concerns the Prince's life: his campaign against Il Toro, the siege of his castle, the retreat, the peace, the celebratory dinner, and the poisoning. Another story involves the Prince's love adventures, and still another the experiences of the Princess in her debauchery and remorse. Then, there are the continuing story of Bernardo and all it signifies, and the instructive love tale of Angelica, with its commentary on guilt and innocence. And running throughout are the social themes characterized by the rise and fall of Renaissance society, the plague, and the questions of punishment for the guilty.

III *Point of View*

To bring this all together under one head and to make it operate as a "measured probing of the ways of evil," a "lay[ing] bare with the utmost precision the ways of evil on the human scene,"[5] Lagerkvist required a technique more subtle than anything he had attempted before. Miss Scobbie has properly related it to his argument in *Word Art and Picture Art* "that a work should be 'mathematically constructed.'" But her view that the characters in the novel are "grouped around the main figure, revealing by contrast or comparison a further facet in the picture of evil" suggests an allegorical interpretation that ultimately undervalues Lagerkvist's method.[6] For him no single character or statement can reveal a truth that can come only out of the totality of human experience. *The Dwarf,* through its use of a persona, demonstrates altogether successfully the cubist principle of "dividing and relocating aspects of reality in order to arrive at a deeper and less obvious reality."[7]

The Dwarf, functioning as an "unreliable narrator,"[8] allows Lagerkvist to explore the complex relationships of good and evil and the nature of illusion and reality in the human experi-

ence. At the same time, he provides unity for the novel through
a rhythmic function of point of view. His shifting capacities
as allegorical and symbolic character hold the novel together
and give it a depth of meaning and unending interest. Nowhere
in Lagerkvist's work do his fundamental ideas find a richer
embodiment or a more intense interest than in the first of his
novels.

The significance of point of view—one that rhythmically develops Lagerkvist's theme of the manner in which evil, a natural
part of man, distorts reality—is signaled by the way American
publishers have set up the very typography which opens the
book. The warning comes of the Dwarf's perspective in the
initial "I," standing well above the rest of the lettering in a
sentence which ackowledges the Dwarf's height as "twenty-six
inches tall." The context casts doubt on the further statement
that the Dwarf is "shapely and well proportioned," and it is a
doubt reinforced by the qualifying: "my head perhaps a trifle
too large" (D. 5; 5).[9]

Lagerkvist, in the opening pages, makes it apparent that the
Dwarf's comments are not to be taken as truth without strong
supporting evidence. "My face," the Dwarf says, "is beardless,
but otherwise just like that of other men." Yet he himself
soon qualifies this description and notes, it "is not quite accurate, for it is very lined, covered with wrinkles." The nature of
his distortion of truth here is explained when he says, "I do
not look upon this as a blemish" (D. 5; 5-6). Clearly, the Dwarf
sees reality only in terms of his own ego, an ego that later becomes recognizable as that of an evil genius.

Such is Lagerkvist's technique with point of view throughout the novel. Placing himself above other dwarfs, Lagerkvist's
persona describes his race as the butt of jokes by their masters
and guests, but insists that he has never so demeaned himself.
Nevertheless, before long he recalls his mock baptism, "done
as a joke" (D. 10; 13), a joke that has continued currency in
court over the years. Or again, this Dwarf, who insists that his
"very appearance forbids" others from making him the object
of "ridiculous pranks" (D. 5; 5), soon describes the laughter he
provokes in court as he is lifted by others to their knees so
that he may pour wine. And yet again, in a moment of anguished confession about his parents' having sold him, after

"turning away in disgust" (D. 11; 15) from the object they had
borne, he notes his purpose in court as that of a jester, born to
entertain because of his misshapen body. Proud as he struts
after his master, he nevertheless acknowledges—he whom nobody
would dare ridicule—that the people "throw dead rats and other
foulnesses from the muck-heaps at me." And when he angrily
draws his sword, "they roar with laughter" (D. 13; 17).

To evaluate the information that comes from such a narrator,
then, requires a close reading, playing off statement against
statement and checking back and forth in the novel. What makes
judgment particularly difficult is that the Dwarf does perceive
truth, one kind of truth, that in itself would be difficult to dis-
pute. He describes, for example, the conduct of the astronomers,
whose predictions "always accord with the Prince's wishes" out
of fear of chastisement (D. 44; 62). He ridicules the peasants'
attempts to foster the fertility of the earth by pouring wine and
oil on it. With the most accurate observation, he depicts mankind's morality as it manifests itself in the lust and ravages of
war.

Indeed, the Dwarf speaks only the truth—or so much of it
as Lagerkvist accords to any man—[10] in much of his social commentary. He understands, especially well, mob psychology, the
weaknesses of men in a group, their selfish concerns which lead
to a betrayal of morality. Whether he is correct in his assessment of Don Riccardo's character, he is certainly perceptive in
noting that subordinates find it "agreeable to be in the service
of . . . a careless and extravagant master" and that crowds find,
"while starving themselves, [it is enjoyable] hearing about the
carefree extravagant lives of others" (D. 108; 157). Morality
in its heroes, the Dwarf remarks, has nothing to do with the
public's approbation of their conduct. Whatever wins, deserves
the cheers. "The people," he declares, "do not avenge their
princes, why should they? Their life is the same under them
all and they are thankful to be rid of at least one of their tor-
mentors" (D. 112; 162). The Dwarf recognizes how the suffering of others can lead not to pity but rather to a sense of dis-
comfort on the part of those more fortunate. The refugees coming to the court for help after the war's devastation prove un-
wanted, a burden offensive to those sufficiently provided for, a
threat in their disease.

IV *Allegory and Symbolism*

In treating point of view in *The Dwarf*, Lagerkvist shows the uncertainty of truth in the human experience, the thin line between illusion and reality. The Dwarf himself, however, functions on both an allegorical and symbolic level as Lagerkvist makes a more profound statement about the duality in mankind itself. An example of Lagerkvist's theme about the nature of true evil which, unable to find anything but ugliness in man, fails to see any potentialities for good in humanity, the Dwarf, through his relationship to other characters, demonstrates the complex interplay between good and evil within man.[11] The Dwarf's deformity allegorically represents evil—a common image in Lagerkvist's work—but the Dwarf also functions symbolically in his relationship to other characters.

Lagerkvist makes clear the Dwarf's allegorical role as the character describes himself in relation to those who surround him:

I have noticed that sometimes I frighten people; what they really fear is themselves. They think it is I who scare them, but it is the dwarf within them, the ape-faced manlike being who sticks up its head from the depths of their souls. . . . They are scared when anything rises to the surface . . . out of some of the cesspools in their souls. . . . (D. 21; 29-30)

To demonstrate the accuracy of the Dwarf's assertion that these others "are deformed though it does not show on the outside" (D. 21; 30), Lagerkvist develops his relationship with other characters. His identification is clear with the Prince, who logically cannot take part in a war without bringing his Dwarf along. It is no slip of the tongue when the Dwarf proclaims, "Our—that is to say, the Prince's—army" (D. 53; 76), just as he knows what he is talking about when he declares that the court astronomers' instruments turned upon him would give the impression "that I was he" (D. 13; 18). As a basic part of the Prince's will, he can indeed guess his master's "desires before they have been uttered, perhaps before he has formulated them to himself . . ." (D. 102; 148-49). From the evidence that supports the accuracy of the Dwarf's assessment, it is easy to understand his conclusion that his incarceration is only temporary.

Yet one entire aspect of the Prince's conduct remains inaccessible to the Dwarf's understanding. The Prince is capable of duality, of being other than evil, as the Dwarf is not. When the Prince, after seeking Don Riccardo's death, rushes to his rescue, the Dwarf, baffled, asks, "Surely one cannot hate and love a person at the same time?" For him the answer lies in "human beings [as a race of] strange dissemblers" (D. 71; 101-102). In a way, they are. The Prince, having gained by the Dwarf's poisoning the dinner guests, must no doubt be pleased with the outcome; but, as he avoids the Dwarf, he reveals a conscience incomprehensible to the latter. For Lagerkvist, the Prince's conduct suggests man's duality; for the Dwarf, it is simply hypocrisy.

In the same way, the Dwarf can cope with only one side of Teodora's character. He sees her through the torment of his own frustrated desires; her beauty attracts him, but makes ludicrous his longing for her. He wants to find his own evil ugliness in her, and is most satisfied when he finally can say—as she succumbs to his power as a mock deity—that she is a hypocrite, mourning for Riccardo, not truly penitent for her sins. He understands her as he plays the role of messenger in her secret trysts. He knows her in her deceit and betrayal, for then he is part of her, his own allegorical representation of evil manifesting itself in her character.

Yet because she is human, Teodora is something more than evil. She is unlike those minor characters, Boccarossa and Fiametta, whom Lagerkvist uses as incarnations of evil and whose conduct is fully accessible to the Dwarf's understanding. When he describes Boccarossa, the images are animalistic, just as his description of Fiametta places her outside the pale of humanity, a woman uninfluenced "by the horrors of life, instead she rules over them; she can even make use of them" (D. 136; 197). Teodora displays the duality characteristic of mankind, and the Dwarf is puzzled.

With Teodora, Lagerkvist's technique displays the full complexity of point of view that comes out of a narrator functioning both allegorically and symbolically. When she admits that the Dwarf's mock communion service had deeply impressed her, indeed that "there had been something dark and terrible about it which had appealed to something within her" (D. 20; 29), it is plain that the Dwarf symbolizes that part of her nature which

is evil. Yet, in the Dwarf's relationship with the Princess, Lagerkvist intends more than mere allegory. As she moves from skit-
tishness to sanctity, as she gets beyond the Dwarf's understanding, Lagerkvist shifts from the Dwarf's representational to his
functional value.

The characteristics of allegory are static; those of symbolism
are accretive. When the Dwarf represents the evil inherent in
Teodora, he is allegorical, but as he functions as a character,
becoming an instrument for producing change, he is being
used symbolically. The effect that the Dwarf has in altering
Teodora's behavior introduces Lagerkvist's balanced view of the
part that evil plays in the development of humanity. The effect
is in the Dwarf's point of view as a narrator: his ambiguous
presentation of Teodora's character reflects Lagerkvist's theme
of the duality in human nature and the multi-sided qualities of
truth.

The same duality in point of view that emerges from the combined allegorical and symbolic function of the Dwarf is apparent
in Lagerkvist's treatment of Angelica. Again, the allegorical evil
of the Dwarf's deformity emerges from his accurate comments
on the blindness of adults who perceive no difference between
a dwarf and a child, and thus are incapable of distinguishing
pure innocence and pure evil. But the emphasis is on the role
the Dwarf plays in Angelica's maturation. Lagerkvist properly
characterizes the differences between them when the Dwarf
declares, "a dwarf is the opposite to a child . . . he is born old"
(D. 14; 18). Now the misshapen figure of the Dwarf no longer
represents only the inherent ugliness in man's nature, but has
become as well the experience that destroys innocence in the
world of men. Angelica, with her "big blue eyes" and untested
innocence, has never been truly comprehensible to the Dwarf
whose own deformity has obscured his perception, but he
guesses accurately the change that has taken place in her when
in her romantic attachment to Giovanni, no longer with the
purity of the child, she becomes conscious of evil. The Dwarf
contrasts his view of her innocence, which he can no more tolerate than comprehend, with her sense of guilt as he approaches
her: "I saw that she dropped [Giovanni's] hand when I approached and I also saw how she paled, presumably because she
feared that I had discovered their shameful secret" (D. 101;

147). To be sure, the Dwarf reads into her actions a malevolence
that comes from his own corruption, but it is also true that
experience has changed Angelica, and while it is a change necessary if one is to live, it is also the transformation from unsullied
innocence which brings to Angelica, as to all mankind, death.[12]

With Angelica and Teodora, the symbolic use of the Dwarf
may not always be distinct. The Dwarf's narration concerning
Bernardo, however, makes the symbolic level clear and demonstrates the complexity of Lagerkvist's use of point of view. Here
Lagerkvist uses the Dwarf not only as an incarnation of evil, not
merely as an instrument for examining other characters, but to
indicate, albeit frequently through irony, the author's own attitude, the values he seeks to bring forth from his novel. With
Bernardo, Lagerkvist makes clear that the Dwarf's distortion of
reality—his judgment in terms of absolutes in a world where
truth is only relative—is his real deformity, and, in fact, it is that
distortion that commands the cubist literary technique and
establishes the theme of the novel.

Bernardo is not pure innocence. The inventions that he contributes to the art of war, his sense of his own imperfection
plainly mark his deficiencies. Yet Bernardo, although he sees
the futility of all attempts at human perfection, does not cease
his efforts to achieve it, while for the Dwarf the impracticability
of human culture becomes a reason for denying it altogether.
The Dwarf is incapable of understanding Bernardo's two por-
traits of the Princess—one, the prostitute, the other, the saint.
Yet this is the balanced view of existence that is at the heart
of Bernardo's understanding. Human beings are neither angels
nor devils, good nor evil, but they are both angels *and* devils,
good *and* evil. Their very complexity suggests the reasons for
Lagerkvist's choice of symbolism rather than simple allegory
in the construction of his novel.

For Lagerkvist in *The Dwarf,* point of view, allegory, and
symbolism combine to present a cubistic picture of the human
experience. No statement and no character in itself can present
the truth, which can emerge only out of the assembling of man's
total experience. The technique in *The Dwarf* is simply Lagerkvist's method of expressing his own dedication to the search
for truth, a search which is not to be dissuaded by the harshness

of reality or thwarted by the sort of distortion presented in
the deformity of the Dwarf's body and mind.

V   *The Character of the Dwarf*

Because the Dwarf is not merely allegorical, but also functions
symbolically in the novel, Lagerkvist develops him in such a
way that he becomes a verisimilar character. While some of this
development comes through the Dwarf's relationship to other
characters, Lagerkvist contributes to the characterization by
offering in the Dwarf's own words the motivating force behind
his bitterness.

The pathos is genuinely moving as the Dwarf reveals the
source of his true anguish—that of the rejected child, the offspring
of parents only too anxious to be rid of him. Despite his earlier
boastfulness about not regarding his wrinkled face "as a blemish" and about his having "nothing against belonging to a different race from the present one" (D. 5-6; 6), he turns quickly
to his view of the dwarf as an outsider, not by choice, but by
circumstance.[13] His comments begin with generalizations about
the race of dwarfs, but move on to a sense of personal anguish
and an expression of bitterness, as the spurned child spitefully
rejects his natural parents:

We dwarfs have no homeland, no parents; we allow ourselves to be
born of strangers, anywhere, in secret, among the poorest and most
wretched. . . . And when these stranger parents discover that they
have begotten a creature of our tribe they sell us to powerful princes
that we may amuse them with our misshapen bodies and be their
jesters. Thus did my mother sell me, turning away from me in
disgust. . . . She was paid twenty scudi for me and with them she
bought three cubits of cloth and a watchdog for her sheep. (D. 11; 15)

Lagerkvist underscores the Dwarf's pathos by having his narrator conclude: "I sit at the dwarfs' window and gaze out into
the night, exploring it as they do. I need no tubes nor telescopes,
for my gaze itself is deep enough. I too read in the book of the
night" (D. 11; 15). But what is it that the Dwarf reads in "the
book of the night"? His own torment does not permit him to
"interpret it"; he sees no stars, no romance, only darkness, and
darkness provides his protection, for the light of truth would be

more than he could bear. Although Miss Scobbie correctly
compares him with the minor character in *The Secret of Heaven*
who is "self-satisfied and incapable of any thought above the
purely material level,"[14] the Dwarf has chosen this point of
view because it alone offers security.

As he describes the court's fascination with seeking out the
mysteries of nature, the Dwarf refuses to identify himself as
"self-satisfied," but instead remarks on human hubris: "They
think that they can read in the book of nature, that it is lying
open before them. They even believe that they can look on
ahead in the book and read the blank pages where nothing is
written. Heedless, conceited lunatics! There is no limit to their
shameless self-sufficiency!" (D. 29-30; 42). To put to rest any
doubts of why the Dwarf adopts this point of view, Lagerkvist
has his narrator immediately relate his comment to his own
personal situation, to the circumstances of his birth: "Who
knows what nature carries in her womb? Who can even guess
at it? Does a mother know what she has conceived? How could
she? She bides her time, and eventually we see the thing to
which she has given birth. A dwarf could tell them about that"
(D. 30; 42).

How it gnaws at him, this rejection by his parents, this isola-
tion suffered because of his deformity! It is the source of his
evil, an evil Lagerkvist makes understandable because it is no
mere abstraction, but rather a concrete emergence from the
Dwarf's particular circumstances. Nowhere does the Dwarf have
more pathos or better indicate the depth of his sense of apartness and personal anguish than in the scene with Bernardo, who
asks him to unveil himself. "I have never hated the human race
so much as during that ghastly hour," the Dwarf proclaims
(D. 32; 46). He whose very rhetoric has been designed to keep
his true image from himself is now forced to offer up his freak-
ishness for human study. "Unspeakable humiliation," "deepest
degradation," "ignominy" (D. 33; 47) is the way he describes
it.

He identifies his resentment with a hatred for humankind;
he sets up his anti-Christ parallel with Christ, and at the heart
of it is his natural resentment of his parents' dismissal of him.
He compares Christ's relationship with the Madonna with his
own treatment by his mother, and insists upon the unfairness:

He has always been encompassed with love, nourished Himself on love—while I have been nourished on hate. From my birth I have sucked the bitter juice of hate, I have lain at a breast filled with gall, while He was suckled by the mild and gracious Madonna and drank the sweetest mother's milk that ever was. (D. 33; 47)

As he leaves Bernardo, his rage is one more reminder of the deep hurt that motivates his conduct: "Soon You are going to be sold for a few scudi to the noble, high-minded people, You as well as I!" (D. 33; 47).

VI *The Dwarf as Anti-Christ*

Out of this anguish that provides the Dwarf's motivation, Lagerkvist develops a motif that works closely with his main concern, the relationship of good and evil in mankind's experience. The Dwarf's torment and suffering suggest a sense of martyrdom that allows Lagerkvist to create in his persona the figure of an anti-Christ. But, as the comparison between Christ's infancy and the Dwarf's indicates, Lagerkvist's anti-Christ is no mere contrast to Christ, but also a comparison, and this comparison, as Lagerkvist would have it, blurs the line between good and evil. It is a blurring that clearly represents Lagerkvist's attitude toward the relationship of good and evil in man's world.

The identification of Christ with the Dwarf comes early in the narrative when the persona, describing the Princess Teodora's "submersion in the world of the crucifix," characterizes Christ as, "The tortured little man on his toy cross . . ." (D. 17; 24). Then, as the Dwarf plays out the role forced on him by the courtiers at the carnival and goes through a mock communion service, his sermon makes clear this relationship: " 'Here is your savior,' I declared in a sonorous voice, my eyes flaming with passion. 'Here is the savior of all the dwarfs, himself a dwarf, who suffered under the great prince Pontius Pilate, and was nailed to his little toy cross for the joy and ease of all men' " (D. 19; 26). It is important to note in the Dwarf's comment "my eyes flaming with passion," for as he assumes the role in the mock ceremony, he grows more intense, more committed, and it is an intensity and commitment that grow into the final scenes with the Princess, where the Dwarf is indeed the anti-Christ and functions in the peculiar manner necessary to Lagerkvist's purpose.

It is also significant that the Dwarf has not chosen his role. As he says, "I was compelled to officiate . . ." (D. 19; 26). What Lagerkvist points out is the duality in man even in his most spiritual concerns. "I am no blasphemer. It was they who blasphemed, not I," the Dwarf declares. Yet they who have placed him in this position for their own amusement are "very upset, almost scared" (D. 19; 27), because as he has gone too far, he has pointed out their own insecurities, their own insufficiencies. Even the Prince, who punishes him, seems confused about his own responsibility and terminates the punishment early, though he has diffiulty later in looking at the Dwarf or being alone with him.

But it is with Teodora that Lagerkvist spells out this anti-Christ role of the Dwarf and the way in which for humankind there is no clear line between good and evil. Lagerkvist prepares early for the Dwarf's climactic scenes with her. Not merely does Lagerkvist make an early identification between the Dwarf and Christ in the narrator's comments on "the little man" (D. 17; 24) on the Princess's crucifix, but immediately after the mock ceremony the Princess's reaction suggests the dual nature of man to whom evil appeals as naturally as good:

. . . when at last she spoke she admitted that my communion service had made a deep impression on her, that there had been something dark and terrible about it which had appealed to something within her. How had I been able to penetrate to her secret depths like that and speak to them? (D. 20; 29)

Indeed, it is the Princess who, early in the novel, forces the relationship of the Dwarf to Christ, when she asks this peculiarly martyred dwarf, "what I thought it felt like to hang on a cross. To be scourged, tortured, to die?" (D. 21; 29).

It is at this point in the novel that Lagerkvist's persona suggests how much he is a part of mankind, how much of their dual nature he composes. Here he speaks of their fears about the dwarf within them, their fear of its surfacing and revealing an ugliness that they would rather hide. Seen in this way, the Dwarf is a natural part of mankind, inseparable from the good which exists alongside his evil. His shriveled face is the wrinkled portions of their souls. His evident deformity is their hidden ugliness.

Not surprisingly, then, when the Princess in her greatest anguish cannot find solace in Christ, she turns to that other side of the mystery of existence for comfort, for salvation. The Dwarf, "conscious of the power which I sometimes exercise over human beings" (D. 143; 208), hears her confession, her plea for salvation. His role in mankind's drama is made evident by Lagerkvist. His function in the moral scheme of the universe is made plain, as he berates her, forces her to confront the truth, mercilessly exercises his "terrible power over mankind," "dispensing [as he puts it] justice!" (D. 143; 208). Whatever his motivation, that motivation that makes him more a symbolic than merely allegorical figure, his conclusion seems accurate when he ponders, "Maybe she was right when she said that I was a scourge of God" (D. 144; 209). Just as there is a duality that exists in Christianity because of its origins in the terrible awesomeness of the Hebraic tradition, there is a duality in men's souls, making evil as natural as good to mankind. The Dwarf, as anti-Christ, is inextricably tied to Christ Himself.

VII Art and Mankind

No discussion of Lagerkvist's concern about good and evil and the mysteries of existence in the novel should obscure the fact that *The Dwarf* is rich in its variety of subject matter. Among the complexities of Renaissance society, with which the novel deals, nothing so fascinates the modern imagination as the art of that period. Lagerkvist makes that, too, an essential part of his novel, a part that again contributes to the larger theme of mankind in all its contradictions and possibilities.

Bernardo, the Da Vinci-like figure, is Lagerkvist's portrayal of the consummate artist, and Bernardo's relationship to the Dwarf provides a picture of the role that art plays in human society. The Dwarf is scornful of that role. For him, poets deliberately lie: "They laud the lofty purity of the human soul, great events and heroic feats. . . ." Their treatment of love becomes the particular object of ridicule: "Above all, they sing the praises of love, which is quite as it should be, for nothing else is in such need of transformation into something different"

(D. 9; 11-12). Repeatedly, the Dwarf comments about his repulsion at the physical characteristics of love, the appalling sexuality of humankind, and he is incapable of discovering any spiritual characteristics in human relationships. In the same way, he indicates the limits of his imagination—that imagination which in normal man makes him a special kind of animal—when he denounces religious artists, whose purposes he sees as deceptive so that people "may have something to worship which is not poor and dirty like themselves . . ." (D. 10; 12).

Through the Dwarf's distorted vision, man's aspirations through art are transformed into the basest hypocrisy. Bernardo's relationship to the war effort appears not as a symbol of the duality in man's nature—a nature whose potentialities are symbolized through art—but rather as an example of man's hypocritical pretensions. Bernardo's art and imagination baffle the Dwarf. Why does Bernardo fail to finish what he begins? Why does he not do one limited job at a time? These are the questions the Dwarf raises, questions that indicate his lack of comprehension of what the novel presents as man's saving grace: a desire to continue on, to live life despite the failures to reach perfection.

The Dwarf's nature is static. "I," he says, "am always the same, . . . quite unalterable . . ." (D. 39; 55-56). Unwittingly, he indicates his own inadequacy, particularly when his statement comes in response to Bernardo's expression of his philosophy. "Are we the happier because we seek the truth?" Bernardo asks. "I know not. I merely seek it. All my life has been a restless search for it. . . . It is the fate of mankind, the inescapable destiny of all human effort and all human achievement" (D. 38; 54). In itself the statement is gloomy, the latter part not far removed from the Dwarf's view of man. But ultimately, it is the mark of difference between the Dwarf's attitude and Bernardo's. Bernardo acknowledges man's failures and limitations, but does not accept the Dwarf's hopelessness. Bernardo's comment pays tribute to man's imagination, his questing spirit, the one thing that gives meaning to human existence. As Lagerkvist has said elsewhere, it is man's determination to find the meaning of life in living itself that is essential. Naturally, since it takes in all experience, the good and the evil, it leads to the apparent contradictions in mankind and is an expression of the dualities in man's nature. Nowhere does the Dwarf show himself less able to com-

prehend that duality that makes a man a man than when, in his
outrage at Bernardo's treatment of him, he finds it "incredible
that the same man should have done the Christ, sitting so pure
and transfigured at His table of love" (D. 34; 49).

VIII   Rhythm through Symbol

Man's questing spirit and the Dwarf's failure to understand
or appreciate it is underscored by Lagerkvist through his rhythmic use of the symbol of the campanile. The bells are excellent
as a symbol of man's dualism. These bells, for all their spiritual
meaning, will doubtlessly peal in response to military victories,
and yet Lagerkvist significantly attributes the delay in their completion to the war, almost as though to say that the evil in man
represents only a temporary setback to his striving.

For the Dwarf, the campanile at the outset stands as symbol
of man's preposterous aspirations. As work begins on it, he ridicules the notion that "It will tower high above the dome of
the cathedral, and when once the bells ring they will echo up to
heaven." The Dwarf sees the design as nonsense, "a pretty
thought, as thoughts should be," or, in other words, the grandiose
impractical hopes of man. He predicts that it may never be
completed, another of man's "ruins of some great conception"
(D. 12; 16).

With obvious delight in his own wisdom, the Dwarf, when
the campanile has been abandoned because of the war, smugly
notes, "It has all turned out exactly as I said" (D. 140; 203).
Even when the work is finally completed and the campanile is
consecrated, the Dwarf will not relent. The court servant
Anselmo's report on the event makes clear the beauty of the
finished work of art: "They sounded so beautiful that every-
body was deeply affected and listened in silence to the in-
describable peal which seemed to come from heaven. It echoed
over the town and all felt happier for having heard it" (D.
157; 227). But the Dwarf will have none of it, as he says, "That
is how Anselmo described it." For the Dwarf himself, "they
sounded much as most bells do, there was nothing special about
them. I was glad when he shut the door again and left me in
peace" (D. 157-58; 228).

With the campanile, as with all else in his relationship with men, the Dwarf is mean-spirited, his vision limited to earth. For all of man's faults, Lagerkvist will not despair because the striving, the effort, that in itself is meaningful; that is the significance of life. The rhythmic function of the campanile—a symbol providing one more element of unity in the novel—reinforces Lagerkvist's theme, that the duality in man's nature is ultimately not defeating, and if there is a dwarf in every man, every man is finally more than a dwarf.

CHAPTER 3

Barabbas: *The Bible as Modern Literature*

I *Beginning of the Pentalogy*

WITH the novel *Barabbas,* published in 1951, in the year he received the Nobel Prize,[1] Lagerkvist placed his dialogue of the soul in a Christian setting that was to serve as background for a series of novels that includes *Sibyllan* (*The Sibyl*), *Ahasverus död* (*The Death of Ahasuerus*), *Pilgrim på havet* (*Pilgrim at Sea*), and *Det heliga landet* (*The Holy Land*). The pentalogy, "focused on the event and significance of Christ's crucifixion,"[2] marks Lagerkvist's successful arrival at "the ideal form for his vision of life," which had been his quest from his earliest writings in poetry, drama, and prose. His prose style has a trimness and simplicity that rival those of imagist poetry. Nothing is wasted in its language and syntax; classical control governs his expression at every point. Yet the form expresses subject matter highly romantic in its mystical quest and in its turning to the dark and mysterious past. As a result, his novels are neither classical nor romantic, but contain elements of both, and become, in this way, an exemplar of the kind of dualism that Lagerkvist believes to be characteristic of all life.

At the same time, the very idea of a pentalogy—five responses to a theme, each incomplete without the others—carries on Lagerkvist's dialogue of the soul. The novels serve as points in a debate which permits no listener to conclude that one argument holds all the answers, but instead forces him to accept that each offers a partial truth. Not even in *The Holy Land,* where the pilgrim arrives, does certainty exist. The very vagueness of the place argues against assuredness. It is only together that the novels reveal, as Lagerkvist notes in *Pilgrim at Sea,* man's need to recognize himself as a pilgrim who can know only the journey itself and who must willingly accept the uncertainties of life.[3]

64

Within themselves, too, each of the novels presents the dualism of human experience in a form intended to convey that very inconclusiveness, tentativeness, and uncertainty fundamental to Lagerkvist's point of view. Throughout the pentalogy, Lagerkvist joins form and content in such a way as to make uncertainty and ambiguity in the human experience the theme of his work. Whereas in *The Dwarf* Lagerkvist presents "continually . . . opposing views" through a single character, in the pentalogy there is an "interaction of various contradictory statements and viewpoints from a series of different characters. . . ."[4]

Lagerkvist's manner of expression, for all its seeming simplicity, repeatedly casts doubt on what appear to be statements of fact, allowing the reader to come to his own conclusions. Does Barabbas, for example, see a halo around Jesus? Lagerkvist says rather, "Barabbas *thinks* he sees a halo around Jesus."[5] When Barabbas falls to his knees at Sahak's death, the narrator notes it is "as though in prayer," leaving—as does the ending itself— "the ultimate verdict ambiguous."[6] Once more, the influence of cubist art on the novelist is apparent throughout the pentalogy and unquestionably the many words of ambiguity chosen by Lagerkvist are intended to convey the author's sense of "the mystery of life" and the effect is to allow the reader "to accept or reject the appearance of things,"[7] consistent with the author's own view of the dualities that characterize human existence.

II *Summary of Plot*

Even in the plot summary of *Barabbas*, the first novel of the pentalogy, the complexity of Lagerkvist's seemingly simple technique is apparent. Although the biblical Barabbas is scarcely more than a name, Lagerkvist provides him with a history and personality designed to allow the author to explore—through parallels and contrasts between Barabbas, Jesus, and others— the complex relationships of good and evil in mankind's experience. As Barabbas, the thief in whose place Christ died, becomes inextricably involved in his quest for Christian truth, Lagerkvist develops his theme of the inseparability of good and evil, the duality of man's nature, and the insolubility of the mysteries of existence. By their nature these questions, involving metaphysics and ethics, are complex, and yet Lagerkvist, in his customary style, chooses the simplest narrative framework to set them forth.

Released from the dungeon instead of Jesus, Barabbas finds himself inexplicably following the Cross, watching the Crucifixion at Golgotha, and witnessing the miracles at Christ's death and entombment. Together with a harelipped girl, who is sworn to bear witness for Christ, Barabbas returns to his dissolute friends. He is unable to shake free of Christ's memory, however, and, seeking to affirm his observation of the darkness that descended after Christ's death, he receives no satisfactory answers.

To no avail, Barabbas indulges himself physically in an attempt to return to his world's reality. He cannot tear himself away from Jerusalem with its underground Christian society. From a Christian leader—the unnamed Peter—he learns about Christ's purpose, His expected rising on the following day. Together with the harelipped girl, Barabbas is present at the Resurrection. For him, the experience is vague, questionable, but Lagerkvist, through his use of the omniscient-author technique, lets the reader get the same action through the believing eyes of the harelipped girl.

Still Barabbas cannot feel free of Christ and remains in Jerusalem, seeking out the company of Christians. They take him to meet Lazarus (unnamed by Lagerkvist). Barabbas's response is not acceptance of Christ, but once again an attempt to escape Him through sensuous indulgence, almost as though the expense of physical energy is the only means to assure him of his existence. And yet, Barabbas cannot escape a sense of Christ's presence. He returns to the Christians, but they have discovered his identity and now express their hatred of him.

At a Christian prayer meeting, Barabbas observes the sect's disdain for the harelipped girl as she bears witness for Christ. He draws closer to her and her needs, and when she is betrayed as a Christian, Barabbas stabs the man who cast the first stone at her. He carries off her body to be buried alongside that of her stillborn child, and he recalls his earlier relationship with her: how she had helped him in his need, borne his child, been cast out of her home, and turned to Christianity. For Barabbas her death represents Christ's betrayal of her devotion.

Barabbas returns to his own people, a band of robbers he had formerly led. Lagerkvist, in a style that almost parodies the

Gospels, presents Barabbas's earlier history. A child of Eliahu and a Moabite woman whom the band had captured, Barabbas had become the leader of the group after he had slain his father, of whose identity he was unaware. An outsider, Barabbas had always been enigmatic to his followers, but now he was even stranger, more remote, uninterested in leading them. Just as they are planning to do away with him, he disappears as suddenly as he had returned to them.

Masking Barabbas's life in the kind of mystery characteristic of the Gospels, Lagerkvist skips to a time when Barabbas is in his fifties and a slave to a Roman governor. He has served in the underground hell of a Cyprian copper mine, chained to Sahak, a Christian who is awed when he discovers that Barabbas has witnessed the Crucifixion and Resurrection. Through Sahak, Barabbas, for a time, becomes a Christian convert, wearing a mysterious medal that Sahak inscribes for him. It is through Sahak and his influence over a Roman guard that Barabbas is released from the mine and becomes the governor's slave.

As slaves, Sahak and Barabbas remain together as though still chained. Barabbas's own faith in Christianity, however, has waned, and when they are betrayed by another slave, Barabbas denies belief in Christ. Sahak, affirming his faith, is crucified, and Barabbas again bears witness to a Christian crucifixion, this time without miracles, although for Barabbas, the anguish is greater than before. His conduct has been a betrayal of Sahak's trust.

Barabbas, now a household slave, accompanies the governor to Rome. He detests Roman life, Roman religion. After a dream about Sahak praying for him, Barabbas turns again to an interest in Christianity and its secret societies that exist in Rome. He risks his life to seek out a Christian meeting in the catacombs. Lost in the underground maze, Barabbas follows flashes of light to blind alleys until finally he emerges into the night's darkness, knowing, as he has never known before and feeling as he has never felt before, the despair of his own loneliness.

Returning to Rome, Barabbas sees a fire blazing and believes it is the Christian insurrection. He joins in the action, wildly attempting to destroy Rome in the name of Christianity. The fire, however, is simply a Roman plot to ensnare the Christians, and he is cast into a dungeon with Christians marked for execution. Barabbas recognizes a white-bearded old man as the unnamed Peter, whom he had met in Jerusalem, and Peter informs Barabbas that his worldliness has led him unwittingly to serve his false god. Rejected by the Christians, Barabbas is separated from them even as he goes to his execution. After the others have died, Barabbas lingers on, until at the end he utters his words into the darkness and delivers up his soul.

III *Style*

The deliberate ambiguities evident in the summary of its plot suggest the overall difficulties in *Barabbas*. Despite the seeming simplicity of its narrative technique, the apparent clarity of its style, and the clearcut tripartite structure of its plot,[8] the novel is in some ways the most complex of Lagerkvist's works. Certainly it has been the subject of wide discussion and varied interpretation, and the disagreement about its conclusion in itself has provided a continuing critical debate. Whether the hero finally commits his soul to God or speaks out to the darkness has yielded an argument that has continued without resolution since the original publication of the novel.

The surface simplicity of Lagerkvist's narration, combining as it does the voices of a biblical narrator and popular storyteller, serves as a warning that what is involved has its antecedents in the ambiguities characteristic of allegorical-symbolic tales. Modeled as it is upon the techniques of the Bible and the Gospels, *Barabbas* demands the same kind of exegesis and commentary as those works.

Even the superficial clarity of Lagerkvist's style turns out to be more puzzling than his classical expression at first suggests. The passage most frequently commented upon, of course, is the penultimate sentence of the novel: "When he felt death approaching, that which he had always been so afraid of, he said out into the darkness, as though he were speaking to it:—'To thee I deliver up my soul'" (B. 161; 180).[9] As André Gide observed years ago, the words "as though" create an ambiguity that can be resolved only by a painstaking investigation of the entire work.[10] Indeed, considering the varied interpretations of the conclusion, perhaps it is not, in a conventional sense, to be resolved at all. Like so much of his work, the novel applies the principles of cubism to literature, and Lagerkvist's ambiguity seems a deliberate attempt to link style to content so that the stylistic ambiguity proves an integral part of the theme itself.

While the passage has been most discussed, it merely represents the climax of Lagerkvist's stylistic ambiguity. The use of "as if," "seems," "as though," previously noted,[11] runs throughout the novel even as it does in the entire pentalogy. That Lagerkvist relates this style to the meaning of his novel is abundantly clear. Irene Scobbie, for example, has demonstrated that the brevity of the final section of *Barabbas* serves to reflect the climax "by attaining a degree of intensity greater than in any other section of the work."[12] More specifically, she has shown Lagerkvist's deliberately vague use of point of view as earlier Barabbas stands in front of Christ's tomb. The passage reads: "But he did not pray, for he was an evil-doer and his prayer would not have been accepted, especially as his crime was not expiated. Besides, he did not know the dead man" (B. 16; 12). As Miss Scobbie suggests, it is impossible to be certain whether these words are the narrator's or Barabbas's, although the "colloquial style suggests . . . Barabbas's train of thought." For Miss Scobbie, the passage, which she finds "typical of Lagerkvist's writing," represents the "strength and the weakness of his prose." Important for creating "mood" and "suggesting the very fiber of the figure in question it simultaneously detracts from [Lagerkvist's] otherwise lucid character studies" and leads to the "various ingenious interpretations" of his work.[13]

But, in any ordinary sense, the characterization is not "lucid"; and, for Lagerkvist, the "various . . . interpretations," "ingenious" or otherwise, are the very heart of his matter. Lagerkvist's stylistic ambiguity reflects the theme and values of his novel. To talk about his techniques without relating them to the meaning of his novel is surely a critical absurdity. To be sure, Lagerkvist should not be approached as though he were a philosopher.[14] Nevertheless, it is equally dangerous to treat his work as an esthetic vacuum. Lagerkvist's technical vagueness expresses the value system of his novel. Despite much of what the critics have argued, good and evil, faith and doubt, even light and darkness are not distinct entities in *Barabbas*. "It is the measure of Lagerkvist's success," Gide has written, "that he has managed so admirably to maintain his balance on a tightrope which stretches across the dark abyss that lies between the world of reality and the world of faith."[15] For Lagerkvist, Christians do not have all the virtues and Barabbas all the vices; faith does not exist without doubt; doubt cannot have meaning without faith. Death and life, love and hate, fidelity and betrayal—these exist simultaneously for mankind. The deliberate ambiguity of Lagerkvist's style reflects his view of existence.

IV Structure

The true complexity of Lagerkvist's theme develops particularly from the novel's structure, which itself appears at first to be the epitome of simplicity. Built upon three crucifixions—Christ's, Sahak's, and Barabbas's—and suggesting a movement or a rhythmic progression in the central character, the structure actually poses a series of inescapable comparisons and contrasts between characters that prove more important to the theme than does the progression itself. In one sense, certainly, Miss Scobbie is correct to note that in Lagerkvist's design, the characters are "placed in a symmetrical pattern around Barabbas," a pattern which yields a comparison or—as she puts it—a contrast between Christ the dead man and Barabbas the released man, between one's halo and blinding light and the other's darkness, between one's "love and meekness" and the other's "hate and violence."[16] It is not necessary to accept the conclusion Miss Scobbie draws from her facts to note that there is a kind of truth to the facts themselves.

Miss Scobbie has written interestingly about the "contrasting characters in *Barabbas*." Her arguments about the placing of characters around Barabbas sees the technique as allowing them to "serve as direct contrasts" to him, with Christ as his "main antagonist."[17] Nor does she stand alone in viewing the novel this way. Criticism has generally regarded Barabbas as the anti-Christ, the force of evil, to whom "darkness" is the natural element. Jöran Mjöberg, for example, sees the contrasts between love and hate, between man's saintliness and bestiality.[18] Yet Lagerkvist's intent is not so didactic, not so positive in its conclusions as the idea of contrasts suggests. Good and evil, love and hate, these are not truly dichotomous in the novel, and Lagerkvist's use of cubist techniques allows him to present fragments of truth within characters and in their relationships in such a way as to provide a truth larger than to be found in any part of his novel. Lagerkvist is not concerned with abstract principles, but with man and mankind, and absolutes are not characteristic of mankind's experience. Consider, as just one instance, the major Christian principle expressed in the novel —"love one another." To be sure, Barabbas cannot accept this, but if the novel demonstrates anything, it is that Christians, not to say mankind, cannot live by it.

What Lagerkvist does, then, in *Barabbas* is not simply to contrast characters, but also to compare them—not so remarkable a practice, since contrast in itself necessitates comparison. It would seem better to describe Barabbas's relationships to other characters as *pairings*. He is paired with Christ,[19] Sahak, the harelipped girl, the unnamed Lazarus, the unnamed Peter. Indeed, the structure is more complex than that. The harelipped girl, for example, belongs to Barabbas as well as to Christ. Just as Christ has raised Lazarus, he has in a sense raised Barabbas. If Christ has Mary and Mary Magdalene, Barabbas has the harelipped girl and the Fat Woman. Even stylistically, there are comparisons to be made. Lagerkvist presents the genealogy of Barabbas and his experiences, particularly in the later sections of the novel, as though the author were a gospel writer. Surely, too, there is an irony in the very opening paragraph of the novel in the fact that "Everyone knows" about Christ (B. 9; 3), and that Lagerkvist's book chooses to be about Barabbas, which is as much as to say the story of one is not complete without the story of the other.

V *Barabbas and Christ*

Quite naturally, the most important pairing in the novel is that of Barabbas and Christ. To be sure, Lagerkvist draws apparent contrasts between them. Barabbas's strength is opposed to the "lean and spindly Christ" (B. 10; 5). Love surrounds Christ from family and followers; hatred and distrust characterize Barabbas's relationships. Christ's innocence is compared with Barabbas's criminality. When Christ dies, He is in the company of those He loves; even on the cross, He is not isolated. Not so Barabbas: even his crucifixion marks him as a man apart; he

goes to the cross "last in the procession, not chained to anyone";
the cross itself is "furthest out" (B. 161; 179).[20]
And yet the pairing is no simple contrast. Consider first the
final words of the two men. Lagerkvist has chosen among the
Gospel versions not Luke's, which has Jesus crying out "with a
loud voice": "Father, into thy hands, I commend my spirit";
but rather Mark's, "My God, my God, why hast thou forsaken
me?" which concludes, "And Jesus cried with a loud voice, and
gave up the ghost." Alongside that, Barabbas's "To thee I deliver up my soul" (B. 161; 180), though it be spoken into the
darkness, has a tone of affirmation, a decisiveness and commitment that make one wary of describing his philosophy as no more
than negation and despair. The two passages should serve as
warning that what Lagerkvist is doing in the novel offers no
easy dichotomy between good and evil, faith and despair.
    Even the often cited distinction between Barabbas as a figure
of darkness and Christ as the bearer of light is not to be understood in such simple terms. Christ's own light is one that fails
to illuminate. The blinding light that is his at the time of the
crucifixion yields to the darkness at his death. The change suggests not only the sorrow associated with his dying, but also
the ultimate failure of Christianity to change radically the world.
At the same time, if, as has been suggested,[21] Lagerkvist intends
Barabbas's "natural element" to be "darkness," why, after Christ's
crucifixion, is Barabbas afraid of the darkness, "And glad when
it began to get light and everything became a little more normal" (B. 15; 10)? Or, why, when he returns to Jerusalem and
is pushed into the drinking room with the harelipped girl, does
Barabbas, whose natural element is supposedly darkness, have
difficulty in seeing, "until his eyes had got used to the semi-
darkness" (B. 18; 14)?
    To be sure, for Barabbas's relationship to Christ, Lagerkvist
uses light and darkness symbolically, but it is less blatant than
a simple dichotomy suggests. Just as the darkness at Golgotha
and everywhere combines sadness at Christ's death with His
ultimate failure, the frustrated hopes of Christianity are indicated
at the climax of the novel as Barabbas seeks the Christians in
the catacombs. He follows the gleams of light through the twist-
ing corridors to blind alleys and ultimate darkness. He makes the
connection between these lights and those he had seen "long, long

ago." It leaves him in doubt: "Whatever kind of light was it he had seen? *Wasn't* it a light?" Finally, there is only "an endless, icy darkness surrounding him," and when he comes out of the catacombs, he looks "up at the dark void of heaven. It was dark now everywhere. In heaven as well as on earth. Everywhere . . ." (B. 147-48; 163-64).

It is, of course, possible to argue that Christ is light, and Barabbas's failure to find him simply underscores the fact that the two are extreme opposites. However, such a meaning ignores the true relationship between the two characters, one to which the ambiguities in the light and darkness symbolism clearly point. In Christ's light, the darkness represents failure; in Barabbas's darkness the light symbolizes the questing spirit, the hope that continues in mankind whatever the disappointments. Lagerkvist has used the relationship between the two characters to make his argument about the relationships between good and evil, hope and despair in mankind's experience.

The inseparability of Christ and Barabbas is emphasized in every way. If they are "two sides of a coin,"[22] it is the *same* coin, and together they make up man's experience in the world. Barabbas is inevitably drawn to Christ, describes His power over him at the crucifixion, a power that continues throughout the novel. Christ has literally died for Barabbas, and as Lagerkvist says, "no one could deny it" (B. 55; 57). At the same time, Barabbas, released in Christ's stead, can in one sense be regarded as "The real chosen one. . . ." Barabbas may insist that Christ is of no concern to him, that Christ has "nothing to do with him," but after his release he watches Christ's martyrdom "hour after hour" (B. 12; 6), and never becomes free of Him again. Christ does have some effect on his conduct, on his way of looking at life. It had never disturbed Barabbas that people did not care for him, but, "He had not known until now that it rankled" (B. 53; 54). To be sure, Christ does not finally make up the whole of Barabbas's character, but no more has He managed to make a thorough conversion of the Christians. For all their pronouncements of brotherhood, they reject the harelipped girl as Barabbas does not. For all the injunctions to "love one another," they are suspicious of outsiders, scorn Barabbas, the man saved by Christ Himself, and even as they await their death, Barabbas remains "an utter stranger" (B. 154; 172) to them.

VI Barabbas, Peter, and Lazarus

Although the pairing of Barabbas and Christ is most crucial to the novel, Lagerkvist's subsidiary pairings provide a rhythmical development of his theme in Barabbas. Never is there simply contrast between his characters—they share experiences with Barabbas, but respond differently, and even where the result of the experience should make Barabbas a believer, he remains in doubt. His skepticism vies with their faith, but their faith, too, has been in some way affected by skepticism. For Lagerkvist, faith and skepticism are as natural a part of this world, of man's experiences, as good and evil, life and death, light and darkness.

Two Christians—Peter and Lazarus, both ironically unnamed by Lagerkvist—offer meaningful, if minor, pairings with Barabbas. Peter's character has been described as being "at variance with Barabbas's on every point." His "large frank blue eyes," his "honest, open character" have been contrasted properly with Barabbas's black eyebrows and "eyes too deep-set, as though they wanted to hide."[23] And yet Peter is part of that group of suspicious Christians. Even as he first meets Barabbas, it is clear that Peter "didn't trust these people here in Jerusalem, not an inch, he made no bones about it, he was sure most of them were downright robbers and scoundrels" (B. 31; 29). If it is argued that Peter has just cause to be suspicious and to assay his surroundings as he does, it nevertheless becomes a comment on the fact that Christianity can be no simple thing in this world. Peter's distrust, inconsistent with Christian charity and faith, suggests that in the world of men goodness and belief do not exist separately from evil and doubt—which is precisely Lagerkvist's point in the novel.

For Lagerkvist, then, Peter is one more example of the blurring of lines between the absolutes in man's experience. It is ironic that, although professing his faith in Christ, Peter can agree with Barabbas that it was "strange" that the "Master had to be crucified," and no more than Barabbas can Peter see "the point of it." Indeed, Peter seems more appalled that Jesus

had died "in such a horrible way." He confesses that for all his
faith, he, too, *at first* had believed that "the fact that he was
crucified proved that he had no special power." Ironically, Peter
assures Barabbas that if he had known Christ, he would have
experienced His power: "You too would simply have followed
him" (B. 32-33; 31-32). But Barabbas *has* known Him, more
immediately than Peter has, and he has *not* "simply ... followed
him," nor has Peter himself resolved all doubt after having
followed Christ.

When Miss Scobbie, in arguing the contrast between Barabbas and Peter, describes the latter's opening his heart to Barabbas,
she unintentionally shows the close tie between good and evil
in the fictional world Lagerkvist has created.[24] Peter's act serves
almost as a confession, and apparently in this world there is
no great difference between opening one's heart to Barabbas or
Christ just as there is no great difference between Barabbas's
doubt and Peter's faith. One does not exist without the other.

In the same way, Barabbas paired with Lazarus, that other
unnamed biblical Christian, demonstrates Lagerkvist's view of
the close relationship between good and evil in mankind's
experience. Lazarus, witness for Christ, and Barabbas, supposedly the anti-Christ, share the experience of having been
"raised" from the dead by Christ, for surely Barabbas, no less
than Lazarus, has been a "dead" man. Lazarus, in fact, when
asked about the realm of the dead and what it was like to be
dead, replies, "... death is nothing. . . . The realm of the dead
isn't anything. It exists, but it isn't anything" (B. 60; 63). And
then, when Barabbas's eyes question him further, he adds, "But
to those who have been there, nothing else is anything either"
(B. 61; 63). Barabbas knows well enough that "nothing else is
anything either," and Lazarus's speech is, in effect, not far removed from Barabbas's final words out into the darkness. To
what, after all, is he then delivering up his soul? That death
which is in darkness is no more nor less than Lazarus's nothing.

From the relationship between these two characters, Miss
Scobbie concludes that Barabbas accepts "Good Friday but not
Easter Day." She sees in Barabbas's sharing bread with Lazarus
"surely a deliberate contrast to the Lord's Supper."[25] These
seem accurate but incomplete conclusions. What must be added
is that the episode with Lazarus demonstrates once more the

inseparability of Barabbas and Christ. Barabbas shares in the Christian ritual, which in itself contains the ambiguity of a Good Friday and an Easter, a communion service in which the corpse that Barabbas tastes is the living Host. These are not separate entities in Lagerkvist's world. Together they make up the experience of man. For Lagerkvist, these are not contrasts, but rather parts of the same whole.

VII   Barabbas and Sahak

With the character of Sahak, too, Lagerkvist makes the same point about the relationship between faith and doubt, good and evil in the world.[26] It will not suffice to argue that Sahak and Barabbas are presented merely as contrasts. No doubt Lagerkvist is repeating the general pattern he established in Barabbas's relationship to Christ, for the very crucifixion of Sahak and Barabbas's role in it have obvious parallels to those with Christ.[27] Barabbas is described once more as "the acquitted" (B. 135; 149); here, in another spring, he watches in semi-hiding, and is moved by the events. And yet there are meaningful differences between the two scenes. At Sahak's death, there is "nothing great or uplifting" (B. 135; 150); as Lagerkvist notes, there are no miracles, there is no darkness.

What can the reader make of this episode? Certainly, it does not indicate the efficacy of Christ in this world. Sahak, although he does not, might well have cried out like Jesus, "My God, my God, why hast Thou forsaken me?" The scene gives no evidence that the world has been changed by Christ's coming—the Roman soldiers, upon Sahak's death, "lay playing dice just as they had done that time so long ago." As for Barabbas, although he is strangely moved by the experience and sinks "down on his knees as though in prayer," "he was not in fact praying. He had no one to pray to" (B. 137; 151-52). Barabbas's inability to do anything is matched by Christ's failure to come to Sahak's aid. In this world, there does not appear to be much difference between faith and doubt; they are continuing processes in life, and Barabbas as much as Sahak is a seeker. Indeed, for Lagerkvist, Christ himself is more a striving for truth than a resolution of this world's difficulties.

As Lagerkvist develops the relationship between Barabbas

and Sahak—in the copper mine and then above ground—the two are more appropriately paired than contrasted. To describe them as "chained together ... only in the physical sense"[28] is simply not accurate. Surely, Lagerkvist makes them dependent upon each other, first as he notes the oddity of Barabbas's finding comfort in "being hobbled together with another person"; then when he remarks that after coming out of the mine, "They had grown so used to keeping together, and used to the chain that was no longer there. When they woke up in the dark at night and felt they were not shackled together they were almost frightened, until it dawned on them that at least they were lying side by side as before. The knowledge was a relief" (B. 118; 129-30). Finally, Lagerkvist makes clear their relationship in the crucifixion scene as Barabbas suffers Sahak's pain and shares his agony:

Barabbas heard every breath right down where he was standing. He too breathed jerkily and heavily, and his mouth was half-open like his friend's up there. He even thought he felt thirsty, as the other undoubtedly did. It was remarkable that Barabbas could feel as he did, but he had been shackled together with him for so long. He thought he still was, for that matter, that he and the crucified man were united again with their own iron chain. (B. 136; 150-51)

No, this is no mere chaining "together but only in the physical sense." No more is it a description of two men who are simply being contrasted by the novelist. They, who have served in hell together and have—each in his own way—sought faith, serve each other, share a need for each other. Lagerkvist calls them inseparable, "twin slaves" (B. 98; 107), whose knowledge of each other sometimes leads to "frenzied hatred," but whose ties to each other help them to "endure their servitude." If Sahak has been responsible for Barabbas's release from the copper mines, Barabbas serves him as having been a witness to the living Jesus. If Barabbas cannot believe in Christ even after having witnessed the Crucifixion, Sahak cannot even bring himself to discuss the event with the man who had seen it. No less than Sahak has Barabbas the desire to believe, for as he tells his inquisitors, he wears the symbolic, engraved Christian disk not because he has faith in a god, but because he desires that faith.

Neither Sahak nor Barabbas is complete in himself. Together they constitute the human experience.

With Sahak as with the other pairings in the novel, Lagerkvist has applied his cubist literary technique to exploring the manysidedness of truth, the blurrings and overlappings that constitute man's character. No single part is in itself sufficient. Together they make up the substance of Lagerkvist's theme, which is finally expressed in the very ambiguity of his conclusion. The voices of faith and skepticism have been vying with each other throughout the novel. Neither light nor darkness, good nor evil belongs exclusively to either Christianity or its opposition. The ultimate gesture of Barabbas combines the two. Indubitably he delivers himself up to the darkness, not to Christ, but the act is one of faith, wrought on the cross, performed with Christian intensity, consecrated in Christian language. Instead of making a choice, Barabbas has become a believer in his skepticism, while remaining a skeptic in his belief.

VIII   Barabbas *and Existentialism*

Lagerkvist's view of these ambiguities in human existence and his rejection of an either/or philosophy place his writing well within the modern tradition of existentialism. Like Camus and Sartre, Lagerkvist rebels against the severe rationalism of classical philosophy, with its universal and enduring truths and its hierarchy of values. Instead, he relies on a truth that is formed by a subjective intensity of passion, a truth conveyed well by a cubist literary technique that depends on multiple individual and sometimes contrary truths to add up to a larger reality. Lagerkvist recognizes that man exists *in* the world and is inescapably related to it; his great concern is with the significance of death, its inevitability and finality; and yet Lagerkvist maintains that the individual is always becoming, is constantly involved in choice, risk, and thereby freedom.

With *Barabbas* and the Crucifixion pentalogy, the existentialist character of Lagerkvist's writing—present throughout his earlier work—becomes more clearly pronounced. Lagerkvist's emphasis upon the quest is clearly related to the existentialist's awareness of man's existence in a world that does not offer to provide the answers to the reasons for existence. He accepts, though not without protest, the existential formula for this, the fact that existence is without essence, and, consequently, he is aware of the dangers and uncertainties to which it leads, the questioning not only of oneself, but also of the world. The groping of Barabbas, even in the final moment, the desire to accept the darkness and the attempt to give it meaning are an echo of the existentialist's cry in the night heard at least as long ago as on Matthew Arnold's "darkling plain/ Swept with confused alarms of struggle and flight,/ Where ignorant armies clash by night."[29]

As an answer to the question of utmost importance to Lagerkvist, the question of being that dominates the Crucifixion pentalogy, *Barabbas* is the first part of Lagerkvist's statement rejecting both orthodox faith and facile skepticism; it is an existential response to the fact of existence. Its concluding ambiguity represents the existentialist's desire to believe in that which he cannot accept. Barabbas, the outsider, is an ideal existential hero. He is in quest of the one important answer. His subjectivity becomes in itself a philosophy, and it is a philosophy of belief in the moment. Barabbas is seeking the objective information of others, but this must always be meaningless for him. Lagerkvist describes him as he makes "his way back to the city along the nocturnal Via Appia." Surrounded by the dead in the catacombs, he has come to see the darkness in heaven as well as on earth, and now,

he felt very much alone. Not because no one walked beside him on the road and no one passed him, but because he was alone in the endless night that rested over the whole earth, alone in heaven and on earth and among the living and the dead. This he had always been, but it wasn't until now that he realized it. He walked there in the darkness, as though buried in it. . . .
And he was immured in himself, in his own realm of death. How could he break out of it? (B. 148; 164-65)

The experience is the moment of existential vision, but the answer has yet to come. When it does, it is in terms of accepting life for what it is, being affirmative even in the face of total negation. Barabbas reaches out into the darkness, not to Christ, and to it he delivers up his soul. It is not an act of resignation or rejection, but the knowledge of the particular moment. This is the existentialist's reality.

IX *Deformity as Rhythmic Symbol*

In order to underscore this existentialist theme in the novel,
to stress Barabbas's position as an outsider, and to enhance the
unity of his work, Lagerkvist uses deformity as a symbol, rhythmically developed. As symbol, deformity provides Lagerkvist
with one more means for the exposition of his theme. He contrasts both Christ's attitude toward the unselfishness of the harelipped girl and her conduct with the unchristian behavior of
supposedly Christian disciples, sound and unsound. There are
the blind man's lack of sympathy for the lepers, his unchari-
table opposition to their cure, and his fear for his own safety.
There is the uneasiness of Christ's followers who find in her
testimony for Christ only a mockery of their Lord. For them,
Lagerkvist says, "it was as if she had ridiculed what they were
about. And perhaps she had. Perhaps they were quite right. Their
only thought after this seemed to be to put an end to their
meeting as soon as possible" (B. 74; 78).

She had indeed ridiculed their belief by unwittingly exposing
their hypocrisy. They are out of all charity with her, ashamed of
and embarrassed by a being whose own conduct was as self-
less as Christ's own martyrdom. Instead of asking Jesus to perform a miracle for her, she would not trouble Him with anything so trivial. There were others, she felt, "who really needed
help; his were the very great deeds" (B. 41-42; 42). And what
had been His response? He had asked her to bear witness for
Him. It is a measure of the difference between Christian ideals
and those who profess to practice them that Christ had no difficulty in understanding her, but her words of testimony for Him
fall like a jumble on their Christian ears. What is so important
in the mean view of men is of no consequence in the sight of the
God they worship. As Lagerkvist describes her after she has
been stoned to death, the "scar in the upper lip had become so
small, as though it didn't in the least matter. And it didn't either,
not now" (B. 81; 88-89).

Significantly, Barabbas himself is never closer to Christianity
than when he is in her presence. She acts as a lure, and it is
apparent that he, the outsider, wants to believe. Yet how can he
believe in the value of Christian doctrine when he has witnessed
Christian behavior? After her testimony has been rejected and

scorned by the Christians, after their platitudes about faith, Barabbas turns away, and he is "glad to be well away from it all. The mere thought of it made him feel sick" (B. 74; 79).

For the outsider theme itself, Lagerkvist also uses deformity as a symbol. The scar, flaming red, marks Barabbas's apartness. The boldness and daring that have come to him only after this disfigurement are related to his break from his father. If it is a sign of his maturity in an active life, however, it is also a measure of the variations in his faith. When Barabbas is closest to yielding to Christianity, the scar pales and becomes unnoticeable, a symbol of his turning from the ways of men, deep in blood, to the ways of Christ. But with the negation of his belief in Jesus, the scar on Barabbas's face grows burning red and signifies once more his individuality. It is an indication of Barabbas's inability to accept Christ that the final mention of the scar, after his imprisonment, marks him as a man apart.

X Role in the Pentalogy

Barabbas is both complete in itself and part of a larger statement. It presents Lagerkvist's view of the ambiguities of human existence. It offers a clear enough picture of the author's fictive creation of a world without certainties, without answers from either faith or skepticism, with only the hope that existence itself can be made meaningful by man. Yet *Barabbas*, in Lagerkvist's fictional portrayal of man's struggle to come to terms with his existence, is only the first part of his pentalogy concerned with Lagerkvist's dialogue of the soul. Each of its parts—including the arrival at the Holy Land—is only a fragment of the whole, which even in its entirety can offer no more absolute conclusiveness than a picture of man's struggle to give meaning to existence and to find life itself, for all its uncertainties, the only certainty he can know.

CHAPTER 4

Sibyllan: *A Dialogue on God*

I *Background*

PUBLICATION of *Sibyllan* (*The Sibyl*, 1956) was heralded
by at least one critic as "perhaps the capstone of [Lager-
kvist's] work, a summary and a complete and daring culmina-
tion."[1] The novel, of course, was hardly that, for the trilogy still
lay ahead, and Lagerkvist was engaged in what critics could not
yet perceive as the creation of a pentalogy about the Crucifixion, a work begun in 1950 with *Barabbas* and concluded only
in 1964 with *Det heliga landet* (*The Holy Land*). Yet at the
time of its publication, *The Sibyl* did serve as an opportunity for
reviewing Lagerkvist's achievement and the novel did provide a
clear view of a "basic philosophy" running through all his work
and giving it a unity of which individual poems, essays, dramas,
and stories are merely component parts.[2]

Whether *The Sibyl* is compared to the earlier travel book
The Clenched Fist or to the novella *The Eternal Smile*—always
allowing for changes in tone and distinctions in articulation—
unquestionably Lagerkvist's world of fictional values remains
essentially the same and his ultimate purpose stays focused on
a single objective.[3] Lagerkvist the seeker shares a philosophy not
only with the existentialists, but with the modern saint of India,
Mohandas Gandhi. His work in literary rather than in Gandhi's
political terms perceives that man's truths "must always be relative, changing according to human contacts, developing as men
understand better each other, their circumstances, and themselves." Like Gandhi's political and life struggle, Lagerkvist's
personal and literary aim is "a continuing quest for Truth as
manifested existentially, a quest that could never end because
human understanding was incapable of comprehending the Absolute."[4] *The Sibyl*, standing at the heart of Lagerkvist's work,
indicates clearly the nature and the necessity of the quest; the
82

novel sheds light on what has gone on before in Lagerkvist's writing and forecasts what is yet to come.

The Sibyl also illustrates how, despite the apparent variety in Lagerkvist's works, not merely content but form itself displays a remarkable unity. Literary cubism and the esthetic ideas expressed in *Word Art and Picture Art* play a pervasive role throughout his writing, and they have shaped a style and technique well suited to convey the dualities that constitute his subject matter. The blend of form and content are apparent in Walter Gustafson's description of the pattern in Lagerkvist's writing:

simplicity of style and organization, characterization through general traits, focusing of the scene on a central point, totality of effect through a fusing of opposites, merging of objects of reality with the world of spirit, spiritual resignation to the mystery of life (the archaic smile), and absolutes presented in a time of crisis.[5]

Although Gustafson's individual points are debatable,[6] the general outline suggests well enough Lagerkvist's continual attempt to find an appropriate form to express the dualities characteristic of his subject matter.

To bring forth these dualities in *The Sibyl*, Lagerkvist also uses a specific technique that has served him well in his earlier writing. Through a device resembling Hebrew antiphonal poetry, he raises the separate voices of the Wandering Jew (representative of the Hebraic-Christian tradition) and the Delphic priestess (epitomizing the classical religious world) to come together finally in a single meaning, a meaning not to be derived from its separate parts. To be sure, it is not a resolution of man's dilemma, for Lagerkvist neither here nor in the pentalogy to which *The Sibyl* belongs arrives at any absolute conclusions. That is not a possibility for mankind. What the novel does offer, however, is another suggestion that whatever meaning existence has for man, it is in the totality of the human experience and not in any individual or particular truth.

II *Plot*

The novel, like life itself, "is a fusion of many opposites: it is like an old legend as well as a modern pessimistic critique of

life; it is both peaceful and violent, revoltingly physical as
well as spiritual, and a song of despair and a paean of victory."[7]
Its form is a reflection of life's ambiguities and dualities, and
these emerge plainly even in a plot summary of *The Sibyl*.

Turned away from the Delphic Oracle from whom he had
sought to discover his destiny, the Wandering Jew has been directed by an old blind beggar to a former priestess of Delphi
who lives with her witless son up in an unused mountain pass.
He finds this ancient priestess, whose sins against her God and
everything sacred have driven her from society. To gain her ad-
vice, he tells her his story.

He describes his happy life with wife and child until the time
he denied Christ permission to rest against his house. Christ's
curse—eternal wandering—worked gradually into his soul until
it consumed him. No longer could he find joy in his work or
family or they in him. The Wandering Jew set forth on his
endless journey into the world's misery. He learned of the
growth of Christianity, but rejected it, particularly its message
of love. He no longer can keep track of time, but he knows that
years ago his wife had died of old age and long before that his
son had fallen victim to the plague.

His story completed, the Wandering Jew accompanies the Sibyl
into her dwelling place, a home unlike that of any other human.
Although uncomfortable in the presence of her mysterious son,
he persists in questioning her about her life, hoping to find in it
a key to his own destiny. She is reluctant to speak, but the stir-
ring of old memories leads her into her narrative.

Born to simple peasants who worked to support the temple
although their own simple worship was devoted to everyday gods
of fertility,[8] the Sibyl grew up in loneliness, her mother her
closest companion. She was a strange child, given to visions, but
outwardly no more than an ordinary, somewhat dull peasant girl.
The temple authorities chose her for their new pythia precisely
because these qualities suited their purpose. For her, wallowing
in self-doubt, uncertain of her belief, but feeling that somehow she had betrayed God, the selection brought the excitement of the prospect of peace and security through her devotion.

Awed by the temple and the thought of being God's vessel,
she was shocked to discover the foulness of the holy pit reserved
for her receiving God's will. She learned as well that reverence

for the temple derived less from religious than mercenary reasons. Yet at her initiation, despite the sickening odor of goats and the terrifying presence of snakes, she felt the ecstatic joy of God's entry into her soul. Drugs and starvation had eased His access, but her own longing to yield herself to God's spirit had been most responsible for the wild fervor that had overwhelmed her. Although the priests were delighted by her performance, the Sibyl herself, after her initial experience, soon recognized that she was not to find her desired "security and repose and rest," for God "was unrest, conflict and uncertainty" (Si. 53; 52).[9] Despite her continued longing for Him, she knew that He used her even as the priests did.

From both the old woman who attended her and her own experience, the Sibyl learned more fully of the corruption surrounding the temple. She discovered, too, that despite her privileged position, she was an outsider, regarded with a kind of contempt by the priests and ostracized by society. Not even the poorest women desired the job, and the priests had been fortunate to find someone so suitable and with parents too simple to know how to reject it for her.

The Sibyl recalls how these discoveries raised such doubts in her mind that one day she could not experience God. Only the kindness of a temple servant, who expressed his own love of God by working for Him, restored some of her faith. At the next festival, her ecstasy returned, seldom to fail her in the future, but always leaving her with dismay when it did. Still, her reputation increased, and she lasted beyond the customary tenure of pythias.

At the same time, she became more and more remote from society, estranged even from her parents until the day she was called to her mother's deathbed. The dying woman scarcely recognized her daughter dressed in her ceremonial gowns. Suffering from guilt at having become so remote from her parents, the Sibyl remained on in her father's household in order to care for him after her mother's death.

While caring for her father, the Sibyl met a one-armed soldier, back from the wars. They had known each other as children, but now they were immediately in love. She turned to him for the security she had not found in God. At their third meeting, he took her to the river banks, and she gave herself to him with

the same passion she had yielded to God. She lived in dread of
God's retribution and of her lover's discovery of her true identity.
For him, however, her being a pythia proved unimportant, and,
despite her awareness that her increased passion would cool his
ardor, she could not control her ecstatic response to him any
more than she had been able to repress her emotions in receiving
God's spirit.

Recalled to the temple, the Sibyl went secretly. This time God
possessed her with unparalleled fury, and later she learned that
her lover had invaded the sanctity of the temple to gaze at her
in the aftermath of her frenzy. All was over between them. The
Sibyl understood that no man could take a woman after having
seen her in such full possession by God.

For a while she remained on her father's farm, but recalled
again to the temple, she experienced her most terrifying encounter with God. In the form of a black goat, He ravished her,
bringing her a strange new delight, but leaving her with a feeling of self-revulsion. At the same time, her lover had been mysteriously drowned in the sacred river, which the Sibyl regarded
as an act of God's vengeance. She managed to keep their relationship secret until her female attendant, discovering the Sibyl
was pregnant and somehow linking it to the dead man, betrayed
her to the priests and townspeople of Delphi.

Awaiting sentence, the Sibyl was rescued from an outraged
mob by the little temple servant, who led her into the sanctity
of the temple. There she felt the serenity of God for the first
time, and when she left, she was able to walk by her tormenters.
Not until she departed from the sacred paths did they dare to
stone her, and finally they permitted her to take refuge in the
mountains, apart from all humanity.

The Sibyl endured the hardships of winter—foraging for food
and stealing when necessary. Her spirit thrived on the hopes of
a child who would unite her with her dead lover. With the turn
to spring, her circumstances improved: animals were naturally
drawn to her and goat's milk was readily available. Yet, as summer arrived, the Sibyl was disturbed because the child was
overdue. Not until summer's end, however, did the childbirth
begin. During an assault of lightning and thunder, mysterious
goats appeared and led her out of the storm to a shelter high up
in the mountain. There, amid the same goat odor familiar to

her in the recesses of the temple and surrounded by animals apparently sharing her anguish, she gave birth to her child.

Now, as she has told her story, the Sibyl reflects on it and questions the paternity of her son, a witless, smiling idiot. She cannot believe he is the child of her lover conceived in their last unpassionate meetings. Although the time of pregnancy dates to the occasion of God's assault on her, she cannot bear to think that this jest of humankind is God's son. Yet she does wonder, at times, if this idiot child is not indeed a God smiling down at his whole creation.

During these reflections, the Sibyl discovers that her son has disappeared. Together with the Wandering Jew, she frantically searches for him and high in the mountains she finds that point where his footprints vanish as though into air. She accuses herself of having driven him away, and she believes that, although he had never given any indication of doing so, he had understood her.

For the Wandering Jew, the Sibyl's story and the final experience demonstrate God's malevolence. He identifies them with his own bitter existence and assures the Sibyl that he knows how much she must hate God. However, she responds that she can neither hate nor love what she does not understand. It seems to her that God is neither good nor evil, darkness nor light, but a combination of both which is simply beyond human comprehension. Angry, the wanderer repeats his purpose in having come to her: to obtain a prophecy of his own destiny. Although she cannot answer that, she points out that he is not altogether a hollow man. His heart is filled with despair and somehow God will always be inextricably involved in his destiny. As the Wandering Jew leaves her looking down at the temple city, a young woman, dressed in a sibyl's garments, is making her way to the holy place.

III *The Wandering Jew*

Neither the story told by the Wandering Jew nor that by the Sibyl can in itself provide the answer to the mystery of existence. Even together, they achieve no resolution to man's quest, but in unity, they do demonstrate the inevitability and necessity of man's struggle to understand the nature of existence, the common

humanity that binds all men, the function of love in the human
experience, and the duality that characterizes every aspect of
living.

In the tale of the Wandering Jew, Lagerkvist follows the general outline of the legend, but elaborates upon it to suggest,
among other things, the true failure of the very Christianity
that the original is intended to celebrate. The Wandering Jew—
described in *The Sibyl* only as "the stranger," but identified in
the next novel of the pentalogy as "Ahasuerus"—portrays that
self-love that Christianity is intended to change, but that,
through the enigmatic character of its God and its commitment
to ritual, it fails to alter.

The Wandering Jew is involved in himself. His refusal to
allow Jesus temporary respite from His burden proves to be no
peculiar aberration in his conduct, but rather a symbol of his
general feeling toward humanity.[10] When he rejects Jesus' request, the Wandering Jew knows nothing of His divinity, and
indeed would have turned away any sufferer. To be sure, the
effect of his "revelation" is to make him see himself as an
"outsider," a "stranger" to his own wife and child (Si. 20; 17).
However, he describes himself more broadly as "not a loving
man," "loveless," never truly "concerned" about his wife, never
"particularly attached to [his son]" (Si. 28, 34, 25; 25, 31, 21-22).
If ultimately, in the next novel, Ahasuerus is permitted to die
"in a semblance of peace,"[11] it is only because through his
experiences he has come to have a sense of compassion and kin-
ship toward his fellow man.

Lagerkvist, however, does not limit the figure of the Wandering
Jew to a simple representation of a "loveless" man. The character
himself insists that for all his being an outsider, he is no more
"loveless" (Si. 39; 31) than the rest of humankind, and if he
is "all want and evil ... evil and loveless" (Si. 27; 24), so too is
the rest of the world as he has come to know it. How, he asks,
does Christ Himself differ from others? Rewarding those who
love Him, destroying the rest, Christ proves "exactly like ourselves, just as good and just as bad." Christians may praise
their Lord for His "signs and wonders," but for Ahasuerus, the
sign is evil, "the eternal unrest of my soul" (Si. 28; 25), and
if God hopes to convert man through pain and suffering, the

wanderer insists, "Unhappiness does not make a man good" (Si. 25; 22).

Lagerkvist's sense of duality is such that the Wandering Jew, indeed, displays characteristics that argue sympathetically for man in his battle against cosmic fate. Ahasuerus's stubbornness conveys man's determination. As he is to do throughout *The Death of Ahasuerus,* he maintains, "I will not bow" (Si. 145; 147). Confronted by ignorance of his future, he prefers to face the truth, "Tear down the veil and let me see, however terrible it may be!" (Si. 30; 27). He becomes, in a moment of defiant rage against his curse, the classical figure of the rebel:

Why did I not rebel against the power within me and say: I will not! I will not! I will live, I will live exactly as others live and be as I have been. I will be like everyone else! I will live.
And when I had said this . . . it was as if the curse fell from me like a heavy garment; I felt a relief, a liberation such as I had never known before during all the time that had passed. (Si. 22; 19)

Although that particular moment recedes into despair, even that despair is better than nothingness, superior to acquiescence. Looking into his eyes, the Sibyl can see that they "were not empty. They were full of despair" (Si. 149; 151). Whatever has happened, he is not without something, even if that something is despair, which itself may become a motivating, driving force. She recognizes how that power functions in the Wanderin Jew:

He is your destiny. Your soul is filled with him; through his curse you live a life with god. You hate him, you mock and revile him. But judging by your indignant words, you care for nothing in the world but him, and are filled with him alone . . . your experience of the divine. (Si. 149; 152)

Ahasuerus sees in these words the significance of the struggle itself: "perhaps [that] would make it even less endurable. [But] it no longer seemed quite as meaningless and hopeless as before. Perhaps not even as unchanging as he had thought. But that was something to which his endless wandering must give the answer . . ." (Si. 150-51; 153). The plight of the Wandering Jew is in some ways the quest of mankind.

IV   *The Character of the Sibyl*

Complex as the character of the Wandering Jew and his tale
are, they appear relatively simple alongside those of the Sibyl
with whose experiences the novel is mainly concerned. The Wandering Jew comes to her seeking information about his destiny,
but through telling him her story, she comes to recognize the
truth about herself, or at least such truth as mankind may comprehend. Like the pronouncements of the Delphic Oracle itself, the Sibyl is enigmatic. As the Wandering Jew looks at her,
hoping to find the answer to his initial question, her physical
appearance suggests her enigmatic character. He peers into her
"furrowed face, as if to read in that old book which, for all its
plain script, was so difficult to decipher. It was as if it had been
written in an ancient tongue which was no longer spoken" (Si.
14; 10). She is the passionate outsider longing to be like ordinary mortals. She is simple and wise, a peasant girl who has
shared God's existence. In an odd way, she has found both ful-
fillment and frustration in her relationship with man and God.

In some respects, the Sibyl resembles Ahasuerus, for it is
important to Lagerkvist's purpose that, as the parallels between
the Christian and ancient myths reveal, their experiences add
up to the general questing nature of mankind. Certainly, their
overall situations correspond. Like the Wandering Jew, the Sibyl
has discovered, "There is no joy in seeing God" (Si. 30; 27).
When the beggar describes the Sibyl's condition, he might very
well be depicting that of Ahasuerus: "One who has been in such
contact with the divine must find it hard to die, with such power
as must yet remain within her ... though he remain only as a
curse" (Si. 14; 10). The Sibyl, like the Wandering Jew, becomes
"an outcast with whom no one would come in contact or even
speak" (Si. 62; 61); to her own family she is a "stranger" (Si.
39; 37). She herself acknowledges her condition as that of an
outsider, and with a plaintiveness similar to the Wandering
Jew's, she asks, "Why couldn't I be like the rest?" (Si. 101; 102).

Yet Lagerkvist's treatment of the Sibyl creates a character far
more complex than the portrait of the Wandering Jew. Whatever the latter may finally become, in this novel he is in the
process of learning. The Sibyl, through her own ambiguity and
her own comprehension of the duality of God's nature, provides

instruction for Ahasuerus. Her struggle to balance love of God and man, however unsuccessful, offers him an object lesson that he later carries into his experiences with Tobias. It prepares Ahasuerus for some understanding of the relationship between Tobias and Diana in *The Death of Ahasuerus,* and when Ahasuerus can finally feel closer to Tobias than he has ever felt toward any other man, that experience will allow him to die in some semblance of peace.

Lagerkvist spells out the Sibyl's ambiguous relationship to God and man. Even her emotions toward God alone present this duality. She cannot do without Him, and yet He brings, instead of ultimate satisfaction, anguish and pain. Worse than the doubt and uncertainty about God is the uncertainty without Him. When He does not come to her in the temple, "it was as if I stretched [out my hand] into perfect vacancy and boundless desolation" (Si. 65; 64). Experiencing Him, she knows only "anguish" and "pain" (Si. 57; 56). Even when she is most His, willing to give herself to Him, she finds no satisfaction: "I was no longer I, I was his, his alone; it was terrible, terrible and nothing else." If "without him all was nothingness and void" (Si. 51-52; 50-51), being possessed by Him brought afterward a terrible loneliness and depletion of emotion. He frightens her, and yet she longs for Him. She knows, "One ought not to feel uneasiness, hesitancy or doubt in one's soul, for then one could scarcely be received into his arms." And "Yet how could one be without dread, without doubts? How could one approach god without them?" (Si. 68; 67).

The source of duality in the Sibyl's character, however, goes beyond questions of the nature of God and emanates mainly from her attempt to reconcile love and devotion to God with the ordinary business of life and her feelings about man. "I was chosen by god; I was god's elect. But I was also chosen by the life of this earth, by ordinary human life, to live it" (Si. 88; 88). After her initial innocence of the world, she becomes well aware of the corruption in mankind. No fool, she recognizes the hypocrisy of the temple woman who attends her; she observes the faithlessness of priests whose ire at her sin has less to do with God than with loss of prestige and profits. She sets in perspective the townspeople's view of her guilt, the wrath of those who "lived on god" (Si. 47; 45), when

she indicates the order of their concern about "the shame I had
brought upon the city, the temple and god" (Si. 116; 117).

And yet her tie is to mankind. For all that she has experienced,
she still can ask whether "men [are] really so wicked" (Si. 55;
54). For all the evidence about "each [man's being] engrossed
in his own affairs" (Si. 10; 4), and her perception of the evil in
the faces of townspeople intent on destroying her, she cannot
derive an "enduring hatred for mankind" for she knows that
"this was not the whole truth about them" (Si. 117; 118). As
Sibyl, committed to God and temple, she cannot yield herself
wholly to them. She expresses anguish at having to remain in
service at the very time her mother lay dying: "The great festival which I could not leave . . . —the wildness, the rapture, the
obsession—what was that compared to the peace in a human face,
and to the possession of that peace?" (Si. 78; 77). Part of the
Sibyl remains tied to humankind, and that results in an ambiguity in her devotion to God.

V *Human versus Divine Love*

Nowhere is that ambiguity better demonstrated than in the
Sibyl's love affair. That human relationship becomes as holy
to her as her dedication to God. She and her lover are brought
together in what amounts to a ritual performed at a "holy
spring." Their act of drinking together becomes symbolic of
their union: "There was nothing extraordinary about this, and
yet I felt that it was a singular act we were performing together" (Si. 82; 82). In terms that can only be intended to contrast the naturalness of their relationship with the unnaturalness
of her devotion to God, the Sibyl stresses that their lovemaking
always took place outdoors, "We loved each other wherever
we happened to be, but always in the open, like the animals,
like all nature" (Si. 90; 90). It would be difficult not to recall
at this point that when receiving God the Sibyl was entranced
by drugs, artificially prepared to be stimulated by Him, and
confined to the foul-smelling pit of the temple.

Throughout her description of the love affair, the Sibyl clearly
juxtaposes love of man with love of God. She is not a full person until she has found her earthly lover:

For the first time I experienced love—the marvel of not being alone, of another person being in me. The marvel of embracing another and being myself embraced, and of feeling a profound, wild satisfaction in my powerful body which, without always knowing it, had always longed for this.

. . . .

This was human happiness, this was what it was to be a human being. I was as happy as such beings can be. I was just like one of them. (Si. 86; 86)

In no uncertain terms, she regards her lover as God's rival. When she learns of his death, she attributes it to "god's vengeance on human happiness and on his elect, who had betrayed him and had not been willing to live for him alone" (Si. 103-104; 104). She delights in discovering her pregnancy, believing the child to be the offspring of her human lover. She calls it a "triumph over death itself. Over the death of love and over death itself" (Si. 106; 106). She relishes the human life she feels in herself; she senses that its blood is hers, "the blood with which I had loved him, love's human blood of which the gods know nothing." Still unaware of the divine paternity of the child, or at least that possibility, she concludes, "So it was. So our struggle with god had ended" (Si. 124; 125).

Whether it is only a psychological manifestation in the guilty mind of the Sibyl or a supernatural occurrence, the character of her experience with God after she has "sinned" with her lover gives every evidence that the conflict between her love of man and God is real enough. The Sibyl cannot interpret her experience as anything but a struggle between the demands of seeking God and the needs of being human. Returned from her lover to the temple, she is taken up by God in such a way as to make evident the duality in His nature, that awesome combination of good and evil that characterizes the fullness of divinity: "never [, she says,] have I known such anguish, never had he treated me so savagely, with such utter fury; but never had he brought me to such a pitch of frenzied ecstasy" (Si. 96-97; 97).

The act itself combines the attributes of delight and despair. The frenzied sexuality has all the passion of a human relationship with something that goes beyond the merely human. Foulness and the sublime join in intimacy as the Sibyl describes being "violated by god." He comes to her "in the shape of the

black goat," which "threw itself upon me and assuaged itself
and me in a love act in which pain, evil and voluptuousness
were mingled in a way that revolted me." Using sexual metaphor to express the dualities of man's experience, whether human or divine, Lagerkvist notes the Sibyl's "delight" during the
act itself and the "revulsion and self-disgust" that follow the
climax (Si. 102; 102).[12]

Sex, indeed, has been used metaphorically throughout the
Sibyl's story to represent the unsuccessful quest for the classical
ideal of balance. In her zeal for God, the Sibyl has been excessive.
Human nature requires mortal as well as divine satisfaction.
When she turns to human love, the Sibyl again fails to respond
in proportion. She cannot control her passion for her lover even
when she realizes that her frenzied responses threaten to cool
his ardor and drive him away. Her passion for him proves as
unbalanced and as unnatural as her zealous relationship to God.

VI *The Mysterious Son*

In the Sibyl's story, Lagerkvist has presented the voice of
classical antiquity raised to suggest one kind of quest for the
meaning of existence. In itself that quest must end in failure
just as any other such quest does. Together all men's quests
lead, according to Lagerkvist, to the conclusion that the meaning of life is in living itself. Spiritual journeys, by their very
nature, must be made by the self; no orthodoxy that represents
an abstract, though particular, point of view can be satisfactory.
Out of the combined experiences of Christianity and paganism,
as they put together the individual lives of people, the significance of the human experience—although not likely to be recognized by any one person—comes forth.

To bring together the voices of Christianity and pagan antiquity and to demonstrate the relatedness of their quests, Lagerkvist uses the character of the Sibyl's son. Walter Gustafson has
demonstrated Lagerkvist's use of the Bible in the story of the
Sibyl's son to mark the parallels between the curious man-child
and Christ. Gustafson cites the manner of birth, the simplicity
and happiness surrounding both the Christ child and the Sibyl's
child. To match the shepherds and angel hosts around Mary are
the concerned wild goats that eat the Sibyl's afterbirth. The

Ascension of Christ, Gustafson notes, resembles the mysterious disappearance of the Sibyl's son.[13]

Actually, Lagerkvist accentuates the parallel throughout the Sibyl's narrative. When the Wandering Jew describes Christ, the Sibyl is more curious about the woman who bore God's Son. She wants to know whether Mary was happy about it, how "god treated her" and she concludes, "How happy she must have been" because she was "chosen for it" (Si. 33; 30-31). Describing her own experiences, the Sibyl leaves no doubt about her identification with Mary. Of her selection as pythia, she uses words recalling the language she chose for her questions about Mary: "Chosen to be his instrument, to speak his words—words inspired by him—I to be filled with his spirit . . ." (Si. 41; 39). The mystery about the parentage of the Sibyl's son parallels the ambiguous legend of Christ's birth—Joseph and the Sibyl's lover serving as God's surrogates. In the conditions surrounding the birth of the Sibyl's child, it would be impossible not to recall the story of Christ in the manger. Finally, at the disappearance of her son on the mountain top, the Sibyl uses language that accords with the description of Christ's Ascension: "he has thrown off the garments in which he hid, his earthly husk, and become again what he really was. The father has fetched him home . . ." (Si. 142; 144).

To leave no doubt of the identification of the Sibyl's son with Christ, Lagerkvist allows the Wandering Jew to bind the two stories, although noting the differences between them:

He reflected that the son of god who was the source of his own appalling fate . . . was said to have ascended into heaven from a mountain, too, and was received by the father-god in a cloud. . . . But he had first been crucified, which according to them made him extraordinary and his life full of every sort of meaning and significance, for every age. Whereas this son of god seemed to have been born merely to sit at the dim entrance of a ruinous goat hut and look out over the world and the breed of men and their many inventions, and his own magnificent temple, and laugh at it all. (Si. 144; 146)

If, as Swanson argues, the Sibyl's son differs from Christ in Lagerkvist's treatment of them, "because Christ knows evil as well as love," while the Sibyl's son, like Dostoevski's Prince

Myshkin, seems a "conventional idea of goodness," one with "total inexperience in the world's evil,"[14] their significance proves identical. For Lagerkvist, both represent God's enigmatic character, the truth of which is impossible for man to know. Whether the observation belongs to the Sibyl or the Wandering Jew, whether it comes early or late in the novel, the view remains the same: like Christ, the Sibyl's son, remote from humanity, stands beyond man's comprehension. From the outset, the Wandering Jew remarks on the "enigmatic" smile, "neither a good nor a wicked smile" (Si. 31; 28), that characterizes the Sibyl's son. At the end of the novel, Ahasuerus identifies it with the image of god in the temple at Delphi:

an ancient image standing somewhat apart as if to make room for newer, finer images. It had the same smile, enigmatic and remote, at once meaningless and inscrutable. A smile neither good nor evil, yet for that very reason frightening. (Si. 144-45; 146-47)

The Sibyl herself suggests that he "is a god sitting here beside me with his perpetual smile; sitting here looking down at his temple, his Delphi and the whole world of men—just smiling at it all" (Si. 138; 139).

VII *The Meaning of the Smile*

That smile is the eternal smile that Lagerkvist uses in his earlier work to express God's inaccessibility to mankind. The Sibyl's son is no more comprehensible to man than is Christ's message to mankind. Neither has much to do with the way men lead their lives, and yet what both represent is man's endless quest for absolute knowledge. The Sibyl expresses this directly when she speaks of her child as "this witless son, who is a mockery of man—of reason and of man . . ." (Si. 136; 138). It is difficult to find in these words justification for Linnér's conclusion that the smile "stands for reconciliation, peace, and acceptance of life."[15] Gustafson, calling the smile a symbol of "the mystery of life,"[16] seems closer to the truth, for Lagerkvist's use of the smile recalls John Keats's famous words to the urn, that taunting mystery that "dost tease us out of thought/ as doth eternity."[17]

Perhaps what Linnér intends by his comment is to note what

Miss Scobbie terms "a new note of resignation" in Lagerkvist's later work.[18] At any rate, the description seems inapt, for the old anguish continues in *The Sibyl* as in the trilogy that succeeds it. To be sure, the Sibyl's words to the Wandering Jew express Lagerkvist's theme of man's *need* to find the purpose of existence in the living of life itself, but the message bears nothing of the tone of either reconciliation, peace, or resignation. God, for the Sibyl, offers no "security and repose and rest," but rather "unrest, conflict, and uncertainty" (Si. 53; 52). Despite man's need for Him, "The divine is not human; it is something quite different. And it is not noble or sublime or spiritualized, as one likes to believe. It is alien and repellent and sometimes it is madness. It is malignant and dangerous and fatal" (Si. 135; 137). She repeats these words at the conclusion of the novel, and what she offers the Wandering Jew is no more comfort than the need to continue the quest:

He is not as we are and we can never understand him. He is incomprehensible, inscrutable. He is god.

And so far as I comprehend it he is both evil and good, both light and darkness, both meaningless and full of a meaning which we can never perceive, yet never cease to puzzle over. A riddle which is intended not to be solved but to exist. To exist for us always. To trouble us always. (Si. 147; 149)

Only the little temple servant, who finds God through his work, seems untroubled by questions about existence, but he represents, like Lagerkvist's grandfather in *Aftonland* who could find security in the one star shining above his home, a lost faith beyond the reach of modern man.

VIII   *The Existential View*

Lagerkvist's resolution is no resolution. It is the existential response to anguish and uncertainty that insists on a continued pursuit of existence in the face of absurdity. Resignation, reconciliation, and peace stand outside the vocabulary of such a philosophy. The Sibyl, as Lagerkvist's spokesman, can offer no absolute responses. Although the old blind beggar describes her as "One who can answer all that man can ask" (Si. 13; 9), her answers are clearly not much in terms of the metaphysical problems that most trouble men. As spokesman, the Sibyl can hardly be expected to give ultimate answers. She cannot even speak with certainty about why the crowd did not kill her as she walked forth from the sanctity of the temple after her sin had been discovered.

The Sibyl is one more point in Lagerkvist's endless existentialist dialogue of the soul. Lagerkvist has been quoted as saying, "I constantly conduct a dialogue with myself . . . one book answers the other."[19] And so it does, but no one answer can be sufficient. If all the individual parts are put together, the total would, of course, be the meaning of the human experience and of existence. But no part can be finally instructive in itself. Intended to convey to the Wandering Jew some understanding of his own Christian experience, the Sibyl's tale *must* seem too particularized to him. The lesson is her segment of truth. Even after she has explained its significance, he says "The things that bring you comfort and meaning hold nothing for me" (Si. 149; 151). His journey will continue, even as the dialogue does in the next three novels, but the resolution must ultimately prove no resolution—vague and unsatisfying, it is man's destiny to struggle after an absolute knowledge that is beyond him. All that he can finally know is the need to try to live the life that is his.

CHAPTER 5

Tobias's Pilgrimage: Lagerkvist's Trilogy

I Relation to the Pentalogy

WITHIN the Crucifixion pentalogy, Lagerkvist has created a trilogy, whose unity he has emphasized by reprinting the novels under the collective title of *Pilgrimen* (*The Pilgrim*, 1966). To be sure, close resemblances in content and form tie the trilogy to the earlier novels, since Lagerkvist obviously continues the dialogue of the soul that began in *Barabbas* and continues in *The Sibyl*. Like its predecessors, the trilogy relates the endless struggle of man for absolute answers in a universe in which the questions themselves seem the only reality. Like them, too, the triumvirate rejects the "conventional concepts of God and Christ and . . . the validity of the Christian Church."[1] Again as in the earlier novels—indeed as in all of Lagerkvist's major work—he argues, as he had in his essay *The Clenched Fist*, "one can be a believer without faith" or "One must follow a private road, an uncharted way. The mystery of the divine cannot be structured and mapped out for us. God, Christ, and the church—in their conventional forms—play no significant or meaningful part in our spiritual quests."[2]

Even in technique and form, the trilogy resembles *Barabbas* and *The Sibyl*. Two forces or two kinds of experience create the structure of the novels: in *Barabbas*, the skeptic hero and the Christians; in *The Sibyl*, the Delphic priestess and the Wandering Jew; in the trilogy, Tobias and his counterparts, whether they be Ahasuerus, Diana, or Giovanni. Lagerkvist's narrative method throughout masks the complexity of his subject matter behind simplicity of diction and sentence structure. For all the airs of artlessness, his style is calculated to create an ambiguity consistent with his "views of reality [that] have now become almost infinite."[3] In all five novels, Lagerkvist renders the dualities of existence through a style that repeatedly questions reality—appearance is reduced to "as if" in such a way as to cast doubt

99

on the actuality of what is occurring and to reflect "the mystery
of life."[4] The very shifting of point of view in these novels conveys the author's sense of the endless possibilities and uncertainties in human existence and the futility of finding absolute
answers where the only meaningful statement can be that all
man can know is that for him the only reality is of the moment
and that life itself "is the one thing conceivable among all that is
inconceivable."[5]

Yet for all these likenesses between the trilogy and the other
two novels, a clear line separates them.[6] The trilogy centers upon
the character of Tobias. It takes him, as an interlocking character between parts, from his meeting with Ahasuerus, through
his pilgrimage to the Holy Land, to his death in a land whose
description is so vague, tentative, and unreal as to suggest that
it exists solely within man's mind: a vision that allows him to
set a goal toward which the struggles of existence are directed
so as to give some semblance of meaning to life. Tobias acts like
Everyman; his experiences become man's relentless quest for
answers to the mysteries of existence. His quest for peace and
certainty involves him in the dualities of good and evil, order
and chaos, faith and reason, life and death. The three stages
of his adventures stand as three steps in the soul's pilgrimage,
moving from despair and doubt to a peacefulness that comes not
from certainty, but from recognition that uncertainty is the
state of human existence and that life's meaning is in the living
of life itself.

II Ahasverus död

What ties the trilogy formally to the two previous novels is
simply the character of Ahasuerus, the Wandering Jew of *The
Sibyl* with whom *Ahasverus död* (*The Death of Ahasuerus*, 1960)
begins. The introduction to Tobias comes through the eyes of
Ahasuerus as he enters an inn filled with pilgrims awaiting a
boat for the Holy Land. Yet despite this initial focus and the
title, the novel clearly belongs to Tobias. Ahasuerus serves as
an observer and commentator. The action concerns Tobias, and
even Ahasuerus's death proves significant ultimately not for
Ahasuerus's story, but for the trilogy that develops through Tobias's quest for the Holy Land.

III   *Complexities in the Plot*

The plot of *The Death of Ahasuerus* seems simple enough until reliability of information, motivation of characters, and symbolic functions of details come into question. Ahasuerus, entering the inn, chooses to sit with the forbidding figure of Tobias. When Diana joins them, she initiates the story of Tobias and their relationship. She describes how Tobias long ago had come upon her in the forest, raped her, taught her to drink, and brought her to low company. After pleading with Tobias not to be angry with her, she chides him with having deserted her. She abuses him for having taken her from her natural freedom in the woods and recalls how he had given her the strange name she detests.

It all seems honest and simple enough, but when Diana leaves the table, Tobias recounts and elaborates on the story. Her view appears only relatively true. When he had come upon her, her mocking smile had led him to rape this beauty adorned only in a deer skin. According to Tobias, she had enjoyed it and their life together, and when he returned to his army unit, she willingly followed him. Tobias then describes her life as a camp follower, sleeping with others as well as him. Although repelled by her physical change, Tobias says, he feels bound to her for what she once was. When the war ended and he joined a bandit gang, she followed him. Finally, Tobias says, he could tolerate neither his fellows nor Diana and longed for something else.

Differences between Tobias's and Diana's views of their experience pose one kind of difficulty in evaluating the novel. When Tobias continues his narrative in response to Ahasuerus's question about the reason for his pilgrimage, the difficulty is of another order. Tobias indicates an inability to understand either himself or the story he presents. Separated from his fellow bandits, he wandered to an oddly cultivated but deserted place where he discovered a dead woman with a dog beside her. Intrigued by the stigmata that she bore, he passed the night in vigil at her bedside and, for some inexplicable reason, promised to make a pilgrimage. He buried her, and the dog, the same ugly animal that still accompanies him, went along with him on his journey. Tobias's uncertainty leads to a discussion with Ahasuerus about Christ's power, and the latter argues that Christ had used the dead woman to force Tobias to go on a

pilgrimage. All that is clear from the episode is that both Tobias
and Ahasuerus are determined to remain independent of God.

The simple narrative continues with the following day, but
even his use of setting hints at Lagerkvist's concerns beyond the
superficialities of plot. In contrast to the terrifying lightning
storm that accompanied Ahasuerus's arrival the previous night,
the day dawns bright. The pilgrims in their departure activities
are seen by Ahasuerus, the outsider, as a motley group, remi-
niscent of the gathering Lagerkvist described in *The Eternal
Smile*. He underscores the special qualities of the day by comparisons with the days of Creation and Resurrection. But from
all this, Tobias is missing; he has decided not to join them.
When Ahasuerus questions him about it, the enraged Tobias
kicks the dog to death. Immediately repentant, he returns
morosely to the inn, gathers his belongings, and sets forth.

Ahasuerus, feeling guilty, either because of the dog's death or
because he has turned Tobias from the pilgrimage, goes with
him. When Diana appears, Tobias rejects her, but relents when
she rebukes his unchristian conduct. They seek a pilgrim's shelter, but it is Diana, now returned to her element, who finds it.
She delights in their being snowed in because she opposes his
pilgrimage. But eventually they come forth, leave the wilds, and
enter the countryside. During their investigation of an over-
turned carriage and the body of a wealthy dead man, Tobias
becomes the target for a mysterious arrow, but Diana inter-
cepts it and sacrifices her life.[7] Her final request is that Tobias
call her by the name she despised. He does, and with her death,
she is restored to purity. They bury her beneath an evergreen
oak, which is symbolically Diana's tree.

Much in these events raises questions beyond the simple answers of the narrative, and indeed appearance gives no sure
evidence of reality. Whether Tobias is responsible for her death
or whether, as Ahasuerus says, the arrow was meant for her to
save him, nothing in the story allows for a definite conclusion.
Even the source of the arrow remains mysterious, although
plausibly it had been shot by one of the bandits who had at-
tacked the dead man. Only the effect on Tobias and Ahasuerus
is clear: one suffers guilt, even about the illegal acquisition of
his money, and despairs of reaching the Holy Land; the other
longs for death.

When they finally arrive at the pilgrims' harbor, the ships have departed, and Tobias appears to be without prospect of making his pilgrimage. He disappears, but Ahasuerus finds him bargaining with some unsavory characters for passage to the Holy Land. Although Tobias gives them all his money, Ahasuerus has little hope for his success. The remainder of the narrative is devoted to Ahasuerus's monologue—a moving lyrical passage—assessing the meaning of his experience and the nature of divinity. Then he dies in light, the familiar light of earth, a manner of death with larger significance in the trilogy as a whole.

IV Point of View in The Death of Ahasuerus

Lagerkvist's deliberate ambiguity, apparent even in a plot summary, becomes compounded and more complex through an examination of his techniques with point of view, characterization, and symbolism. His treatment of point of view allows Lagerkvist to present man's uncertainties about the world in which he lives, his alien condition in an environment he does not control, and therefore his impossible attempts to gain absolute knowledge. It follows naturally enough that Lagerkvist's characterization offers neither motivation for his characters' conduct nor their self-awareness of the reasons for their actions. Added to these complexities is Lagerkvist's symbolic use of characters to convey a sense of man's impossible quest for ultimate knowledge through the myths of Christianity and pagan antiquity.

Point of view immediately creates a perplexing ambiguity. In the very opening pages, whether information comes from an omniscient author or through the eyes of one of his characters, it is tenuous or uncertain. Ahasuerus entering the inn is "a man who *seemed* chased by lightning, for when he flung open the door the whole sky blazed up behind him; rain and wind hurled themselves at him..." (Ad. 5; 5).[8] Was he indeed being "chased by lightning"? Lagerkvist's very real use of natural detail only complicates the ambiguity of his statement. When, shortly after, one of the people in the inn looks up "at the stranger who seemed pursued by lightning" (Ad. 6; 6), is the repetition of the phrase from the narrator's or character's point of view? The author's point that "No one else took any notice of him" would appear to suggest that the repetition represents a charac-

ter's point of view. Seemingly from the omniscient perspective,
Lagerkvist describes Ahasuerus, who "seemed to be wondering
where he was." Is the statement verified by entering the character's mind or is it simply reinforced by the narrator in the following phrase: "What *was* this place?" Certainly matters do not
become clarified when the perspective is clearly that of a character. It is evident that Ahasuerus, looking at the pilgrims kneel-
ing in the inn, reflects, "They looked as if they were praying . . ." (Ad. 5; 6). But not only does Lagerkvist convey Ahasuerus's uncertainty here, he is himself commenting satirically upon
the Christianity of this assembled group of dubious Christians.
When he later characterizes the assemblage in their varied
hypocrisies, this earlier phrase takes on an ironic intention not
immediately present in Ahasuerus's doubts.

Ambiguity in point of view, even as in *Barabbas* and *The
Sibyl,* runs relentlessly through the novel.[9] Whether the words
are describing Diana as "evidently drunk" or Tobias who
"seemed not to care about [the movement of the dog at his
feet], or perhaps never noticed that it had moved" (Ad. 7; 7-8),
they never speak with assuredness of the actions they are presenting. Lagerkvist's deliberate refusal to enter the minds of
Tobias and Diana, his decision to stand either outside the
action or alongside Ahasuerus who is watching it, these lead to
non-judgmental comments. When Tobias withdraws into silence,
his motives can be described only in terms of "it rather seemed"
or "He may have felt . . ." (Ad. 63; 76). His anger with Diana,
seen from outside, comes in terms of its effect on her: "He
seemed in such a passion that she was amazed, bewildered";
and his physical appearance at that point is perceived by either
the narrator or Ahasuerus in terms of his eyes which "looked as
if they might easily turn savage . . ." (Ad. 14; 16).

Perhaps the primary reason for this uncertainty in presenting
information derives from Lagerkvist's use of Ahasuerus as his
focus. Ahasuerus himself, a seeker torn by doubts and inde-
cision, cannot render positive decisions. Looking at the pilgrims, he is puzzled by their holy expression, for, after all, it is
alien to his own personality. His own questions about Christianity, questions that have led to his predicament, prevent his offering an objective view of the pilgrims' actions and their homage to Christ. Mournfully, he watches them bear the cross

"through that mighty landscape as if the whole earth belonged
to it..." (Ad. 56; 68). As he reflects on the pilgrimage, their
motives are ignored for the sake of his own doubts:

So many had been crucified on that Golgotha, that little hill to
which all now made pilgrimage. Yes, on the same cross as he—the
cross they called his, and worshipped as the holiest thing in the
world; on this many others had been tortured, for it was used as long
as it was serviceable. Then there were all the other crosses before
and after his, and all who suffered on them. (Ad. 56; 68-69)

In a world seen either through Ahasuerus's eyes or from a
vantage point close to him, nothing is certain and appearances
are most deceiving. The innocent-looking girl who earns her
money by giving her body to men presents a single example of
deception, and who knows what she really is? After all, as
either the narrator or Ahasuerus declares, "Many things ... de-
pend on the distance from which one beholds them...." If one
could get close enough to see, "in her eyes there may have been
a glow which was not to be discerned at such a distance" (Ad.
54; 66).

Yet one never gets close enough to see, for that is exactly
Lagerkvist's point. Man never knows what truth is in this world,
if by *truth* is meant something absolute. Lagerkvist's characters never can be certain of their own motives, let alone what
is going on around them. Characterization, like point of view,
leads only to ambiguity. In the summary of plot, it was clear
from Tobias's and Diana's covering the same ground from different perspectives that truth is anything but absolute. When
details of character are examined closely, the conclusion is
reinforced.

V *The Characters of Tobias and Diana*

Tobias, who is the central character of the trilogy, informs
the reader that nothing he says or does is likely to be unambigu-
ous, for "how little a person knows of himself..." (Ad. 33; 38).
His story about the mystical experience that has somehow driven
him to his pilgrimage is filled with his uncertainties about what
has happened. The details are vague, contradictory, or even
hallucinatory:

All that happened—somewhere about midnight, I should think—
was that a horse came along the road; it must have been a horse.
That's what it sounded like. And it was lame. It couldn't put its
weight on one leg; one could hear that plainly—more and more
plainly as it approached. When the road ended it turned up the
path to the dead woman's home, sniffed at it—at the end wall,
the window; it went all around the house, and at last sniffed for
a long time at the door. It was as if the animal had been in the
habit of coming here and doing this. It may have known that one
person was left here. . . . (Ad. 35-36; 41)

Even Tobias's reason for going on the pilgrimage must remain
obscure for so it is to him, "oh, it's complicated, and I don't
really understand it. . ." (Ad. 35; 40). Did he willingly bind
himself to the woman's fate or did she somehow bind him to
herself? Too proud to kneel before anyone, he has indeed knelt
before the dead woman, and if she was in fact God's agent, he
has knelt before God, but surely not willingly. What kind of
pilgrim is he, after all? Diana contrasts him with the other
rogues, and says that they, at least, are "honest," while he is
"a rogue only, [and they are] not a mixture of rogue and half-
saved fraud like you" (Ad. 44; 51). If Diana is not to be accepted as judge, there is other evidence. When Tobias is absent
from the company of pilgrims, "No one asked after him or thought
of awaiting him, for no one knew that he was a pilgrim, and he
was not really of their company" (Ad. 55; 67). When he arrives
after the pilgrims have departed, in contrast to him they are
described as "the real, the true pilgrims [who] had sailed" (Ad.
81; 100). He himself, having gotten the money for his journey
dishonestly, compares himself to the girl who sells her body to
make the pilgrimage and asks, "Am I a real pilgrim? Am I?"
(Ad. 78; 97).

No more than Lagerkvist's other complex seekers can Tobias
rest with uncertainties, even though that may be the only kind
of truth. He is reluctant to go on a pilgrimage that would indicate his subservience even to the Christ he seeks, and yet when
he believes that the journey is impossible, he regards the prospect
as the loss of all hope, and it fills him with despair. The goal
itself, as for all Lagerkvist's seekers, seems less important than
the quest:

What he had lost, what he was not to attain, what he had not been chosen to experience, stood forth to him as the only goal—the only thing worth living for—living and dying for. To lose it was to lose his soul and virtually to exist no longer, either here in time or in eternity; to lose all hope. (Ad. 81; 100-101)

There is determination in Tobias's complex character, a sense of commitment that he cannot explain even to himself, and Lagerkvist uses small details as well as larger purpose to display this aspect of his character. Tobias, for example, shows his determination, regardless of whether he comprehends it, by his tie to the dead woman and to her dog—even as earlier he had to Diana.

No less than Tobias, Diana as a character presents a series of contradictions and ambiguities. Lagerkvist uses Tobias's comments on her to set up a series of paradoxes never resolved in terms of human characterization. Tobias confesses, "I no longer understood her. But that I'd never done, nor had anyone else" (Ad. 23; 27). Impressed by her natural beauty and purity, he had named her Diana, and when he ceases to call her that, presumably it is because she has lost her chastity. Nevertheless, as Tobias notes, she somehow remains intact; giving herself to anyone, she gives herself to none. "She was like a virgin whom no one could utterly possess" (Ad. 20; 24); "no one can gain any real power over her" (Ad. 23; 26). Though Diana in her degradation as camp follower "became like the rest . . . she could never be altogether like them" (Ad. 25; 28-29). She sleeps with other men, but despises them, her object evidently "to possess" them. Her personal relationship to Tobias suggests something of her allegorical function; for this queen of nature, uprooted from her forest, Tobias becomes a necessary part of life: "without someone who knew of her past—knew who she really was" (Ad. 26; 30), she cannot endure.

Diana's name, description, relationship to Tobias, and role in the narrative action pose endless ambiguities, and if she is to be understood at all, it is in her function as a symbolic character.[10] The same proves true of Ahasuerus. Identifying the character with the Wandering Jew of biblical legend, Lagerkvist casts him in a symbolic role. Lagerkvist's description of him places him outside the bounds of ordinary human nature. "How queer you look," Diana says to him; "you look as if you died long ago" (Ad. 44; 51). Whereas Diana's eyes are symbolically "earthly as a hunter's" Ahasuerus's are "ancient, ancient eyes" and "alien to her" (Ad. 68: 82). As in *The Sibyl*, Lagerkvist uses the pair of characters to represent two distinct traditions, and Ahasuerus, even as Diana, is not to be understood in terms of human characterization. For Lagerkvist throughout the novel, Ahasuerus is "the stranger" and an instrument for presenting the theme.

VI   *Christian and Pagan Allegory*

The theme of *The Death of Ahasuerus*, the first part of a trilogy devoted to man's quest for ultimate knowledge in an unresponsive universe, is the ambiguity in human existence. The ambiguities in point of view and characterization deliberately underscore man's condition in the universe. The novel is built upon the conflicts between Christianity and paganism, between belief and uncertainty, and between quest and frustration.

Lagerkvist juxtaposes Christianity and paganism in a manner that emphasizes the inadequacies in both and yet demonstrates man's need to strive toward some holy goal. In Ahasuerus, he presents the failure of Christianity, in Diana the flawed paganism of antiquity. Tobias stands between the two, satisfied by neither since neither can satisfy, and yet their very existence somehow drives him to pursue the vague ideal of a holy land.[11] Tobias, acutely aware of the mysteries of existence, speaks of them to Ahasuerus:

if you think that time is over now—I mean the time when one could experience unbelievable things, incomprehensible, quite inconceivable things, things that the human mind could not grasp—then you're wrong. Really wrong. (Ad. 22; 25-26)

Puzzled by men's concern for "what they're to live on" rather than "what is one to live for" (Ad. 28; 32), Tobias himself has no answers. But where is he to turn for answers? Ahasuerus, after all, is the classic example of the skeptic who has rejected Christ. Diana, in her intuitive response to the world around her, may recognize that "Everyone must live," but she adds, "though why it should be necessary who knows?" On the Holy Land itself, she says, "I suppose one must call it something" (Ad. 9;

10). From the two, Tobias will gain no ultimate knowledge; instead he must make his own pilgrimage of the soul, which ironically enough will lead to the conclusion that there is no absolute answer and that whatever meaning life has is in the living of life itself.

Exploring his theme of ambiguity in man's experience, Lagerkvist constructs a thesis and antithesis out of which he himself draws no synthesis. The technique indicates his long-standing commitment to literary cubism. Diana, representing one part of Lagerkvist's dialectic, embodies a paganism that provides no answer except to insist upon the durability of nature. Raped by Tobias, she cannot be conquered. At the point of death, she is restored to her original purity, and the tree beneath which she is buried, "Diana's tree," has an "immemorial greenery [which] distinguished it from everything else up here—from all that surrounded it" (Ad. 75; 93-94). Within the Christian world of Tobias and Ahasuerus, she remains essentially unchanged. Christianity may use her, as indeed it did, and she may die so that Tobias may go on, but she shares none of the Christians' purpose. She opposes Tobias's pilgrimage, and even in her dying words, the pilgrimage has nothing to do with her: "I hope you reach the land you long for" (Ad. 74; 89). Her life in nature has been brought to an end by Tobias's—Christianity's —intrusion into the sanctity of nature's domain. Her existence presents one kind of experience, but can never provide answers in itself to the mysteries of life.

No more, though, can Tobias find satisfaction in the antithesis of Christianity. The other pilgrims are a mixed lot, but they offer the varied contradictions and weaknesses in the established Christian faith. Their practices suggest the failures of the church. Gathered for their holy journey, the rich and poor live separate lives, eat apart from each other, travel according to their means. Servants accompany their masters out of necessity rather than faith. Wherever pilgrims gather, there is a coming together of "all kinds of riff-raff" (Ad. 45; 52). What kind of comment on pilgrims and pilgrimages is it that a young girl must sell her body to men to satisfy her spiritual need? And yet Diana, puzzled as she is by this girl's ability to "hold her body of no account" in relation to her soul (Ad. 11; 13), can believe in the girl's innocence. After all, Diana has yielded her own body without yielding herself. In both what is demonstrated is the individual's own need to strive for a goal, to live one's life, regardless of the dictates of others and their codified religious demands. Tobias, in the end, will find the need to make his own journey.

In the Christian material of the allegory, Elizabeth, housekeeper and manager of the inn, is a key figure. She stands as a kind of Virgin Mother amidst the realities of the world. Weary with all that she has witnessed, she has come to appear as a divine confessor to those around her. Diana asks her forgiveness, and she responds, "I shall have to, I suppose." And yet, when Diana says, "Yes, you forgive everything," Elizabeth admits her weakness and limitations: "Oh no, I don't. Don't run away with that idea. Though most people do. It's just that I leave judgment to someone else. He may be stricter than I am, but then he knows much more. I don't know enough to judge" (Ad. 47; 54-55).

For Tobias, this figure of mercy, unknowing and incapable of judgment, can provide no satisfaction. Lagerkvist has placed limits upon her. In his characteristic use of physical deformity to suggest aspects of character, he has provided her with a limp. When she finishes talking to Diana, Elizabeth is described as returning "back into the darkness as she had come" (Ad. 48; 56). Watching the pilgrims depart, she appears as no divine figure, but rather a pathetic mortal who has watched it all before and for whom the Holy Land is remote, an "inconceivably far country, of which she had heard so much but would never see" (Ad. 55; 67). Her look—the point of view is that of Ahasuerus—is "grey" and the observer can only guess at her emotions, indeed only guess if she had ever made the pilgrimage herself. Despite her ability to elicit words from others in the hope that she will comfort them, Elizabeth does not have that effect on Tobias, "Not even she could get him to say anything..." (Ad. 62; 75).

VII *The Importance of Ahasuerus*

Within the Christian portion of Lagerkvist's allegory, no character, of course, is more important than Ahasuerus. Yet it is clear that because of his philosophy, rooted in reason and bound by self-love, he can provide little direction for Tobias. In fact, as he says in the final monologue or apostrophe,[12] Ahasuerus has learned from Tobias, learned that there is "Something so important that it were better to lose one's life rather than one's faith in that thing" (Ad. 89; 114). It is not sufficient to raise him beyond the earthly limits to which he has been committed, but it is enough to allow him to die, to die in "tranquility" removed from the storms that had surrounded him, but still in "the light so familiar to earth" (Ad. 92-93; 118).

In some ways, Ahasuerus "articulates a great deal of Lagerkvist's theological thought."[13] Certainly, Ahasuerus reflects Lagerkvist's view of orthodox religion and his belief in the importance of one's personal goals:

Beyond the gods, beyond all that falsifies and coarsens the world of holiness, beyond all lies and distortion, all twisted divinities and all the abortions of human imagination, there must be something stupendous which is inaccessible to us. Which, by our failure to capture it, demonstrates how inaccessible it is. Beyond all the sacred clutter the holy thing itself must exist. That I believe, of that I am certain. (Ad. 89; 114)[14]

Lagerkvist clearly shares Ahasuerus's view that "god is what divides us from the divine" (Ad. 89; 115).

Yet for Lagerkvist, Ahasuerus has omitted the most important element of all. In the peculiar attraction that Ahasuerus feels for the lay brother who attends him at his death, Lagerkvist hints at the need that one has for the sense of human love, that something that transcends self.[15] When, finally, Tobias dies at the end of the trilogy, his death reflects the difference from Ahasuerus's—the light is not the familiar light of the world. Throughout his monologue, Ahasuerus indicates the increase in his understanding, but *not* in his feeling. He still does not *feel* what has been wrong in his failure to allow Christ to "lean your head against my house" (Ad. 85; 109).[16] Tobias, in *The Holy Land*, will discover the importance of love in the human experience. It will not resolve the dualities and ambiguities in existence, but it will allow man to live with them and to find life's meaning through his way of life.

VIII   Pilgrim på havet

So well-contained is each unit of Lagerkvist's trilogy that, after the conclusion of *The Death of Ahasuerus,* the continuation of Tobias's journey in *Pilgrim på havet* (*Pilgrim at Sea,* 1962) seems somewhat surprising. Ahasuerus had witnessed Tobias's deal with unsavory looking pirates, and it had appeared inconceivable that the negotiations could conclude in anything but Tobias's death. Nevertheless, *Pilgrim at Sea* begins with Tobias aboard the ship, resting with "A peace such as he had never known" (Ph. 5; 5),[17] despite the raging weather outside. Tobias's journey continues, and the purpose of the second part of the trilogy is to present him, through the experiences of Giovanni, with more evidence of the dualities in man's existence and with additional knowledge of man's need to strive toward an ultimate goal regardless of the seeming impossibility of ever reaching it.

In technique, *Pilgrim at Sea* fundamentally resembles *Barabbas, The Sibyl,* and *The Death of Ahasuerus.*[18] Its use of point of view to underscore the ambiguity of the theme continues the literary cubist practices in the earlier novels.[19] More particularly, its structure parallels that of *The Sibyl* and *The Death of Ahasuerus.* Just as the Wandering Jew's arrival permits the voice of the priestess to tell her story, Ahasuerus's confrontation with the former soldier Tobias allows the latter to relate his tragic romance with a pagan goddess and his mystical experience leading to his pilgrimage. Now, in *Pilgrim at Sea,* Tobias himself meets a defrocked priest who recounts his tale of personal tragedy, his fall from the state of innocence. In all three novels, the new character serves to instruct the other, but the meaning comes not from the speaker alone, but from the combined experiences of two lives that have been brought together by the accident of fate. To achieve this dialogue of the soul, Lagerkvist requires a fictional framework that makes natural the possibility of the inset, and that is the function of the plot.

IX   *Function of Plot in* Pilgrim at Sea

When Tobias awakes aboard the pirate vessel, Giovanni is at his bedside, asking him questions although he already seems to know the answers. Aware that Tobias is not like the pilgrims, whom he despises, Giovanni advises him not to worry about goals, not to concern himself with the Holy Land, but rather to reconcile himself to not knowing and uncertainty. Although the sea will not afford security, find peace in it, Giovanni advises him. Then, acting as guide to Tobias, Giovanni points out on deck the ship's crew and evaluates them—particularly the tyrannical captain and the brutal helmsman. From one of the crew, the rodent-like Giusto, Tobias learns about Giovanni himself— a defrocked priest, a blasphemer, but a good man.

Together with Giovanni, almost as though fated to be with him, Tobias shares the gruesome experiences of life on board a pirate vessel. Giovanni is apart from the rest even when engaged in the same activities. As they come alongside the pilgrim ship in a harbor, Giovanni berates the passengers and keeps their attention, while the pirate crew pillages the vessel. Yet Giovanni's activities are sincere and have little to do with his shipmates' purpose. He is more concerned with Tobias, goading him into joining the pilgrims, but obviously satisfied when he refuses. Giovanni and Tobias again stand apart from their shipmates when their vessel comes upon another in distress. As the pirates overwhelm their victims and Giusto is forced by his captain to execute the captain of the survivors, Tobias and Giovanni refuse to participate, and Tobias pleads unsuccessfully for mercy toward the victims. Already bound somehow to Giovanni, Tobias is finally indebted to him for saving his life when Giovanni disarms an assassin and throws the murder weapon into the all-encompassing sea.

As they stand alone on deck, it seems natural enough when Giovanni relates the tale of his life. The story begins with a childhood in a household obsessively dedicated to God and religion. Dominated by his widowed mother, Giovanni unquestioningly entered holy orders. Unfortunately, he heard his first confession from a married woman obsessed with thoughts of her "lover," and the young, inexperienced priest could only offer to join her in prayer in this and subsequent meetings. Drawn to her, he found no comfort or protection in religion and became as obsessed as she. Finally, he followed her home and in the darkness took advantage of her mistaking him for her "lover." When she discovered the truth, she resisted, but as he reached for her locket, it led to an ecstatic sexual experience. Their clandestine affair, abundant in physical attraction, of-

fered no other joys of love. She continually bemoaned her betrayal of her husband and "lover," while Giovanni became
involved in a pattern of lies to his superiors, colleagues, and
mother. After his mother discovered the truth, Giovanni was able
to see her in all the ugliness and harshness of her spirit. She
consigned him to the devil with the same fervor that she had
given him to God. Their venomous relationship culminated in
her persuading his unwilling superior to unmask him. Excom-
municated as a result, Giovanni was far more bitter about what
he regarded as his lover's betrayal of him and her distortion of
their relationship in her testimony. While she was confined by
her husband until later allowed to make a pilgrimage, Giovanni
was oppressed by his townsmen and forced to escape to the sea.

When he has finished his story, Giovanni reveals that he had
taken the lady's locket only to discover that it was empty. He
finally realized that her "lover" existed only in her imagination.
In answer to Tobias's question, Giovanni says that she had died
on her pilgrimage to the Holy Land, never having arrived there.
Tobias equates this with her failure to find her lover, calling it
"a dream [which] cannot survive reality." And yet, Tobias insists
"that it does nevertheless exist. That perfect love exists and the
Holy Land exists; it is just that we cannot reach it. That perhaps we are only on our way there—only pilgrims at sea" (Ph.
113-14; 116).

X   *Giovanni's Relationship to Tobias*

It is, then, Giovanni's relationship to Tobias that provides the
theme of the novel. Giovanni's character, experiences, and attitudes become the means of enlightening Tobias and allowing
him to proceed one step further on his journey of the soul.
Through Giovanni, Tobias learns once again of the inadequacies of orthodox Christianity. In Giovanni's response to his
experiences, Tobias can see the weaknesses in a negative philosophy even as he becomes aware of his own inclination to accept
that philosophy and to share the attitude of a man whom he
regards as a kindred soul.

For Giovanni to serve in this manner, Tobias must come to
see him whole, to recognize his strengths and weaknesses, to
understand their points of similarity and differences. Lagerkvist

presents Giovanni as a good man whose experience in the world
has driven him into refuge and whose knowledge of love has
been unfortunately limited. Not only is he named "after the
disciple [God] loved most" (Ph. 22, 56; 22, 58), but his goodness is underscored by Giusto's description of him and by his
own conduct. Giusto calls him as "godless a man [as] I've ever
met in all my life," "a blasphemer and lecher." Yet Giusto also
points to his kindness, and even while insisting, "He's a terrible
sinner, no question of that," concludes, "but a *good* man ..."
(Ph. 20-21, 22; 21-22). Giovanni's blasphemous expressions and
"coarse laugh ... sounded strangely false, coming from him"
(Ph. 31; 32). Even as Tobias listens to Giovanni taunting the
pilgrims, and his "embittered, agitated" conduct seems to belie
"those memorable words to him, below, in the bowels of the
ship," Tobias "perceived his true face" under "the mockery
and wrath." For Tobias, "That face was dear.... He would
not be parted from it" (Ph. 30; 31).

Tobias quickly recognizes the significance of Giovanni for
him, even as Giovanni immediately perceives that Tobias is
unlike the "real pilgrims" and that "a cross wouldn't suit hands
like [Tobias's]" (Ph. 9, 11; 10-11). Even before Tobias knows
Giovanni's name, he surmises and is drawn to his philosophy:
"To choose unknowing and uncertainty.... To choose oneself
as one is. To dare to be what one is, without self-reproach" (Ph.
15-16; 16). Tobias recognizes that Giovanni has "talked to him
so strangely about things which perhaps Tobias, too, had borne
in his heart, but which he had never thought that a man might
dare to say, or even think. [Giovanni was] the man who had
uttered words that might come to mean much to him—liberate
him perhaps, and make him free" (Ph. 19-20; 20). By the time
he questions Giusto about Giovanni, Tobias regards the latter
as "the big man who had come to him down there in the half-
dark and opened up a new world, as it were, a new life for
him ..." (Ph. 22; 23). Then, when Giovanni has saved Tobias's
life, they seem almost one: "Tobias and Giovanni stood side
by side in the darkness, which was no true darkness, for the sky
was full of stars" (Ph. 53; 54).

Tobias and Giovanni *are* alike. Giovanni has pointed a possible way for Tobias. And yet there are major differences between
them, distinctions evident in their experiences and what they

finally will settle for. Together they will find their way to the
Holy Land, but what they discover there and their manner of
death will clearly distinguish between them and their philos-
ophies.

XI   *The Christian Religion*

On one point, however, they are identical: their belief that
orthodox Christianity offers no hope for salvation and neither
Christian ritual nor practice affords the way to the Holy Land.
In Giovanni's account of his life, Tobias can find nothing to
alter his own views of the orthodox faith, views derived from
his earlier encounter with Ahasuerus and his own experiences.

Giovanni's story condemns the hypocrisy and unnatural demands of orthodox Christian faith. While presenting a sense of
"security and complete certainty," the religious household of his
childhood was "stifling, narrow ... in every room an emaciated
man hung dying for our sake ..." (Ph. 57-58; 59). His mother's
conduct provides the link between God and Satan, good and
evil that Christians pretend are distinct entities. Once she has
discovered that her plans to dedicate her son to God have been
thwarted, she reveals "how violent a nature was hidden beneath
her peaceable exterior" (Ph. 102; 104), and she consigns him
"to the devil with the same ardent zeal as that with which she
had once presented me to god: to his embrace as once to god's"
(Ph. 99; 100).

Giovanni's actions lift the mask of respectability from others
and disclose the ugliness beneath. Recognizing the vapidity of
his own religion, he discovers the emptiness of Christian ritual.
It is a faith that makes natural human passion a sin. The softness
and warmth of human flesh become symbols of corruption, and
prayers can do little to quell normal emotions. For all its "spirit
of sanctity," the church fails to make the divine less complex
or "enigmatic"; its "mysterious power" is shrouded in "dimness"
(Ph. 59; 61). Its inefficacy can be seen in "a city overflowing
with churches and priests and believers and worshippers," yet
virtually barren of "good people" (Ph. 103; 105). What power
has faith over townspeople who offer no Christian charity to
Giovanni after the discovery of his conduct? What meaning has
belief for pilgrims deterred from their journey by angry seas?

For Giovanni, prostitutes who "don't pretend to be anything but what they are" deserve more respect than pious Christian women dishonest in their lovemaking (Ph. 110; 112).

XII *Love and Humanity*

Tobias surely has no disagreement with Giovanni's views on Christian orthodoxy. However, Giovanni's experiences have driven him away from the society of men to seek the peace, if not the security, of the sea. Although that may tempt Tobias, particularly as he finds ease in his situation, it cannot finally satisfy him. Tobias is *not* Giovanni, whatever their similarities. Tobias has known love, while Giovanni, although unlike Barabbas and Ahasuerus who were without love "for another person," has only experienced "being-in-love" in a way that "was more tentative than actual."[20] Even for himself, Giovanni recognizes that what was for him a "dizzying peak of love was past," leading to "passion self-nourished, fed by no new fuel" (Ph. 93; 94).

Even with Tobias, Giovanni's relationship and feelings are ambiguous. He struggles to protect Tobias from the captain and his cohorts, but the struggle seems less human than it does an allegorical battle between the fallen man of God and Satan and his disciples. The captain, with his "chill, reptilian eyes," "unnaturally cold" (Ph. 48, 51; 49, 52), stands apart from those he has satanically driven to evil. He holds some supernatural power over those who are physically stronger, a "singular power to inspire fear" (Ph. 49; 50). When Giovanni has rescued Tobias from the captain's disciple, Tobias himself places the action in an allegorical framework by describing Giovanni as "the elderly man of god [who] had proved the stronger of the two." Even the weapon becomes an allegorical figure of Christian symbolism when it is cast into the "holy sea," "bloodstained, but in the depths it would be cleansed. As everything must be at last" (Ph. 54, 52; 54, 53). Lagerkvist denies any possibility of seeing Giovanni's act as one wrought by feeling of one human being for another. Even Giovanni cannot attribute such purpose to his conduct which is deliberately kept ambiguous: "What made him do that? Had he acted deliberately or on impulse?" (Ph. 52; 53).

Tobias, with the propensity for strong human attachments

described in *The Death of Ahasuerus*, will never be able to accept Giovanni's acquiescence to the sea, his yielding pursuit of all goals. For a while Tobias may find solace, "peace" (Ph. 6; 6), in the sea. It may even be, as for Giovanni, "holy," but he will not be able to accept Giovanni's: "[it is] the only thing I do feel is holy." Giovanni, critical of "restless creatures" who believe "the goal is the meaning and purpose of their life," finds satisfaction in withdrawal:

Until one has learnt to be carried along by the sea, to surrender to it utterly, and cease fretting about right and wrong, sin and guilt, truth and falsehood, good and evil—about salvation and grace and eternal damnation—about devil and god and their stupid disputes.[21]

What Giovanni wants is to "surrender utterly to the unknown—to uncertainty as the only certainty, the only really dependable thing. . . ." (Ph. 14; 14). For Tobias, there is much truth and appeal in this. He comes finally in the trilogy to recognize that the meaning of life is in living, but in order for living to be meaningful, one must not surrender, not acquiesce. Unwilling to kneel to Christ, Tobias is not more likely to kneel before the holiness of the sea. Quest and human love are important to him. He refuses to reject the goal, for it is the motivating force in life: "perhaps we are only on our way there—only pilgrims at sea," but that is not all:

Yet the sea is not everything; it cannot be. There must be something beyond it, there must be a land beyond the great desolate expanses and the great deeps which are indifferent to all things: a land we cannot reach but to which nevertheless, we are on our way. (Ph. 113-14; 116)

Contemplating Giovanni's story, as "the ship glided imperceptibly forward over the endless sea, without a goal," Tobias still has his soul turned toward the Holy Land, "his eyes on the shining stars" (Ph. 114; 116). His pilgrimage will continue, for *Pilgrim at Sea* is a "transitional novel in the pentalogy. . . . Its concern is to present existence (the Holy Sea between life and death) and the nature of the existentialist pilgrimage."[22]

XIII   Det heliga landet

When *Pilgrim at Sea* was published, without hint that *Det heliga landet* (*The Holy Land,* 1964) was to follow, most critics believed it to be the conclusion of a tetralogy that had begun with *Barabbas*. They imagined that the novelist's quest for God could not go beyond Tobias's journey itself, and that Lagerkvist, having described life as being no more than a vast expanse of sea upon which pilgrims were destined perpetually to travel, could never present the Holy Land itself. Obviously, they were wrong. Not only could Lagerkvist bring his questing pilgrim to the hallowed shores; he could do so without violating the theme that he had developed throughout the earlier novels.

In retrospect, it now seems natural enough that Lagerkvist should permit his pilgrim to reach the Holy Land and that the place itself should prove no absolute. Its vagueness, its tentativeness, its very unreality serve merely to emphasize that Lagerkvist's dialogue of the soul, like man's experiences, is continuous and, in fact, endless. Once more the truly remarkable quality of Lagerkvist's trilogy is that each unit, while being complete in itself, goes into the making of a unified whole, even as each man's individual experience is an entity, while together the separate entities create the sum total of human existence.

XIV *The Plot of* The Holy Land

As Lagerkvist resumes his story of Tobias, it is apparent that much time has passed. Blind and useless, Giovanni has been put ashore by the pirates, and Tobias has accompanied him to a desolate, barren land. To protect themselves, they take refuge behind some pillars, the ruins of an ancient temple, where they are discovered by native herdsmen. The primitive herdsmen know nothing about the ruins, the sea, God, or a Holy Land.

Giovanni and Tobias themselves have no answers. They cannot condemn the cruelty and low character of the crew because they regard themselves as no better than their shipmates. They cannot describe the Holy Land because they have not been there. Even Giovanni's locket, which catches the herdsmen's interest, remains inexplicable since a locket's value is in its contents and this one is empty. Yet the locket has taken on special meaning for Tobias, who somehow believes Giovanni cannot live without it. The pair cannot be certain of even the reason for Giovanni's blindness, attributing it either to the crew or to God's punishing Giovanni's blasphemy.

Tobias and Giovanni settle down to a simple life in the ruins. No longer concerned with the sea, Tobias looks to the mountains, mysterious and vague in the distance. When the herdsmen take Giovanni and Tobias to see a baby brought down from there after its mother's death, the mountains take on a new significance. The father had responded to an inner voice when the mother mysteriously had placed the child on her breast as she died. Tobias relates the baby to Christ, a notion rejected by Giovanni. The difference between the two men is repeated when Tobias digs up an ancient god which he disdains to accept because of its appearance of evil and indifference, qualities that make it a perfect symbol of deity for Giovanni.

As a plague afflicts the animals on the island and vultures mysteriously appear, the religious commentary continues. The primitive herdsmen turn to a cruel ritual. Despite their gentle nature, they enjoy the vengeful tearing out of the entrails of a wounded bird. Tobias is shocked, but Giovanni attributes the viciousness to man's nature. While a lamb is vainly sacrificed at the temple's altar, the god unearthed by Tobias stands "smiling its mocking smile at the scene" (H. 54; 46).[23]

Turning from the ancient ritualistic practices to a more Christian strand of the narrative, Lagerkvist introduces a woman who comes down from the hills, speaks to Giovanni, and seemingly knows even his thoughts. When she asks about the locket, Giovanni cannot explain why he wears it. She takes it, and he dies peacefully. Although initially angry, Tobias becomes calm as he sees Giovanni's face. The woman places the locket on Tobias.

On the same day, the baby dies. Although the herdsmen are appalled, the father accepts it calmly like a religious initiate. Only Tobias knows that a snake, borne by the mysterious woman, has caused the child's death. He links the child to men's hopes and questions his responsibility for its death. In the same way, Tobias muses over Giovanni's grave about man's journey, destiny, and continuity. With the end of the plague and the father's disappearance with the child, the shelter is blown away, and Tobias's adventure at the foot of the mountains ends.

Returning to his quest, Tobias enters the mountains. He discovers three crosses on an empty hill. One is Christ's. Tobias identifies them with thieves and murderers, but notes that the crosses will always be together. Going on to a more pleasant side of the hill, Tobias finds a kind of evening land (similar to that in Lagerkvist's fine collection of poems). He believes he sees another man looking in a river, but it proves to be himself, a portent of death for which Tobias is not yet ready. Coming upon a spring, Tobias drinks and quenches forever his earthly tastes. He continues upward to a land not "of dusk but in a bright dimness that was less oppressive" (H. 84-85; 74). Finally, he falls asleep near a wooden statue of a woman with "gentle face" and a "kindly and perhaps rather sad smile..." (H. 86; 75).

At the climax not only of *The Holy Land,* but of the trilogy, Tobias speaks to the Madonna about himself and his quest of a holy land that does not exist. Sadly, she insists that however dim it seems at times even to her, it does exist. As they talk, Tobias reveals his past life. He tells her of the young woman who was his love and who was to bear his child, until his wealthy parents intervened, forced them apart, and caused her suicide. Mary tells him that his love forgives him and does not judge him. As she tries to encourage him, however, he berates himself. Although Mary begins by saying she cannot help, her conclusion is more indefinite, and as he continues, Mary is replaced by his love, who has waited for him. She takes the locket from him, and, whereas Giovanni had died "as if he had found a kind of peace" (H. 60; 51), Tobias's face at death "seemed full of a great peace" (H. 99; 85).

XV *The Role of Ambiguity in the Novel*

Even through a summary of its plot the novel may clearly be seen to belong to the trilogy in its technique, attitudes, and concerns, while new elements in details and insights become apparent. Ambiguity abounds in *The Holy Land* as in the rest of the trilogy—ambiguity of word or phrase that reflects the uncertainties of existence and the dualities in man's experience. Little touches expose the difficulty in judging, whether it be Tobias's inability to discern the age of the herdsmen or the contrast between the nobility of the birds of prey in flight and their obscenity on the ground.

The third part of the trilogy shares with its predecessors a shifting point of view which makes uncertain whether the observations are those of the narrator or characters.[24] The characters' bewilderment about the temple ruins, the god unearthed by Tobias, the child brought down from the mountains, and the mysterious lady are never the subject of direct comment by the narrator, who seems to be no more certain of the truth than they are. When Giovanni and Tobias try to reconstruct the history of the ancient temple, its purpose, and its functions, the very language is that of "perhaps" and "may not have been" H. 41-42; 35-36), and no narrative voice speaks with any greater assuredness.

Lagerkvist, through Giovanni's words, puts in perspective the relationship between this narrative ambiguity and its theme: "All that divinity, if there was such a thing, must be something far more comprehensive, more complex, than men could conceive of, and thus much truer. For the pure and simple was not—could not—be true. Only the complex could conceivably be that" (H. 43; 36).

XVI   A Structure of Contraries

In structure, too, *The Holy Land* resembles the other novels. Tobias and Giovanni represent contrasting forces out of which some semblance of truth emerges. The paganism associated with the ancient temple ruins is counterposed by a kind of primitive Christianity, neither of which offers a definable solution, but both of which indicate man's need to believe, his striving for knowledge even as he is unaware of his desire. Into the main narrative, Lagerkvist inserts, as in the earlier novels, an instructive story: the experience of the father who brings his baby down from the mountains and effects a change in the herdsmen's lives. Tobias suggests the significance of the inset as he associates the baby with Christ and perceives a relationship between the child's death and Giovanni's.

These aspects of structure—working through contraries—continue Lagerkvist's earlier procedure even down to some of the details. The play of ideas between Giovanni and Tobias, neither offering any certainty, has been well prepared for in *Pilgrim at Sea*. The line of distinction, however, is more clearly drawn in *The Holy Land*. As a result of his experiences, Giovanni has become increasingly more cynical, while Tobias, although appearing at times to have given up his quest, retains the sensibility of a pilgrim. When they arrive at the temple ruins, Giovanni suggests that perhaps during their long time at sea all the temples and gods have been destroyed, and the thought satisfies him. His cynical view is gratified to discover the gentle herdsmen's cruelty to the carrion bird. Tobias, on the other hand, still wants to believe. He is disturbed by Giovanni's blasphemy. He refuses to see the temple idol as a god, perturbed by its "contemptuous smile" and its apparent indifference "to the whole world of men . . ." (H. 41; 34-35). For Giovanni, "god, if he existed, might well have that evil night aspect . . ." (H. 42-43; 35).

Even in their response to the baby, the two men differ. "To the blind man [Giovanni] the hut was full of darkness, and he understood nothing" (H. 37; 30). Not so, Tobias. To the admiration of the herdsmen, he contributes his own, and if "perhaps he didn't quite come up to the old men's expectations," it is only because "he was so full of wonder at the scene that his thoughts were busier with that than with what he was saying" (H. 36; 29).

It is, of course, the mark of difference between the two that Giovanni dies bound to this world, while Tobias, following his friend's death, resumes his search for the Holy Land.

Lagerkvist's treatment of pagan and Christian religious practices to show the inadequacies of both and yet man's need to believe in something also has its antecedents in an earlier volume of the trilogy, *The Death of Ahasuerus*. Indeed, this antiphonal use of two religious forms to produce a third possibility has prior treatment in both *Barabbas* and *The Sibyl*. In *The Holy Land*, the ancient religion, symbolized by the temple ruins, has failed. All that remain are scraps and evidence of what it once was. A goat nibbles "the dry grass in the room which might once have been holy" (H. 12; 9). The altar, "the holiest thing" (H. 30; 20), survives because it was made of marble, while the temple, composed of volcanic rock, has crumbled even as the religion has become useless to man. For the herdsmen, a place, described by Giovanni and Tobias, as not "intended for people, but for someone else" (H. 29; 24), seems incomprehensible. Whatever endures of the old ritual has a hideousness resembling the statue of the god itself. The sacrificial lamb is "bled to death as slowly as possible, so as to satisfy both the unknown and [the 'priest']himself" (H. 53; 45-46). As for the altar, it is "soiled with blood, innocent blood. Once again. And doubtless not for the last time" (H. 54; 46).

Primitive Christianity, introduced through the episode of the mysterious child, begins with hope for man, but ends, for the herdsmen, in "an infinite emptiness now that the baby no longer existed in their world" (H. 63; 54). The details of the story make apparent Lagerkvist's allegorical recreation of messianic Christianity. When the herdsmen sufficiently trust Giovanni and Tobias, they seek to share the secret of the baby with them and, like some early Christian cultists, "agreed to initiate the strangers" (H. 33; 27). To view the child, the herdsmen, "as if in reverence to something within, though it may only have been to see better" (H. 34; 28), kneel down, even as Tobias must do. The snake-bite marks on the baby appear as a kind of stigmata. On the death of the child, the father remains calm because "he was in some way initiated" (H. 64; 55). For Tobias, the baby's death raises questions of his own guilt and responsibility suggesting mankind's responsibility for the death of Christ. And finally, even as the child's original appearance in the village bore the qualities of a miracle, so does its disappearance along with its father take on the sort of mystery associated with Christ's Ascension.

XVII *Theme*

Both the pagan and Christian responses to man's need to believe provide Lagerkvist with the means to present through Tobias his own convictions about man's struggle for faith in an existence that offers no positive answers. Tobias, seeking ultimate knowledge, never loses touch with the human condition. Within the temple ruins, he works to make it "more and more like a human habitation" (H. 29; 24). He uses the roots of once sacred trees to build a fire to enable Giovanni and him to survive. With equal concern for humanizing his religious quest, he approaches the Christian revelation by pondering its meaning for men. He cannot rest comfortably with a religion that has "nothing to do with your destiny. That is too trivial, like all human destinies." What is he to make of a God "who deprived men of their hope—their only hope—by means of a little poisonous snake?" (H. 67-68; 57-58).

The quality of Tobias's concern for human feelings and emotions within the quest for ultimate truth provides the two new elements in the final part of the trilogy—the nature of the Holy Land and the function of love in man's existence. Perhaps the most satisfactory comment on the significance of the novel's conclusion has been made by Swanson: "Tobias finds the highest and holiest in life—as a dream. It is in himself . . . . Tobias dies within his dream, within the perfection to which he is on his way." Swanson contrasts Tobias with Barabbas, Ahasuerus, and Giovanni: "all find true death; but only Tobias finds holiness. For Barabbas, Ahasuerus, the Sibyl, and Giovanni, human love is incompatible with holiness. But for Tobias it is holiness itself; it is that which makes one holy."[25]

If Swanson overemphasizes the finality of Lagerkvist's conclusion, since after all it is in a "dream" that Tobias reaches *his* Holy Land, he nevertheless presents an accurate picture of what has happened. The Madonna cannot herself *give* the Holy Land to Tobias, but he does find it through the experience of love. "Love does not judge" (H. 95; 82), the Madonna says, and she then fades away into the image of Tobias's early lover, a figure of "infinite tenderness," whose words and touch bring to his face in his dying moments an expression that "seemed full of great peace" (H. 99; 85).

With the exception of this new stress on the importance of love, *The Holy Land* does not differ fundamentally from Lagerkvist's thesis from *Barabbas* on. As an answer to the mystery of existence, it holds forth no prospect of ultimate truth for man, certainly not the truth of religious orthodoxy. The human condition, according to Lagerkvist, demands the quest itself, since whatever meaning life has comes through man's struggle for existence. What man must learn is that he should not stand judgment on others or demand that humanity produce more than it is capable of. Men are neither good nor evil; goodand-evil is the nature of man. If life has significance, it is in the living—the final answer is beyond the quick.

The marvel of Lagerkvist's writing is that, given its limited thematic scope in the Crucifixion Cycle, its interest does not pall. To epitomize its theme does injustice to the trilogy as art.

It reduces the rich, full symbolism to sterile allegory; it scants the effectiveness of a prose style ideally wedded to a narrative as simple and complex as the Bible upon which it is modeled.

CHAPTER 6

Mariamne: *The Dialogue Continues*

I Background

WITH the completion of his trilogy, Lagerkvist did not
put aside his interest in reconstructing biblical history
to comment on the human condition, the endless struggle of
man to reconcile the dualities in existence and to find something
to believe in that would give meaning to his life.[1] *Mariamne*
(*Herod and Mariamne*, 1967), a short novel, finds its material
in the years just prior to the birth of Jesus. In a manner similar
to his treatment in the earlier biblical novels, Lagerkvist's Herod
departs from the portrait in the Gospels and history and becomes instead the author's not altogether unsympathetic picture
of an outsider, the Edomite King of Israel who can neither trust
nor love those around him. Lagerkvist simplifies the complex history of Herod, the Romans, and Jews during the involved con-
troversies and partisan struggles at the time of Jesus' birth. In
an unaffected, unadorned narrative, he offers a parable not really
concerned with biblical history, choosing, instead, to relegate
the ghastly tale of Herod's Slaughter of the Innocents to an
anticlimactic addendum. His narrative focuses upon the relationship of Herod and Mariamne in order to demonstrate the manner in which good and evil intertwine in their characters even
as they do in all humankind.

II Plot

Herod, the Edomite, has come to the throne of Israel. With
the help of the Romans he has ruthlessly seized power, destroying many of those who opposed or were likely to oppose him. To
the Jews, he is an outsider, alien in appearance, conduct, and
race. Their hatred for him is increased by his desire to build
a temple more glorious than Solomon's. His degenerate and
lascivious court life outrages their morality.

By chance, Herod first lays eyes on Mariamne outside the Damascus Gate. Fair-haired, beautiful, and regal, she overwhelms him, but he does not know who she is and he is in no position to find out. However, she appears at his court to plead for a young kinsman who has been seized for attacking one of Herod's guards. Impressed now by her courage as well as beauty, Herod frees the boy, a member, like Mariamne, of the Maccabean elite whom Herod had attempted to crush. Only when Herod tells her of his experience at the Damascus Gate does Mariamne instinctively appear defensive.

When people learn of her influence on Herod, they besiege her with requests for intervention, but she is aware that mass appeals will only anger him. Her own family, resenting her conduct, abuses her, particularly the youth she has saved. She pleases those whom she benefits by her repeated visits to Herod, visits that increase his desire for her and convert his way of living at court. Finally, Herod asks her to marry him, and feeling pity for him and concern for her people, she accepts.

As they live together, Mariamne grows more used to him and finds some satisfaction with him. He releases many prisoners at her request. Although this pleases many people who come to regard her as a savior, it further outrages her family, who wish her dead. The boy whom she originally saved returns to the hills to join a Maccabean band, and Herod, already generally suspicious, is especially displeased. Despite his love for Mariamne, he does not confide in her, and neither can give himself fully to the other. She cannot entirely satisfy his passionate, violent nature, and he cannot provide the tenderness and gentleness she requires. Aware that she does not truly respond to him, Herod becomes increasingly more suspicious and watchful.

An uprising by the Maccabees brings Herod into the field. Although he seems to have lost some of his zest for combat, when he meets Mariamne's young kinsman, Herod savagely destroys him and leaves him dead among the defeated Maccabees. Learning what has happened, Mariamne believes herself responsible. She feels that her conduct had driven the boy back to the hills and that her failure to love Herod had outraged him. When Herod returns and casts himself at her feet, she gently strokes his forehead and soothes him.

In time, however, Herod becomes restless, unhappy with her

coolness. He chides her for her lack of feeling before he goes forth once more to battle. Alone, with only the occasional companionship of an old serving woman who secretly defies her family to visit her, Mariamne is calm—subdued in spirit, but content with her quiet life. Although most townspeople gratefully smile at her, her own kinsmen turn away.

On Herod's return, he verbally assails her, describing her kinsmen whom he has slain and reporting on his affairs with other women. He is angry at her failure to respond. Mariamne herself is grieved because she realizes that she misses the sensual satisfaction that he has given her and she sees the loss of her control over him. Indeed, he resumes his tyranny over her people, brings whores to his court, and openly reproaches her for not responding to his atrocious behavior. Finally, he leaves her and avoids meeting with her again.

When she learns that the old serving woman has disappeared, Mariamne fears for the rest of her kin, but Herod has actually begun to plot her own death. Afraid of dying—not in battle, but through other causes, particularly assassination—he no longer trusts her so close to him. He chooses as an assassin someone who resembles him. Yet when the time arrives, having deliberately absented himself from the castle, he repents and rides furiously back to the court to stay the execution. Too late, he sinks beside her, repeating, "Beloved, beloved" (M. 98; 96).[2] She opens her eyes, puts her small hand in his, and dies—leaving him uncertain of whether she knew what he had done and had forgiven him or whether she was unaware of his treachery. In a rage, he slays his hired murderer.

Herod temporarily mellows, but then resumes his tyranny. He crushes the Maccabees, nearly exterminating them. He returns to his dissolute life until it affects his health. Ravaged by disease, he terrifies even his servants. However, when the three wise men come to Jerusalem and to his palace because they believe that the Holy Child must be there, he receives them. He scans the starry skies with them, but they depart when it becomes clear that the special star will not stop at Herod's palace. The wise men continue on to Bethlehem while Herod still gazes into the heavens at the stars that seem to pierce his soul.

Learning about the birth of the child, Herod orders the death of all male children in the town in order to make certain that

no king will arise from among the people. However, the child
and its parents escape the slaughter of the innocents. It is
Herod's last villainy. Deserted by his servants, who no longer
fear the decrepit old man, Herod dies in the dreaded night and
loneliness, crying out for Mariamne, the one good thing in his life.

III *Point of View*

The simplicity of its plot confirms the novel's intentions as
parable. However, like all parables and particularly those of
Lagerkvist, its meaning is complex and elusive. The very mode
of narration assures no simplistic, didactic significance. In passing comments and overall point of view, Lagerkvist makes clear
only the distinction between appearance and reality, only the
difficulty of ascertaining absolute truth. When, for example,
Mariamne has come to live with Herod, and the townspeople
see her as unaffected, unchanged by her new prominence, the
narrator remarks on the limitations of their judgment:

For although she was now queen she dressed as before: simply, it
seemed, but in fact this was not so. Her garments were often em-
broidered with silver thread, her mantle was edged with silver,
and her girdle or sash too was of silver, as were the loops of her
sandals. (M. 50-51; 50-51)

Or, again, when Herod shields his eyes after first looking upon
Mariamne, the narrator comments, people "might think he was
shading his eyes from the sun. But he was not" (M. 23; 23).
    Even the narrator, however, does not speak authoritatively.
Presenting his theme about the complex relationship between
good and evil, he resorts to "perhaps" and "may." In such terms,
he describes Herod's way of life: "A vicious life, no doubt; yet
perhaps not exactly for the reasons given by the people. It may
have been sinful because it was so joyless; for an empty, joyless life it must be where love itself is evil" (M. 19; 19). Not
even on that final point, however, is the judgment absolute, for
indeed "cruelty may bring with it a kind of joy" (M. 19; 20).
    Ambiguity and irony are Lagerkvist's primary tools for deal-
ing with his theme because he desires to demonstrate the duality
in man's nature, the close relationship between good and evil
in man's world. Although believing in the importance of love

to man's existence, Lagerkvist recognizes, as always, its imperfect nature, its own many-sidedness, and, in its transience like man's life itself, its inadequacy in bringing permanent satisfaction to man despite its necessity in making human existence bearable. The ambiguity, therefore, that marks the individual comments and overall point of view characterizes as well Lagerkvist's treatment of Herod and Mariamne and their relationship.

IV *Herod's Character*

Herod proves as complex as any character that Lagerkvist has created. From the opening comment, which sets the general style of parable, the ambiguity in the treatment of Herod's character is apparent:

When Herod the great king lived his life here on earth he was a mighty man, whose like perhaps has never been known. Or so he himself believed—and he may have been right. He was an emblem of mankind; mankind that replenishes the earth but whose race shall one day be erased from it and, so far as may be conjectured, will leave no memorial. But let us now turn from this, and tell his story. (M. 7; 7)

The passage, despite the simplicity of its utterance, presents a complexity of ambiguities. Its tone combines the pessimistic prophecy of Ecclesiastes, crying out against man's vanity, with the grimly ironic note of Shelley in "Ozymandias," despairing about the wasteland that is the legacy of tyrants. Herod, described as "mighty" (at least in his own eyes), stands above and apart from mankind, but somehow the emptiness of his endeavors, the consequence of his struggle to endure, is equated with mankind's ultimate failure. He may seem more wicked than other men; he may appear more powerful than other men, but finally his existential condition does not differ from other men's. Although Lagerkvist pretends that the passage is no more than a starting point for narrative, he returns almost *verbatim* to it at the conclusion, and the story itself provides the supportive detail for this initial observation.

Herod's condition as an outsider among the Israelites parallels man's existentialist position in the universe. "He had no link with the divine. Inwardly he was a wilderness, and the stars drove their cold spears into his soul" (M. 54; 54). Paradoxically, despite his awesome power, he "seemed a captive in his own evil stronghold" (M. 41; 41). Even in battle, he stands remote from the officers and men who serve under him. To overcome his sense of desolation, his fear of nothingness, Herod strives for action, almost as though the activity can reassure him of life's purpose. But the emblems of mortality prove inescapable. He belongs to a desert people who occupy "a land of death rather than life" (M. 106; 102), and "All unawares he bore the desert within him, and at times he felt its vast desolation" (M. 8; 8).[3]

The temple Herod builds becomes a symbol of man's desperate effort to insure his sense of being, to use some kind of religious edifice to reach out beyond the bounds of man's existence. As Lagerkvist presents this episode, using historical reality as a base, he underscores the ambiguity in man's conduct. Lagerkvist repeats the historians' arguments that Herod's purpose was self-glorification, an attempt to surpass the achievements of Rome and of Solomon, "so that his name might be handed down to posterity and he himself become immortal." The narrator asserts, "And surely this was true" for Herod himself "would have acknowledged this . . ." (M. 13; 13). Yet Lagerkvist goes on to show how Herod is drawn to the temple, and when he wants to display it to Mariamne it is because "it was *his*" (M. 53; 53). The narrator describes the odd fact that Herod in having the temple built does so in a way that will not interrupt worshipers, "a consideration remarkable in a criminal, a desecrator of all things holy" (M. 16; 17). And what can be said with assuredness about Herod's motives when the narrator raises questions about Herod's attitude toward the building itself: "Over himself only? Only to glorify himself?" and then concludes, "That I cannot say. I don't know" (M. 105; 101).

If Herod's purpose in building the temple appears vainglorious, if it is no more than a futile gesture to find a link between man and divinity, how does that differ from other men's efforts? To be sure, Herod himself ridicules the efforts of the Israelites:

he mocked both them and the god they clung to and worshipped in their dilapidated old temple, which they revered for its antiquity and in which nothing might be altered either in the building itself or in the lord's service. (M. 11-12; 11-12)

And if Herod is not to be taken as a fair judge, the testimony of the Israelites itself presents sufficient evidence of the futility of their attempts to link themselves with God. Their attitude toward Herod's building a temple, toward its magnificence, was one of outrage. They judge how the Lord *must* respond. With irony, Lagerkvist comments on the hubris of the priests:

One could not be sure. One could never be quite sure what the Lord's will was. But the high priest, who stood nearest of all to Him, was of the opinion . . . [that] the Lord, like his servants, would have preferred everything to remain as it had been in the old days. (M. 15-16; 16)

In what way is their conduct less self-serving than Herod's, their desire to find a link to God less a sign of their hubris, their inability to perceive His purpose, His will any less a sign of their failure and indicative of their limits as men? With what futility in man's quest for God and ultimate knowledge are the words spoken: "The Lord's will was hard to interpret, yet insofar as one could know anything of Him one must believe that this was what He would wish" (M. 15; 15). Such "assuredness" recalls Tennyson's expression of faith in "In Memoriam": "We faintly trust the larger hope."

V Herod's Relationship to Mariamne

In Herod's relationship to Mariamne, Lagerkvist uses love as the only means of man's giving purpose to his life. If existence has a saving grace, it is the divinity of love, and yet, as Lagerkvist presents it here, love itself, like the divine ideal, is only transient for man, never providing certainty, never yielding ultimate satisfaction. It is as much a part of human frailty and ambiguity as anything that enters into man's existence. It may offer hope, provide him with solace, sustain him in his struggle, and, indeed, be the greatest good on earth, and yet it has all the limitations of the finite.

Part of the failure of love to provide salvation for Herod is no doubt attributable to his character. "For in him," the narrator remarks, "love itself was evil" (M. 87; 85). When he asks Mari-

amne to be his wife, Herod cannot bring himself to use the word
"love." "Nor could he even pronounce the word; he had never
used it, and was shy of it. It was no word for him, he felt" (M.
41; 41). He knows that he desires her, and believes "it to be
enough, he believed it to be love." Never having experienced
anything like it before, he does not know even how to respond
to it. "It was foreign to his nature" (M. 57; 57).

Mariamne can exert some influence over him. For her, "He
had cleansed his whole house," and at the beginning of their
relationship, "He had had no woman since he met her" (M. 37;
37). When he looks upon her, "There was no lechery in [his
gaze], as might have been expected from all that was said of
him . . ." (M. 35; 35). For a time, his cruelty diminishes, or at
least appears to have done so. He loses his ferociousness in battle
sufficiently to appear as an ordinary soldier. And yet her influence, the narrator insists, has "failed to alter him" either during
her life or after her death. His mildness is external; cruelty lies
dormant until he plots her murder in "the slimy bed of his
soul" (M. 94; 92).

By presenting love through Herod and Mariamne's relationship, Lagerkvist no doubt limits the possibilities of love as salvation because of Herod's particular nature. Nevertheless, Lagerkvist's opening and closing paragraphs, linking Herod with mankind and his fate, suggest a more pessimistic attitude generally
toward love's power than the attitude expressed at the conclusion of his trilogy. It is almost as though love, like the divine,
lies beyond the reach of man's aspirations. To that dual nature
of man's soul, love remains an enigma that teases men's thoughts
with a purity beyond man's natural possibilities.

That Mariamne brings to Herod a love suggestive of the divine
Lagerkvist makes apparent throughout the novel. She herself is
described several times as needing no temple. Like the very
"trees, flowers, and the beautiful stones to be found along the
shore," "divine service" is within herself (M. 81; 80). Her "worship was within her. . . . She was like a tree which the wind fills
with its secret soughing. She had no need of any sanctuary" (M.
104; 101). As she walks among the people, love pours from her
as from a divinity. She is the epitome of selflessness. Her beauty
emanates from within so that even in sorrow, her face seems
"illuminated from within by grief" (M. 71; 71).

Her meeting with Herod "on the road to Damascus" bears the qualities of a miracle. Life changes completely for him: "the moment when it happened was so different from the moment before that nothing could ever be the same again..." (M. 22; 22). It was "like nothing he had ever experienced." For him, Mariamne is a "vision," "a revelation of something utterly unlike himself" (M. 24; 24). She fills his very being. When he returns to her from battle, having slain her kinsman, he needs her comfort. As though she were a deity, a Virgin intercessor, "he begged forgiveness for his wickedness, for being what he was. Forgiveness from her who could forgive everything." In her gentle stroking of his "brutal brow," "he seemed to find a kind of peace" (M. 72; 72).

Yet Lagerkvist suggests how remote this purity of love is from the nature of Herod, and, in turn, mankind. When Herod turns from her to other women, despite the fact that "it was she whom he loved," he finds in them a "sensual delight in experiencing something so different from her and her purity. Too great a purity," the narrator notes, "can become wearisome" (M. 84-85; 83). How can Herod relate to this figure of martyrdom, who is beyond his comprehension? How can he find satisfaction in someone who belongs to "those who blame themselves for everything" (M. 71; 70), "who continually ask themselves if they have done wrong?" (M. 45; 45). Not only is it unnatural to Herod's own character, it is alien to the nature of man.

Despite this use of Mariamne to represent a love as remote as God from man's comprehension, Lagerkvist also uses her as a symbol of good to indicate that in the world of men, goodness does not exist without evil. In man's experience, reflecting man's nature, good and evil exist in each other. When, after her marriage to Herod, Mariamne returns to the Damascus Gate, the flowers that had bloomed there on her first coming "had withered away" (M. 44; 44). It is as though her innocence, which could remain pure only by denying itself experience, has been lost in her relationship with Herod. Within his household, she may "never really [have] felt at home" (M. 48; 47), but she now belongs there; certainly once there she can no longer return to her people, who have come to regard her as "a disgrace to their lineage" and desire "her death" (M. 49; 49).

Through the metaphor of sex, Lagerkvist suggests the dualities of good and evil. Although she cannot altogether satisfy Herod, in their sexual relations, "she was at times deeply fulfilled. She had to admit this, repugnant though she found him" (M. 47; 46). She does not understand her feelings about him, and although she inclines to attribute them to pity, she asks, "But was it compassion alone?" (M. 43; 43). She knows that she has become "fond of him," but the extent of her feeling finally astonishes her. "He had roused her senses, and once aroused they craved their part in her life—but not as he craved it. She could not respond to him in his way at all" (M. 58; 58). And yet, "She was astonished that after what had happened she could take the smallest pleasure with him; and yet she did" (M. 73; 73). Man's experience allows for no absolute division between good and evil; in the world of men, they are intertwined.

In his parable, then, Lagerkvist continues the dialogue of his biblical re-creations. He demonstrates the manner in which both good and evil function within the characters of Herod and Mariamne even as they do in all humankind. With an insistence that characterizes all these works about the plight of man who seeks faith and is confronted by darkness, he underscores his theme of the separation of man from God, the importance of man's need for self-reliance, remembering his limitations and making the best of them.

CHAPTER 7

Poetic Landscape of the Soul

ALTHOUGH Lagerkvist's reputation rests on his prose fiction, particularly his novels, he has left his mark on Swedish poetry and drama in the twentieth century. The poetry, interesting and important in itself, has the added significance of making clear, through the intensity and conciseness of its form, the conflicts and dualities that characterize the entirety of his writing.

I *The Relationship of* Motiv *and* Ångest *to* Ordkonst och bildkonst

Lagerkvist has had a long and successful career as a poet, beginning with publication of a handful of social and political poems as early as 1909 and extending to *Aftonland* in 1953.[1] Whether measured by the sales that would be the American equivalent of over a million copies of his *Collected Poems* or by the enormous influence that he had upon more than a generation of young and idealistic Swedish poets, his success has been most impressive. Out of his own sense of torment and anguish as a young man turning away from the conventional beliefs of his forefathers, he drew his emotional intensity that struck a responsive note in readers sensitive to the destruction of their own confidence by the catastrophe of a world war. His awareness that the methods of traditional verse could no longer satisfactorily express the emotions of men uprooted from the old faiths drove him to seek new modes of expression and new techniques that helped to revolutionize a Swedish poetry moribund through its ties to nineteenth-century conventions. He turned to the developments in other art forms for his inspiration, and finally he discovered an idiom and manner that brought fresh and shocking sounds to his nation's poetry.

To be sure, he was not alone in shaping an esthetic revolution.

For all the differences among them, such poets as Dan Andersson, Edith Södergran, Harriet Löwenhjelm, Bertil Malmberg, Erik Blomberg, and Birger Sjöberg shared with Lagerkvist a reaction to a universe of "gray and miserable sky, or a horizon torn by war...."[2] Bo Bergman, Vilhelm Ekelund, and Anders Österling, like Lagerkvist, rejected the nineteenth-century poetic fashions of "big, bulging poetical phrases" and a "lyrical oratory no longer supported by and filled with a great and redeeming emotion."[3] Writing in 1917, the year after Lagerkvist's *Ångest* had been published, C. W. Stork makes no mention of Lagerkvist, but cites Verner von Heidenstam as the leading poet of the day and describes the struggle between what he calls "home poets" and "esthetes, individualists, or cosmopolitans," without quite recognizing the poetic revolution that Lagerkvist was taking a major role in shaping.[4]

Yet Lagerkvist ultimately proved to be the most important poet in revolutionizing Swedish poetry in the twentieth century. His aims were deliberate and calculated to overturn the old order. Almost programmatically he went about his business, offering in *Word Art and Picture Art* a clear call for a new kind of poetry, one that combined primitive sources and modernistic cubist and expressionistic techniques.

Although *Word Art and Picture Art* was to have a major effect on Lagerkvist's immediate and later writing, its influence on his work was not initially successful. His first collection of poems in *Motiv* (*Motifs*, 1914), experimenting with cubist techniques in poetry,[5] proved disastrous. As Alrik Gustafson has noted, Lagerkvist had yet to find a way to get beyond the artificiality of a "rigidly controlled cubism, the primitive naïvism, and the violently explosive expressionism" to the more personal voice that would allow him to explore his own conflicts of "affirmation and skepticism, light and darkness, the ideal and earthbound."[6] Lagerkvist himself recognized the failure of *Motifs* and has never included it in his volumes of *Collected Poems*.

Ångest (*Anguish*) in 1916 was another matter. Although Sven Linnér, proceeding from Lagerkvist's comments in a letter to August Brunius in April, 1917, believes that the volume represents the poet's repudiation of cubism after *Motifs*,[7] the evidence suggests that Lagerkvist never entirely rejected the ideas expressed in *Word Art and Picture Art*. To be sure, some personal

crisis combined with the catastrophic effect of World War I
to modify the program Lagerkvist enunciated in his essay, a
modification that resulted in a more personal and less stylized
language in his poetry and produced a more controlled style
which exploited more effectively his tone of "explosive bitterness
and pessimism."[8] However, the basic technique in *Anguish*
remains committed to the cubist principles expressed in the
essay.

Anguish stands as a kind of paradigm of Lagerkvist's general
literary method. Whether viewed through its structure, theme,
tone, or images, the collection offers a universe of dualities and
conflicts unreconciled by the poet, but presented in such a way
that, as in cubist painting, the division and relocation of the
aspects of reality produce "a deeper and less obvious reality."[9]
Thus man's alienation is not simply presented directly, but also
indirectly through the desperation that is expressed in faith:
the pathetic person in "På frälsningsarmén" ("At the Salvation
Army"), rising in spirit, at least, "high up towards eternal stars"
to escape "a shell of poverty" (13-14); the search after human
comfort in "Lilla hand, som ej är min" ("Little Hand, that Is not
Mine"), a groping into the darkness for the consolation of human
warmth (14).

Flodstrom, in a perceptive reading of the poems, sees the
structure of *Anguish* built on a division between the poet and
the universe, between the outer world and his inner existence.
Its major themes and images make *Anguish* a "total picture
which gains definition only as all of the parts fall into place."[10]
Summarizing Lagerkvist's methods in the volume, Flodstrom
sees the poet's purpose carried on in the

arrangement of the poems (a central section of prose poetry dividing
two sections of verse poetry), the emotional variation within the
poetry (ranging from active revolt to passive submission, with the
latter attitude dominating the final poems), and the imagistic and
thematic "population" (the reappearance of certain themes and
images in poem after poem, welding together the diverse poetic
fragments into a poetic totality).[11]

Through his technique Lagerkvist speaks directly to the needs
and attitudes of modern man. *Anguish* makes a clear assault
upon the traditional nineteenth-century Swedish romantic poetry,

its idealism, conventional meters, and stock phrases. Neither romanticism nor naturalism will do any longer. The conventional phrases of "throat's cry" and "heart's wound," he transforms, through a kind of synesthesia, into "throat's wound" and "heart's cry" (8).[12] The measured rhythms yield to deliberate harshness and stridency. The sounds and images of modern life invade the provinces of the old idealistic and charming verse.

Although Lagerkvist's methods differ somewhat from those of the American poet Robert Lowell (b. 1917) and the more recent "confessional poets" who are Lowell's followers, there is a striking resemblance between their thematic interests. The Lowell school places the poet and his emotions at the center of an unfeeling universe and uses his subjective responses as an expression of man's generally anguished condition. While Lagerkvist also places the poet-persona in the same situation, his technique is more objective and he universalizes through devices of abstraction and generalization rather than through the personal and subjective response to man's existentialist position. And yet his theme is essentially theirs: the awful distance between sentient man and the insentient universe. "I tear my blood-stained upstretched hands," Lagerkvist says in the title poem, "Against the frozen rags of the clouds." Man is depicted in his desperate groping after the meaning of existence, reaching out into the cosmos, mutilated in his attempt, while the universe itself remains unconcerned, its sky like "black iron," its earth "cold" (7-8).

If the war accounts in part for Lagerkvist's mood, the fundamental point of view remains characteristic of most of his later work. Well before such celebrated writers as Sartre and Camus, Lagerkvist in *Anguish* was sounding the major theme of modern literature: the unrewarded quest, the futility of man's finding a solution through orthodox faith. Lagerkvist, in this early collection of poetry, regards man in his absurd relationship to the universe and draws conclusions that were to become the dominant note in world literature only after the tragedy of the Second World War.

II Kaos

Less effective than *Anguish,* but significant to an understanding of how Lagerkvist's work develops through variations on a fundamentally unified artistic vision,[13] is Lagerkvist's next collection of poems, gathered under the title *I stället för tro* (*Instead of Faith*) in the volume called *Kaos* (*Chaos*, 1919). The handful of poems in *Chaos* is less impressive than the short play, *Himlens hemlighet* (*The Secret of Heaven*), and the excellent short story, "Den fordringsfulla gästen" ("The Demanding Guest"), included in the volume. *Instead of Faith* seems somewhat more conventional, less shocking than *Anguish*. Lagerkvist's rhythm and language, more traditional than in the earlier volume, appear to reflect a lessening tension in his own situation. At least in descriptive poems set in Denmark, the poet expresses a richer response to earth's beauty.

And yet the ultimate feeling that derives from these poems does not differ from the sense of man's insecurity and his transient relationship to the universe that emerged from *Anguish*. A poem like "Mitt barn, mitt barn" ("My Child, My Child") allows Edfelt to speak of the "belief in life, in spite of everything" that characterizes these poems,[14] and Miss Scobbie emphasizes the volume's break from hopelessness, its enjoyment of the world, and its expression of faith in life.[15] But even the appreciation of a sunset in "Det är vackrast när det skymmer" ("Beauty Fills Us," 28) is underscored by a feeling of man's impermanence, life's transience. The setting sun stands as a reminder of man's mortality, "All is mine, all shall be taken from me." The rootlessness of modern man is merely underscored by earth's beauty ("I shall wander/ Lonely, without trace").

Jöran Mjöberg has pointed to a stanza in one of the poems in *Chaos* that clearly reflects the dualism that marks all of Lagerkvist's work, the constant interplay between light and darkness, sorrow and joy, naked truth and illusion—Lagerkvist's varied views of the meaning of life:

> I am no one. I am a yearning.
> Now for darkness, now for light.
> I was no one, just a yearning
> To be stunned by the powers' fight. (33)[16]

As in *Anguish*, Lagerkvist probes life's ambiguities in *Chaos* and applies the techniques outlined in *Word Art and Picture Art*, techniques by which the varied aspects of the "raw data of poetic experience" are transformed "into some higher, more significant reality."

III   Den lyckliges väg

Superficially, as the title itself suggests, *Den lyckliges väg* (*The Way of the Happy One*, 1921) appears to be a more optimistic expression than anything Lagerkvist had written in his previous years. His verse form is far more regular than before. His rhymes, imagery, and tone, all achieve a greater sense of harmony than in his previous poetry. Emphasizing the importance of love, his ties to humanity, and the quietude of nature, Lagerkvist indeed brings an idyllic and, at times, pastoral quality to his work. Life itself in these poems seems to have more sense of purpose than Lagerkvist had accorded it in earlier volumes.

Nevertheless, the changes should not obscure the fact that these poems, too, play their role in what may be considered as Lagerkvist's continuing dialogue of the soul. Not only should the volume be seen as one poetic fragment to be balanced against a poetic fragment, say, like *Anguish* in order to arrive at a poetic totality that is Lagerkvist's true expression. Although that point is true enough and Lagerkvist *does* regard one volume as a point in a continuing debate with his other works,[17] *The Way of the Happy One* in itself provides a sense of the ambiguities and the dualities that characterize his writing. It offers no resolution to the questions about man's relationship to the universe, no end to man's struggle to learn the mysteries of existence, and no termination of man's conflicts between orthodox beliefs and his individual doubts.

The Way of the Happy One has been most often compared to *Det eviga leendet* (*The Eternal Smile*), the prose work which had been published in the previous year.[18] The comparison, as between other volumes of Lagerkvist's poetry and prose published in the same time periods, is certainly justified. But what does that say about *The Way of the Happy One?* *The Eternal Smile* itself is an assembling of diverse voices raised in a question about the meaning of existence and responded to by no other assurance than that life is a mystery to which man can receive no ultimate answer. Nothing there quiets man's restlessness, insecurity, and uncertainty.

In what appears to be a poem most reassuring about Christian faith—"Det kom ett brev" ("A Letter Came," 55)—Lagerkvist, in fact, underscores the distance between his mother's faith and his own skepticism. The letter comes to him from "afar"; its "sprawling script" is "queer," as much as to say that the old religion and its dogma are no longer decipherable. The security that the poet speaks of belongs to the letter writer; for the recipient, it is still veiled in "O mystery!" If there is any doubt about Lagerkvist's meaning—this contrast between the faith of his ancestors and his own inability to believe—it is only necessary to point out that in *Aftonland,* some thirty years later, the poet is still contrasting the security his grandfather could find in the "single star" shining above his farmhouse with the poet's own need "to seek distant, hidden things, to wander below stars" (254).

The Way of the Happy One, in its own fashion, is yet one more aspect of reality which together with the other aspects of reality in the author's work provides "a deeper and less obvious reality"; it is one more suggestion of the anguish that ultimately signifies modern man's alienation in the universe. It is not to be satisfied even by love which ends with the death of one's beloved and the loneliness of "darkened trees" in the "weird night" (45).

IV   Hjärtats sånger *and the essay* Det besegrade livet

Love itself is the major theme of *Hjärtats sånger* (*Songs of the Heart,* 1926), a volume that some critics have classified as among the best love poems in the Swedish language.[19] Although Mjöberg has described Lagerkvist here as "too pale and impassionate, compared, for instance, with such poets as Karlfeldt, Gullberg and Lindegren," the poems possess power and have a sincerity that Lagerkvist urges as he dedicates the second part of the volume to "E.," Elaine Hallberg, the second wife whom he had married shortly before. Certainly, there can be no question that Lagerkvist desires to see in love the one force that creates, an emotion capable of assuaging man's sense of insecurity. In "Vårt enda hem är kärleken" ("Our only Home Is Love," 92), Lagerkvist offers homage to the power of love:

> She is our mother strict and good,
> Unfathomably great in mood,
> Our truest world, our reality,
> The only certain thing we see.
> The rest are only dreams at best
> and cannot change our cares for rest.

That Lagerkvist in this period was looking at the world with greater hope than he had expressed earlier cannot be denied. *Det besegrade livet* (*The Conquered Life*, 1927), an essay, assails the limitations that reason places on man and celebrates the simple, unsophisticated belief in illusion that allows man to rise above everyday reality and to achieve, thereby, victory over life itself. Lagerkvist exalts the human spirit, raising it above the values of mere worldly knowledge, and he relies upon emotion, man's feelings, rather than upon reason. Within man, he argues, exists a divine spirit, which man needs to liberate to triumph over life. Unquestionably the emotion and feeling that Lagerkvist looks to for hope in his essay is the "love" that he praises in *Songs of the Heart*.

And yet, as always in Lagerkvist's work, another voice speaks in counter-terms throughout *Songs of the Heart*. Whatever the poet may desire to find in love, the man who writes the poems is too aware of life's ambiguities and dualities, as even *The Conquered Life* suggests, to accept comfortably such solution to his anxiety, such resolution to his quest after an unfathomable reality. *Songs of the Heart* presents only a struggle to maintain illusions against a constantly threatening reality, a desire to believe in the unbelievable. Love, in these poems, is complicated by a continuing tone of melancholy; the happiness it offers is, after all, fragile.

Whether in the obviously more personal second section of the volume or the seemingly more impersonal opening, doubt and skepticism accompany the poet's insistence on love's security. "Det blir vackert" ("Beauty Grows," 83), the first of the poems dedicated to his wife, celebrates the poet's love as someone whose presence on earth seems to transform it. She brings to "Earth and path and shore where [she has] walked," a brightness and rejoicing. And yet it only seems "As if earth were smiling," and the poet's love is warned, "Walk on it, . . , But never hard," a reminder of man's insecurity in this world.

"Torso," (67) which opens the volume, is a poem whose language, for all its celebration of love, has clear echoes of "Anguish." It speaks of pain, suffering, and torment—of limbs "lying/ In the gravel of the path/ For all to trample on." To be sure, the poet addresses his love as the sole provider of peace from "the depths of suffering," but it is a love devoid of joyousness, unhappy in its happiness, and intent on reminding the reader of man's uneasy relationship to the universe in which he exists.

V *Confrontation with Darkness*: Vid lägereld, Genius, *and the Travel Essays* Den knutna näven

The same forces are at work in *Vid lägereld* (*By the Campfire*, 1932), although here once more the darkness clearly dominates. Lagerkvist's gloominess in this period is best characterized by "Tanken har intet mål" ("Thought Has Nowhere a Goal," 104), a poem that in itself expresses a markedly nihilistic viewpoint:

> Thought has nowhere a goal,
> Prayer cannot find a father.
> Pain has nowhere a home,
> Longing never a mother.
>
> Born without a navel string,
> Dying without a track,
> Coming from out of nothing,
> And to Nothing turning back.

Yearning, however, remains the key to Lagerkvist's work, and nihilism, no more than easy acceptance, can satisfy him. If depression is most pronounced in the volume, that other voice, that other aspect of reality, exists to counteract it, to give ultimate balance to Lagerkvist's search for values. Addressing nature in "Du stora, vreda Natur" ("Oh Thou Great Wrathful Nature," 120), he acknowledges how it torments him, how it burns within him, and yet how he loves and embraces it. He will not yield readily, but views life as a struggle, something to be conquered and turned into his personal song. Like Barabbas in his later novel, the poet, who cannot find acceptance of the orthodox faith of his forefathers, at least affirms his belief in the darkness. For Lagerkvist, a world that demands a Christ requires a Barabbas for its completeness.

Mjöberg, who has described *By the Campfire* as containing some of Lagerkvist's finest poetry, neatly summarizes the volume: ". . . the poet sets out the barren conditions granted him in the 'desert' of human life, but at the same time, after the deepest depression of his poetical career, accepts these minimal conditions, accepts Life itself, after being its adversary."[20] Many other critics have also argued that Lagerkvist's philosophical development has led him finally to an acceptance of life as it is, but the description is somewhat misleading. Its effect is to portray Lagerkvist's writing as ultimately didactic, and that seems far from the truth. What Lagerkvist offers in *By the Campfire*, as in his other poetry and prose, is a picture of life's challenge. Each work contains within itself a dialectic—opposites that work against each other, from whose conflict the reader can come to a greater understanding of the deeper reality of life. Poem works against poem, volume against volume, and only from the whole can man gain some semblance of understanding of the nature of existence.

Between *By the Campfire* and *Genius*, his next volume of poems, Lagerkvist published *Den knutna näven* (*The Clenched Fist*, 1934), a collection of four travel essays that demonstrate the way in which his inner struggle was related to the external events of the period. Lagerkvist, conscious of the threat to civilization posed by the Nazis, celebrates man's aspirations for the ideal as indicated by cultural history. In the title essay, which describes his journey from Palestine to Athens, he uses the Acropolis itself as a symbol of man's struggle to reach beyond earthly limitations, to create a civilization from an assortment of heterogeneous elements. He lauds the search for human integrity, freedom of thought and action, respect for the individual—a fundamental humanism. And yet, throughout the collection, Lagerkvist is aware of the conflicting forces in mankind —the Apollonian and Dionysian at war for man's spirit reflect the fascist clash with the best values of humanity.

The process continues in *Genius* (1937), in which the forces of darkness—whether ethical, moral, or metaphysical—are pitted against those of light. Lagerkvist ponders life's secrets, particularly man's evil tendencies and his uneasy relationship to the universe in which he lives. The poet celebrates the search for truth, but recognizes that an almost impenetrable darkness seems omnipresent. He argues, therefore, the greater need for man to uncover the unpleasantness that surrounds him, to get beyond the confusion and chaos to the truth. *Genius*, as Edfelt has described it, presents "the eternal drama of the human mind: the light's struggle for liberation from darkness, the rebirth of the mind from night and chaos."[21] Dangerous though it may be to examine what exists beneath the surface, Lagerkvist characteristically cannot be content with illusion. In order to present the conflict, the fullness of the dualities that exist in man's world, Lagerkvist, as he has done in his earlier volumes of poetry, must offer a variety of aspects of reality, playing one off against the other and allowing his "truth" to come out of their relationship to each other.

In the most beautiful poem in the volume, "Mater dolorosa," Lagerkvist expresses the full nature of man's conflict—the mystery of existence that provides man's anguish and the incessant yearning of man to lift the veil that separates him from the truth:[22]

> With face veiled she stands silently apart,
> Her hand rests on the sombre catafalque of malice.
> A nation bleeds to death within her heart.
> Once more she empties the familiar chalice.
>
> Her form is shadowed on the evening sky:
> No-one can scan her features, and her voice is dumb;
> Yet eyes turned upwards through the vacancy,
> Pray for the earth and for the day to come. (128)

The full range of man's anguish is in the poem; the old paradoxes that plague Lagerkvist the man throughout his work make up the volume itself. For all their differences in verse technique —one traditional, the other wildly avant-garde—*Genius* and *Anguish* speak very much to the same problem and are not far removed from one another in their fundamental attitudes.

VI *Poems of Patriotism:* Sång och strid *and* Hemmet och stjärnan

Even *Sång och strid* (*Song and Battle*, 1940), clearly marked by Lagerkvist's fervent patriotic response to the Nazi holocaust,

shares his overall purpose: man's need to confront life's ambiguities, to struggle to give meaning to his existence. Faced by the
oppressiveness of German terror, Lagerkvist places his faith
in the human spirit. Against the evil in man's nature as manifested in Nazism, Lagerkvist sets that other aspect of man's
nature, the imperishable spirit that will one day achieve freedom. Lagerkvist's nationalism is not limited to Sweden, but
extends to the idea of civilization and independence in Scandinavia and its European neighbors. In "Det sörjande Norden"
("The Grieving North," 176), he mourns the fall of Norway,
where nature itself now seems dead:

> No more in joyous carnival
> The praise of life is ringing,
> Hushed is the summer's festal hall,
> And not a breeze is singing.

He describes a Norway "sorely bled," which "Lies low in desperate anguish." Its "northland flowers droop and fade,/ Unmindful of the season." Man's greatest treasure, freedom, has been
"trampled out." Yet Lagerkvist looks assuredly to man's indomi-
table spirit and forecasts freedom's return, "As brave and as
glad as ever."

With more subtlety, in another of the war poems, "Tanken
som byggde en värld" ("The Thought that Built a World," 160),
Lagerkvist deals with the two sides of man's nature and sees
the good as ultimately not to be vanquished. To be sure, those
same intellectual powers that promised so much now threaten
to destroy civilization. Yet, like a two-edged sword, thought has
the power to act in different ways. Even man himself contains
this duality in the bestial and spiritual sides of his nature. What
Lagerkvist seeks is a balance between the destructive and con-
structive forces in being, the power to destroy those illusions
that mislead, that bring spiritual death and sterility, and the
power to seek out the truth in human endeavors. Lagerkvist's
meaning here foreshadows in miniature that of his fine short
novel, *Dvärgen,* in 1944.

Amid these war poems, concerned as they are with a didactic
purpose and written in generally conventional meters, Lagerkvist
nevertheless continues his dialogue of the soul, with its longing
after life's mysteries and its anguish at not deriving any ulti-

mate truth. In "Stjärntimman" ("Star Time," 193), he ponders the mystery of existence, looks, as in his earliest poems, to an inscrutable nature for his answers. The poem begins with the supplication, "Star that falls in the summer night,/ Brighten the soul in me," and goes on to express a desire that heaven's mystery will be revealed by some inward insight. But, in the end, it is too late; the nonbeliever, for all his desire, cannot believe in conventional formulas. The tone, to be sure, is a long way from that of "Anguish" in his first volume, but the theme has not changed, and Lagerkvist continues, after many years, to probe the same spiritual problem.

Like *Song and Battle*, Lagerkvist's *Hemmet och stjärnan* (*The Home and the Stars*, 1942), a volume of poems published during the war, continues the poet's patriotic response to the Nazi terror. Its very title, however, indicates Lagerkvist's continued larger struggle with life's ambiguities. Here faith vies with reason, as in *De vises sten*, a drama published five years later. "Home" in the title reflects his ancestors' orthodox beliefs, their acceptance of a pietistic religion as simple as their lives on the farmland of Småland. For Lagerkvist, even as late as his description of the Sibyl's childhood in the novel published in 1956, something in their quiet faith endlessly beckoned to him. The stars,[23] however, remain a ceaseless torment to his imagination, representing a quest for knowledge no less powerful as an attraction to his soul. To be sure, in their vastness, stars and heaven are "depressive and awesome," but from *Anguish* to *Aftonland*, Lagerkvist could not ignore them.[24]

In *The Home and the Stars*, Lagerkvist seeks to emphasize the virtues of faith. "Folket på kyrkogården" ("The People in the Churchyard," 206-207) depicts worshipers whose hymnbook is "their only power." "Faith with its dazzling white sail/ Sets out over seas of light." Yet a nagging uncertainty characterizes the tone of the poem:

> Toward heaven the windows are opened
> Up high, and resounding bells
> Ring out to the grey, cold rocks and
> The ocean that no one compels.

Death seems to be the only resolution to man's uneasy quest in "Fiskarbegravning" ("The Fisherman's Burial," 207-208), a

poem in which he surely intends to celebrate the simple life.
Lagerkvist speaks gently of "his coffin . . . borne by the same
hands/ he saw every day." The burial service is compared to a
final journey, ironically taken through mountains, that has his
boat "going/ home through a flood of light." But the fisherman's
life has been a struggle against heavy seas and squalls. Death
itself is less a glorious resolution than an end to life's turmoil.
The wanderer finds no answer to his quest other than an end
to playing out and reefing in the sails.

As Jöran Mjöberg has noted, the poems in the volume reflect
the dualism in Lagerkvist's own nature.[25] "Oh foreboding," Lagerkvist says, "which a realm of dusk/ bestowed on me,/ Though
I search for clearness, thou my/ homeland be!" (218). Particularly in "Vår är himmeln" ("Ours Is Heaven," 224), the dualism
is displayed. Lagerkvist describes man's "dream of heaven" as
"a frail illusion"; yet it is not one that man can do without:

> One day all the walls will fall,
> Which we built with our earthly hands,
> But that world, the frailest among all
> Yet is part of the immortal lands.

Lagerkvist offers no genuine resolution, and the poems of
this penultimate volume of his poetry, like those that have
gone before, have the two-sidedness of a debate in which there
can be no victor because for man there is no ultimate truth. At
times one side is favored, at others, its opponent. If there is any
meaning to come forth from the debate, it can only come from
the totality of the arguments, which is, after all, the nature of
existence itself, in which the meaning of life comes through
living, the existential response.

VII Aftonland: *Reflections on a Lifetime*

It is a debate that Lagerkvist carries on into *Aftonland*
(*Evening Land*), his final volume of poetry in 1953. The subject is man's longing after a knowledge of the God he cannot
know, the absurd relationship of man to his universe, the
passionate seeking for answers in a world indifferent to man's
need to know. "Who am I?" the poet cries out; but "Under a
sky, scribbled all over with stars,/ everything is incomprehen-

sible." Man moves through his existence like "an unknown wanderer/ with a nameless goal" (248-49). "Lord over all heavens, all worlds, all fates," he asks, "what have you meant by me?" "Accidental,/ transitory,/ gone in a short while" (258), man is a homeless wretch beneath the vastness of the stars that represent the mystery of existence. And yet man cannot put aside his questioning of "The god who does not exist," for "he it is who enkindles my soul . . ." (259). God's effect on man Lagerkvist presents as a series of paradoxes ("Who are you who fills my heart with your absence? Who fills the whole world with your absence?");[26] man's relationship to God the poet sees as a driving force in his existence; the seeking itself, the endless quest becomes the meaning of life.

Recently, Gunnel Malmström has demonstrated how the five sections of *Evening Land* are unified through its atmosphere and theme. Yet it is a unity that emerges from the relationship between contrasting and conflicting points of view toward a single topic, and what unifies the disparate voices is the fact that only out of the whole does a meaning emerge. In the fourth section, for example, which Mrs. Malmström accurately describes as twenty-four poems with "variations on the same theme, the relationship between mankind and the two powers, death and God,"[27] none of the poems individually represents the poet's point of view; only together do they yield the completeness of his meaning. Even in its concluding section, nine poems offering "recurring motifs" of "loneliness and a sense of alienation,"[28] the effect is no didactic assertion, but rather a small model of the nature of existence which provides experience but no ultimate answers.

For all the differences in tone and manner of expression, *Evening Land* stands at no great distance from *Anguish* in Lagerkvist's created world. Miss Scobbie is correct when she contrasts the "dominant setting" of the final poems—"the endless, desolate wastes"—with that of "the frozen, rugged landscapes of Lagerkvist's expressionistic poems," but, as she herself recognizes, in *Evening Land* no less than in *Anguish*, Lagerkvist persists in his basic theme: seeking the answers to the mystery of life.[29] To be sure, as he progresses from book to book, there are differences. At various stages his work shifts emphasis from expressionism, to naïvism, to pessimism, to politics, to philosophy.[30]

And yet, as Gabrieli argues, for all its changes, Lagerkvist's poetry remains essentially the same. Gabrieli points to the fundamental similarity in Lagerkvist's themes in his lyric poetry: "Identical themes, here and there slightly extended or deepened, reappear ... both as an evocation of the Platonic meaning ... and as a hope in an unexpected epiphany of the divine."[31] From collection to collection, landscapes, visions, emotions—however different—are treated similarly and to a single purpose. "Life," Gabrieli remarks, "is regarded [in Lagerkvist's lyric poetry] as the allegorical pilgrimage of a being who knows neither where he is going on his fatal course, nor why, and who for a brief instant only lingers by a camp-fire, where others have gone before him and others will follow...."[32]

As long ago as 1933 Erik Blomberg recognized this essential unity in Lagerkvist's work.[33] Even then it was apparent that the ideas in *Word Art and Picture Art* provided a guide to Lagerkvist's poetry just as *Modern teater* did to his drama, and the ideas expressed in both essays have continued to influence his development throughout his career. Indeed, although his search for an *"expressive* ideal" has provided an enormous variety in the forms of his art,[34] Lagerkvist himself has acknowledged the unifying thread that binds the varied fabric of his writing.[35]

CHAPTER 8

Dramatist of the New Wave

I Modern teater *and the Idea of Drama*

THE 1966 publication of Thomas Buckman's edition of *Modern Theatre: Seven Plays and an Essay* more than doubled the number of English translations of Pär Lagerkvist's plays and made another dimension of Sweden's Nobel Laureate more fully available to English-language readers.[1] The event was significant, for Lagerkvist's Scandinavian reputation, as the discussion of his poetry has demonstrated, stands on more than the fiction that has made him known in the United States. As he had brought new sounds and rhythms to Swedish poetry, helping along an esthetic revolution in the genre, so, too, did he play an important part in opening Swedish drama to the artistic possibilities of Strindberg's expressionism and avant-garde theater. Long before he achieved fame as a novelist, he had gained recognition as a poet and playwright. Together with Hjalmar Bergman, an older writer upon whom he exerted an influence,[2] Lagerkvist completed Strindberg's break from naturalistic drama, and his overall success in the theater has been such that he has been called "one of the most important Northern playwrights after Ibsen and Strindberg."[3]

Like his poetry, Lagerkvist's dramas helped to shape the development of the genre in modern Sweden. Again like his poetry, his plays bear a strong thematic and tonal resemblance to his fiction, giving his work a remarkable degree of unity and allowing the reader to regard the whole as Lagerkvist's own created literary world.

Together with his poetry, Lagerkvist's dramas anteceded his interest in the novel, although not shorter fictional forms. Probably his enthusiasm for the theater was aroused by the companies that visited Växjö and presented a combination of classical and contemporary drama, including Shakespeare, Goethe, Ibsen,

153

Tolstoy, Strindberg, and Maeterlinck.[4] Among the earliest examples of his writing is *Livet* (*Life*, 1911), a one-act play showing
the influence of his interest in dance, ballet, and music.[5] At any
rate, his original serious concern for the theater—related to his
study of modern painting from 1913 to 1919—along with his
poetry marked his earliest genuine literary involvement. It has
proved no casual interest, producing as it has nine full-length
and six shorter plays.

To be sure, for Lagerkvist the drama has never seemed quite
as consequential as prose, toward which his attitude approaches
the reverential. Nevertheless, he regarded it as significant enough
to devote careful study to its form and development and to write
one of his few critical essays on the subject.[6] In his years in
Denmark during the First World War, he devoted considerable
time to investigating medieval drama, which—together with his
later exploration of classical and Indian theater, as well as an
intense reading of Strindberg and the German expressionists—
strongly influenced his own work. His probing went deep, and
his own work benefited from his study of Sanskrit and Chinese
sources and the theories of Yeats and the practices of the Commedia dell' arte.[7]

What that work was to be was foreshadowed in great part
by his dramatic criticism in *Svenska Dagbladet* and, even more
importantly, in his essay *Modern teater* (*Modern Theater*),[8]
written in 1918. From 1918 to 1919 his reviews and articles,
along with frank comments on actors and productions, offered a
clear enough statement of his values in the genre. He praises
Hjalmar Bergman's antirealism and condemns Ibsen's naturalism,
relegating it to the past. Ibsen, for Lagerkvist, was to be
applauded for his idealism and dramatic intensity, but that
was all. Attacking the decadence of the Swedish theater at that
time, Lagerkvist casts his lot for Strindberg against the realistic
and naturalistic Ibsenism that dominated the contemporary
Swedish stage. The importance of *Modern Theater* cannot be
overestimated, either in its effect on Swedish theater or as a key
to Lagerkvist's work. As Buckman notes, Lagerkvist, through
Modern Theater and his experimental dramas, revitalized a
Swedish drama that was generally in a deplorable state. The
essay, as its subtitle indicates ("Synpunkter och angrepp"
["Point of View and Attack"]), is a deliberate polemic, but Lag-

erkvist understood it to be of central importance to his own dramatic works.[9] Alone of his expository writing, he has permitted it to reappear, with mainly stylistic changes in 1946 and then, in 1956, with a somewhat more conciliatory comment on Ibsen, allowing the Norwegian playwright at least some historical importance.[10]

In *Modern Theater*, the assault on Ibsen is central. Lagerkvist views Ibsen's naturalism and what followed it, not simply as something that has outlived its usefulness, but rather as something that is out of place in the theater, a form of art inappropriate in its production, acting, and expression to what best defines the theater as *theater*. "Naturalism," Lagerkvist says, "means for the theatre constraint and curtailment of its possibilities in many respects, a one-sidedness which once had its importance as reaction, but which now seems only bare and oppressive because, basically, it is incompatible with so much that is essential for the art of the theatre" (I, 26; B. 18-19).[11]

Yet attack is only one part of Lagerkvist's essay; "point of view" implies a more positive side as well. Repelled by what he regards as the failure of imagination in naturalism, Lagerkvist seeks a means of "expression for the violent and abrupt contrasts in modern life, for all of the complexities and the confused and fantastic elements which we see" (I, 26; B. 19). For that Lagerkvist turns to Strindberg, for "Strindberg's newly created dramatic form, despite all its subjectivity, nonetheless corresponds to an artistic instinct in our age" (I, 40; B. 30). What Lagerkvist finds there becomes his own program for creating "A theater which gives the imagination of both dramatist and actor greater freedom of movement and greater audacity, a simpler, more immediate, and more expressive form" (I, 50; B. 38). How well he describes in Strindberg's work what proves to be his own repeated dramatic method when he calls for a drama in which "everything is directed to one purpose—the liberation of a single mood, a single feeling whose intensity increasingly grows and grows. Everything irrelevant is excluded even if rather important to the continuity or to the faithfulness of representation. Everything which occurs is meaningful and of equal weight" (I, 35; B. 26).

With Lagerkvist's drama as with his poetry, there is a remarkable relationship between an early programmatic prose statement and the lifetime's work that follows. No less than *Word Art and Picture Art* had done for his poetry, *Modern Theater* provides an outline to Lagerkvist's dramatic creation. Although later including modified forms of realism and lessening the early overwhelming expressionism in his plays, Lagerkvist retained, as Buckman has noted, the core of his theories expressed in *Modern Theater*:

the unity of artistic effect, the necessity for an inner compulsion to create, art as a way toward deeper personal realization and knowledge, the prerogative of the playwright to create freely and to imply in his work the full use of all the possibilities of the modern stage.[12]

These remain throughout.

Moreover, certain continuous aspects in Lagerkvist's plays emerge from his dramatic method, a method through which genuine intensity is achieved by the playwright's close "emotional and intellectual identification with his characters, representing various aspects of a complex and paradoxical existence...."[13] Buckman notes the significance of the continual presence of a "metaphysical background" throughout Lagerkvist's productions. It is a background against which his characters—however much they "have a convincing reality of their own"—do, at the same time, achieve a certain universality so that the plays seem always "to unify a cosmic perspective with some primary aspects of individual experience."[14] It is not much different in method from Lagerkvist's use of abstractions in his poetry to achieve a larger than personal meaning.

And yet, for all the relatedness of Lagerkvist's entire dramatic production, it is possible, as with his short fiction and poetry, to show different stages in his dramatic career, different interests reflecting the period of composition, and, of course, different degrees of achievement.

II   *The Early Expressionism:* Sista mänskan, Den svåra stunden, Himlens hemlighet, *and* Den osynlige

In his earliest plays, Lagerkvist was finding his way, either guided too frequently by Strindberg or lost in an expressionistic maze.[15] From Strindberg, Lagerkvist apparently developed the sharply contrasting emotions, the clearcut divisions between good and evil, that characterize these works, a technique that he was to modify to good effect in his later writing. His stage atmosphere, weird and too ostensibly symbolic, he borrowed rather incautiously from that part of Strindberg that appealed to his as yet immature artistic judgment. Combined with the shrillness that he drew from German expressionistic drama, these influences from Strindberg led initially to a drama that too often was bewildering in its plotlessness and vagueness. He mistook unbridled passion for effective dialogue and offered personal symbolism as though it had universal meaning.

Lagerkvist's initial failure is apparent in *Sista mänskan* (*The Last Man*, 1917), a short expressionistic play that preceded the ordering of his thoughts on drama in *Modern Theater*. Although the play deals with the perplexing dualities of love and hate, a common subject in his later works, here the treatment is inept. To emphasize his gloomy, pessimistic view during World War I, Lagerkvist has created not so much characters as representative forces in the figures of Gama, Vyr, Ilya, and Omi-Ga. The evil Gama, who has been blinded by Vyr, a figure of love and the life force struggling for existence in a world of hatred, strangles the woman. As a result, the son, Ilya, the very embodiment of innocence, dies brokenhearted. Gama's philosophy is offset in the play by that of Omi-Ga, who, although paralyzed, expresses the ideal of Christian love. Although in his later work, Lagerkvist uses symbols of deformity to express a triumphant spiritual force, here Omi-Ga's paralysis suggests merely the inadequacy of Christian principles in a world directed by deterministic powers beyond man's control.

The philosophy of Lagerkvist's play resembles that of the cruel, deterministic fictional world of Thomas Hardy. Man's position in that world is untenable because his aspirations are beyond his control. That much is clear in Lagerkvist's drama, but overall it lacks clarity, for Lagerkvist had not yet learned to control the abstract elements in his drama, and his symbolism muddles its way through a private labyrinth that ends in obscurity. For example, Gama expresses his anguish by declaring, "I have been groping and groping around me—but never found what I was searching for! Never.... Soon earth will be deserted and empty ... my fingers are slit open far into the flesh!—I am the last man! No, I am the first one! The only one!" (I, 59).[16]

In his later work, Lagerkvist learns to use such ambiguity in characters to the advantage of his theme, but here, as Miss Scobbie points out, he has so emphasized "man's greed, selfishness, and cruelty" that Gama's ambiguity seems more a contradiction in characterization than a suggestion of the duality that Lagerkvist intends.[17] Although Lagerkvist manages to display a sense of theatrical effectiveness and conveys the mood of despair felt in humankind confronted by the end of the world, the play ultimately fails through a lack of unity and confusion of symbolism.

However, with Den svåra stunden (The Difficult Hour, 1918)—three one-act plays concerned with the experience of death—Lagerkvist at least, as Buckman notes, gives evidence of his dramatic ability,[18] an ability that becomes even more apparent in Himlens hemlighet (The Secret of Heaven, 1919), a drama which presents characters trying to "comprehend the meaning of existence through their own limited vision."[19] Both plays demonstrate his early expressionism at its fullest. Like Strindberg's plays, they were well ahead of their time, closer to our modern "Theater of the Absurd" than to the conventional fin de siècle drama or the popular imitations of Ibsen.[20]

The trilogy of The Difficult Hour presents those moments surrounding death during which the significance of life itself is questioned. It is presented in the dark, forbidding atmosphere of the stage, consistent with Lagerkvist's gloomy appraisal of mankind's situation. Colors are dull, and the stark white light in the second part of the trilogy illuminates a death bed, with the full horror of the situation itself. Unlike Strindberg, as Buckman has pointed out, Lagerkvist finds no optimism in the prospect of dying; for him "the transition from life to death [is] from darkness to darkness."[21] Still borrowing heavily from Strindberg, particularly from such later plays as To Damascus and The Ghost Sonata, he has learned how to make the material his own. His language is cleverly ironic and works to control the grim mood, and despite his unconventional and disjointed dialogue, he manages to create a unified effect in a drama that merges melodrama and realism.

In the first play, a Man in Tails experiences the reliving of the most crucial episode of his earlier life. Victim of a railway accident, he is confronted by the shadowy figure of a hunchback, who forces him to recall a love affair filled with doubts about genuine emotion and fidelity and about the role he had played by taking her away from another man. The dialogue builds to an almost unbearable tension until death or the recognition of it brings the episode to a quiet close.

By contrast, the second play, set in a hospital, dazzles with enormous activity on a stage with the contrasting white light and darkness described above. The dying man is surrounded by the bizarre figures of a nightmare, the hallucinatory shifting of scenes, the confusion of people and voices, a wild mixture of the consequential and inconsequential, and the meaningful and insignificant. He, too, is obviously reliving in chaotic fashion past episodes of his life until the shrill whistle of the station master signals his end.

Once more in the third play the stage is dark. A small boy with a candle is wandering about bewilderedly. Confronted by an Old Man and an Old Woman struggling over him, he is lured into darkness and death. Lagerkvist manages a particular anguish in this final episode because the child's innocence, assailed by all the misery, horror, and chilly self-interest of the world, stands as mankind's experience within a universe that drives him out as naked as the day he was born and that has little concern for his needs and desires.

Despite Lagerkvist's insistence that, although published along with *Modern Theater, The Difficult Hour* was not written "to exemplify the principles . . . in the essay,"[22] it is impossible not to see that it does so rather remarkably with its crisis situations and its use of Strindberg's expressionistic techniques.[23] Together with *The Secret of Heaven*, the trilogy most clearly exemplifies Lagerkvist's principles and marks the way in which he was to proceed in much of his drama, although varying and developing his technique from work to work even as he did in his poetry and fiction.

In *The Secret of Heaven*, Lagerkvist's first play produced in Sweden,[24] disfigured and demented characters roam about the bizarre spherical stage (suggesting the vastness of earth), seek the impossible, fail to communicate with one another, and despair of discovering the meaning of their existence. Lagerkvist's use of expressionism is nowhere more evident than in this play, but the obscure symbolism that clouded his earlier work has been cleared through his perception of an existential response to life. His play holds together through his characters' quest for the meaning of existence. Each, in turn, raises the question, and each, in turn, is unable to communicate, to empathize with the others. The young girl seeks the one string that will provide the true note; the man without legs crawls in search of a coin with a hole in it that will distinguish it from common currency; the blind man searches for the foot of the stairs that will lead to heaven.

Nowhere in Lagerkvist's work, either earlier or later in such mature writing as *Dvärgen* or the Crucifixion novels (all of which are foreshadowed by this early play),[25] does he deal more poignantly with the dreadful division between man's desire and capacity to know the nature of his own existence. The despair that characterizes the human condition is summarized in the words of the man with the skullcap, whose answer to the question of existence is, "The meaning, you see, the real significance of it all, it's this . . . it's this . . . that . . . that. . . . Everything whirls around. Everything.—And therein lies the *meaning*, my young friend. Therein lies the real *meaning*" (I, 144-45; B. 82-83).

But it is not sufficient answer for the boy who is the hero of the play. As his inability to identify himself indicates, he cannot provide the answers to the meaning of existence, and, as the dwarf, ironically, says, he is not a whole man. But he tries. He tries to communicate, and he tries especially to love. When that fails, he is confronted with that condition that Camus called *the absurd*. Acting in the one way that will give him control of his own fate and bring him either to the emptiness or significance of life, he leaps to his death. Lagerkvist himself, no believer in the light, describes the young man's action as "fling[ing] himself out into the darkness," even as the man in the skullcap muses, "hehehe, they think there's a bottom . . ." (I, 154; B. 91).

And throughout it all, God, sawing wood and saying nothing, like the workman god in *Det eviga leendet*, is not concerned with providing answers to man's dilemma. The man with the skullcap, surely a symbol of inadequate priesthood, describes that god as unfathomable, more mysterious than the universe itself. The meaning of life, as Lagerkvist presents it in the play, can only be in the very striving, questioning, and seeking that make up man's existence. Perhaps that is no satisfactory answer, but, according to Lagerkvist throughout his work, that is all the answer man can hope for. Clearly, Lagerkvist has tied together his expressionistic techniques here with an existentialist philosophy that makes *The Secret of Heaven* a truly experimental drama for its time and a foreshadowing of such plays as Samuel Beckett's *Waiting for Godot* and *Endgame*. At the same time, the play, with its ties to all his later and earlier work, demonstrates the unifying thread that runs through all of Lagerkvist's writing.

Whatever their limitations, both *The Difficult Hour* and *The Secret of Heaven* possess the great merit of attempted experimentation—a movement away from conventional plot and characterization. Both, too, avoid easy classification of their forms, and Lagerkvist's final play of this period, *Den osynlige* (*The Invisible One*, 1923), continues his forging of new forms in such a way that critics rather desperately try to provide such labels as "a series of ritual scenes" or "oratorio."[26] Like the earlier plays, it continues Lagerkvist's attack on Ibsenism and pursues the direction taken by Strindberg in the theater. But as several critics have demonstrated, Lagerkvist seeks no simple formulae in his drama. Here he attempts to make something new out of such disparate elements as Strindberg's *A Dream Play* and *To Damascus*, medieval allegory, and classical Indian drama.[27]

Once again Lagerkvist is concerned more with forces than with people. His characters—the Invisible One, a seeker and the very spirit of man; the Administrator, a slave driver and a figure of death ruling over mankind; the Hero, fighter for light and mankind against the Administrator's oppression and darkness—all are more representational than individualized. Lagerkvist uses them in a way that foreshadows all his later themes and interests, particularly the dualities of light and darkness, life and death, good and evil. Moreover, his resolution of the conflict —after the Invisible One slays the Administrator and the Hero dies believing his ideals have been illusions—stands very close to the philosophy of Lagerkvist's later work. What the Invisible One discovers as seeker is the indivisibility of good and evil, the inseparability of life and death, the collusion of light and darkness that characterize man's existence.

Although *The Invisible One* is somewhat "more obscure and less intense" than his earlier work, oddly enough it is also more "homogeneous,"[28] indicating that Lagerkvist was preparing to take a major step forward in his dramatic development. It was, however, a development still in line with his theories in *Modern teater*.

III   Han som fick leva om sitt
liv: *A Turning Point*

Han som fick leva om sitt liv (*The Man Who Lived His Life Over*, 1928) did mark a transition in Lagerkvist's dramatic technique, and the play introduces philosophical changes characteristic of the somewhat more subtle thinking of the author in his later years. Indeed, Kay Nolte Smith, describing the plays from 1928 to 1939 as plays of the middle period, summarizes accurately some of the characteristic development in Lagerkvist's technique, a development in which some of his "best dramatic assets emerge":

artfully plain speech which gives great weight to the unspoken; characters inked in broad strokes, yet telling of growing moral awareness with the precision of an etching; exposition brought in at the moment when it acquires moral (and dramatic) awareness in the characters' lives.[29]

What this implies is not a change in kind, but rather a change in degree, a greater artistic maturity in *The Man Who Lived His Life Over*, a play that Alf Sjöberg, the great Swedish director, has called the author's best drama for stage production. That maturity comes especially in Lagerkvist's stylistic development using realistic details.[30] Here, for the first time, Lagerkvist combines the visionary elements of his earlier plays with a setting familiarly realistic. Using his detailed knowledge of Småland types in his characterization and setting, he provides a groundwork for the mystical power that formerly, at times, ran too wildly through his work. Whatever the metaphysical implications of this drama, his characters struggle with the very real problems of living in this world. Out of the action which presents a man whose life lived over proves no more successful than his original existence, Lagerkvist argues that man can only try to make the best of an existence over which he has little control.

Given a second chance to live after his first life, which had been a failure and had ended disastrously, Daniel is determined to pursue what he calls his "own life," to "be victorious" (I, 223; 375).[31] Although he cannot recall it, that first existence had been characterized by his lack of restraint, his yielding to his emotions. Now he is cautious, careful that his actions will not lead to a second defeat. When he meets Anna, a woman positive of the wonderful effects of love and who believes "that everything can be changed . . . if one wants it" (I, 248; 394), he marries her. He works hard as a shoemaker, proves himself a devoted husband, dedicates himself to his family, raises four children.

Through those trying moments when a "double" brings back reminders of his past and the strain seems unbearable,[32] Anna comforts Daniel—almost as much as to say that love indeed can somehow change man's existence. And yet, after his children have grown and three of them are happily settled in their lives, Daniel's chosen way of life for his second existence, his determination to control his emotions, destroys him as surely as his lack of restraint had done previously. His son, Elof, pursues a futile love affair with a woman of bad reputation who does not love him. Daniel, unsympathetic to the boy's feelings, deliberately restricting his own emotions, offers him no solace, and consequently, Elof commits suicide.

The structure of the play—counterposing as it does Daniel's past and present life—seems ideally suited to Lagerkvist's theme of the dualities in man's nature and existence, that omnipresent need to find a balance between reason and emotion, that insistent awareness that good and evil are not separate entities but rather belong to one whole. In Daniel's first life he has yielded completely to his *id*; he has, in Mjöberg's words, "allowed his nature to claim its due without self-restraint." Daniel's second chance follows the dictates of the super-ego, an excessive moral code leading to destruction with the same inevitability wrought by unbridled passion. As Mjöberg has shown, Lagerkvist's play is strongly influenced by classical drama, and in his attempt to discover how "to reconcile the nether powers with the laws of the world," Lagerkvist displays the concern of the classical Greek playwrights.[33]

By no means does this exhaust the thematic interests of a play which, like most of Lagerkvist's drama, closely parallels the form of a philosophical essay without yielding its dramatic intensity. Lagerkvist expresses an existential belief in the need to come to terms with existence, to recognize that man does not ultimately control his destiny, and to accept the fact that he can only live his life as best he can. It is Boman, characteristically one of Lagerkvist's physically deformed characters whose view of existence is healthier than that of the presumably healthy characters, who warns Daniel:

Are you afraid of life somehow, my child? You shouldn't be. . . . Certainly it is difficult . . . yes, yes . . . it can be agonizing. . . . And one doesn't know what is coming . . . what it is that lies in wait for us. . . . But we live as best we can, we do our best. Yes, we ought to do that. . . . You should too! And then no one can ask more of you. . . . Yes, we live the best we can . . . this hard, hard life . . .we put up with it . . . drag ourselves through it . . . day by day, year by year . . . as well as we are able. . . . (I, 236; 384-85)

Out of Daniel's struggle to make his second life more meaningful, to truly exist rather than merely live, evolves this second theme: man's relationship to the indifferent universe, which has the power to affect him, but stands beyond his capacity to strike back. As Daniel cries out for an opportunity to live his "real life," his "own life" (I, 223; 375), it is the existentialist cry in the night that rings out through most of Lagerkvist's major work and, indeed, through much of modern literature. It is his particular achievement, however, that he does not let such philosophical preoccupations diminish his art as art.

IV   The Drama and Politics: Konungen, Bödeln, Mannen utan själ, and Seger i mörker

In the following years, Lagerkvist responded artistically to the catastrophe threatening civilization, and yet his expressionism, his fundamental esthetic interests do not disappear in his political plays of the thirties.[34] Despite its historical setting, Konungen (The King, 1932) presents the brutality apparent in European political events; and however influenced by Sir James Frazer's The Golden Bough, with its ritualistic theories, Bödeln (The Hangman, 1934) makes one of the earliest attacks directly on Hitler's barbarism. For Lagerkvist there is no dichotomy between life and art; there is a concern for the particular in generalization, and a regard for the abstract in the specific.

On the surface, *The King* concerns itself with politics,[35] pitting traditional kingship against the revolutionary spirit. Buckman, in fact, offers an interpretation of its theme that satisfies this ostensible purpose of the play, which he describes as a "philosophical dialogue in a dramatic context," arguing " that a common bond of humanity must be the foundation for building a new world, in poverty and faith."[36] Yet such a reading ignores a good part of the philosophical discussion and suggests a change in Lagerkvist's fundamental concerns that runs contrary to the evidence of the drama.

As a summary of *The King* indicates, Lagerkvist once more assays the nature of good and evil and their symbiotic relationship in man's world. In that world, as Lagerkvist sees it, there are no absolutes, and man's experience should show him, as William Blake recognized nearly 200 years ago, that good often is energized by evil. The very structure of *The King*, built as it is around the characters of a king and his scapegoat, is ideally suited to Lagerkvist's concern for exploring the various dualities in existence.

Replaced by a scapegoat king (Iream-Azu) during a festival for Azu, god of fire and violence, King Amar-Azu expresses his despair with kingship, his sense of frustration with its "mere show." Amar, a truth-seeker who refuses to delude himself, recognizes that truth is neither pretty, obvious, nor absolute. Even the god Azu, whom he serves, Amar has seen through as no more than a means of satisfying man's desire for cruelty and destruction. Not all the persuasion of Sibile, his favorite wife who by coming to him has violated the taboo, or Nadur, a faithful servant equally guilty of breaking the taboo, or the high priest who argues that however accurate Amar's judgment, order requires a continuing pretense—not any of these can change Amar's mind. Life itself has destroyed his belief and brought him to a confrontation with the abyss.

At the same time, Iream-Azu, the scapegoat king, offers a portrait of the proletariat who at first sees in kingship only an opportunity to gratify his desires and who cannot comprehend such values as loyalty and friendship. When a revolution of the

166

PÄR LAGERKVIST

masses occurs, Iream becomes the idol of the people. Meanwhile, Amar, unrecognized by his subjects, has been badly beaten, but as he is dying he bequeaths Sibile to Nadur, recognizing their love for each other, and he calls upon Nadur to hold on to his beliefs and ideals and return to the world of men to serve mankind. It is an ideal that Nadur intends to abide by when, pardoned from his sentence of banishment by Iream, he will not promise to serve the king and his followers, but vows to serve mankind.

Doubt, philosophical skepticism, the uncertainties of human existence—the basic material of all Lagerkvist's work—constitute the primary subject matter here. While critics have argued that *The King* offers "some hope for mankind,"[37] Lagerkvist has actually placed severe limitations on what mankind can hope for in this world. Human love seems at best a "lovely masquerade of souls"; illusion alone allows man to believe in the purposefulness of existence, whereas the truth could lead man to confront the nothingness and terror of the human condition. To be sure, these observations come from a variety of characters in a dramatic situation and cannot be ascribed simply to Lagerkvist himself. Nevertheless, the dialectic of the play leads clearly enough to Lagerkvist's characteristic belief that the only value of life is in the living of life itself, nothing grandiose, nothing comforting, nothing so optimistic as "hope for mankind," at least as that phrase is commonly understood.

Rewritten from Lagerkvist's novella at the request of stage directors, *Bödeln* (*The Hangman*, 1934) was produced not only in Sweden, but also in Norway, where because of its political message, it was received enthusiastically.[38] Yet the play, like the novella and like *The King*, was intended to be more than political propaganda. Not only the Nazis, but racism generally comes under attack. Lagerkvist demonstrates the role played by "nice people" in allowing violence to run rampant in a society where civilization glosses over the basest human instincts. His historical perspective in the drama permits Lagerkvist to comment upon the universality of conduct that indicates man's relationship to the lower orders of nature.

By making *The Hangman* a play whose structure unites medieval and modern barbarism, Lagerkvist uses his expressionistic technique to turn contemporary political commentary into an exploration of the violence and cruelty in man's nature. The violence allows Lagerkvist to create an unusual amount of action for one of his dramas, but his final effectiveness is achieved by ironic contrasts between what may be designated as its two parts. They amount to voices raised separately, brought together not by artificial rhetorical devices, but by the fact that they are expressions of the kinds of violence in man's soul. The old expressionism creates the sense of horror that the play requires, while the realism of the actual political scene allows the reader no escape from a confrontation with the ghastly brutality of the moment. In *The Hangman* are strong echoes of that uncontrolled expressionism in the earlier plays, but tying it to the actuality of contemporary politics, Lagerkvist has now brought it under mature control.

Both *The King* and *The Hangman,* then, carry further Lagerkvist's combination of his old expressionism with a violent kind of realism. His theme remains in both a kind of metaphysical probing after the mysteries of existence or the nature of good and evil. And yet he has truly learned to harness his expressionism in these plays, through more realistic settings, characterization, and dialogue. Attacking, as he does, the particular evils of totalitarianism, he restricts his use of expressionism to the roles of heightening the emotion and enlarging the scope of his dramas.

Even *Mannen utan själ* (*The Man Without a Soul,* 1936)—showing the effects of a political murder on the assassin—indicates how well Lagerkvist could deal with contemporary life without simply yielding to realistic or naturalistic techniques. Although the drama clearly reflects the contemporary circumstances of the Spanish Civil War,[39] Lagerkvist eschews the precise details that would limit the significance of the play. His setting is a world in which chaos appears to be international and in which whatever little sense that could control man's behavior has been relinquished to madness. The radio that informs the patrons of the bar in his first act blares forth a record of the day's mayhem and murder. The people sitting in this conventional retreat from the world can think of nothing better than to lament the sorry state of things or to attempt to shut it out of their lives by talking about other matters. Nothing could be farther from dramatic realism than the coincidence that marks the play's central event. A young man, fresh from a political assassination, takes refuge in a bar at a table occupied by a forlorn young woman who, as it turns out, is the pregnant mistress of his victim. Unaware of his identity and deed, she protects him from the police and spends the night with him. Whatever realism exists in the incident comes not from the event. Even as the man sees the portrait of her murdered lover in her room the next morning, the response hardly conveys the true horror of the situation. Rather the reality comes through a sense of their uprootedness, their anguished despair over giving life a sense of sanity through the significance of human relationships and sex.

Even the conclusion of the play depends less on the logic of dramatic realism than it does on Lagerkvist's ability to convince an audience of the legitimacy of his characters' feelings that go beyond temporal circumstances. The young woman dies in childbirth, but finds her happiness in the victory of life which continues beyond the individual. The young man, having been released from prison by the triumphant rebel forces, can no longer find satisfaction in the limited political cause for which he had killed, and when he is executed as a traitor or deserter, he goes proudly to his death, having discovered a purpose—that sense of life's continuity—more meaningful than anything he had believed in before.

Despite its immediate political concern, then, the play makes its larger point through the repeated struggle for faith, and Lagerkvist indicates that his subject is not individual man, but mankind. Even characterization is developed so that it generalizes beyond the immediate circumstances. The unnamed "Man" and "Woman" belong to the allegorical tradition of *Everyman*, and, as Alrik Gustafson has noted, "we know next to nothing of the mere outward accidents of their existence."[40] What we do know is their existential anguish. The Man tries to find meaning through action devoted to some abstract political cause. As he says, "When there is action, one feels the excitement, the tension, like a wild joy within one! . . . then one lives!" (II, 146; 73). But it is not sufficient without the bonds of *human* relationships, without love. When he insists to the Woman that "We must live!" she responds, "Yes . . . but how?" (II, 179; 97). He has no answer.

Gustafson has argued that "The central emphasis of the play is an ethical one, concerned solely with the moral consequences of a recently committed political murder."[41] To be sure, Lagerkvist's concern is ethical rather than merely political, but as in all his work, ethics becomes metaphysics. In his closing lines Lagerkvist uses a hospital nurse as a choric figure to tell the audience, "one death, and one life. It's often like that.... And still it is life that is victorious, so that it can go on. We must do our best—so that it may go on" (II, 187; 103). The "Evil Man" of the play searches and gropes for an answer, and Lagerkvist turns political observation into metaphysical drama.

In his final play of the period—*Seger i mörker* (*Victory in Darkness*, 1939)—Lagerkvist ostensibly is more didactic than in any other of his dramas. Concerned with a patriotic response to world conditions, he becomes far more conventional than he has ever been before, particularly in the structure of his play. He relies on dialogue, with little regard for scenic effects. Here he gives his characters full names, personalizing them, and he resorts to the kind of psychologizing that he ordinarily detests.[42]

For all that, *Victory in Darkness* retains important elements of Lagerkvist's dramatic values, indeed, of the values that permeate all his work. Originally, he had intended to call the play *Människokällaren* (*The Human Basement*), a symbolic description of the evil and darkness within all men.[43] His plot is designed, as usual, to show the duality in man's nature, but whereas in *The King* he has more or less placed the duality in two unrelated characters, and in *The Man Who Lived His Life Over* he has defined it in Daniel's two lives, here he sets up two stepbrothers, an ideal device for suggesting both the interrelatedness and opposed qualities of good and evil. Spurred by contemporary political events, Lagerkvist uses a political framework in which to play out his battle between good and evil, a battle which inevitably for Lagerkvist, whatever the external forces on him, leads to no clear-cut victory.

Robert Grant, envious of the power and personal life of his brother, Gabriel Fontan, engages in a plot to overthrow the government of which his brother is prime minister. By informing Gabriel's son Stefan of his father's extramarital love affair, Robert wins the youth's support. While Gabriel's government is democratic, Robert seeks to install the dictatorship of a general. Robert ultimately succeeds in his plot, but his victory is undercut when Gabriel and his wife are reunited at their execution and reaffirm their faith in Gabriel's system of government and its future.

And yet, as already suggested, the dichotomy between the brothers is more apparent than real. Lagerkvist, by resorting to the psychology he generally eschews, creates some sympathy for Robert, who feels wronged by the treatment of his brother and his brother's wife. Actually, Gabriel does demonstrate a failure to understand Robert. Moreover, Gabriel's affair with a mistress and his betrayal of his wife, which outrages his son and turns the youth away from him, indicates the underside of Gabriel's nature. So even here, when the political content of the play seems uppermost, Lagerkvist manages to enlarge his probing of his subject in such a way that his work seems more than the specifically didactic publication that was its impetus.

V   *Plays of the 1940's*: Midsommardröm i fattighuset;
De vises sten; *and* Låt människan leva

The didactic emphasis declines or at least becomes subsumed in the more purely dramatic purposes of Lagerkvist's plays of the 1940's. In *Midsommardröm i fattighuset* (*Midsummer Dream in the Workhouse*, 1941), he returns to the idea of drama as he had envisioned it in *Modern Theater*: a form in which imagination, movement, and audacity must have free play.[44] In what has been called his finest blending of realism and fantasy,[45] he allows old Blind Jonas to create a dream world of hope for a young girl, turning at the same time his depressing surroundings into an enchanted dream of his own.

The real world around Jonas oppresses through its every detail of human poverty, deformity, and despair. Characters like "The Murderer," Lame Fredrik, and Deaf Anna people the workhouse, which in itself festers with ugly gossip, rumor, and unhappiness. Even Ellen, the Matron, is a hollow woman, a shell whose unhappy life has emptied her of all sense of joy and hopefulness. Against this squalid background. Lagerkvist sets the power of fantasy to transform Jonas's life and surroundings. In Jonas's dream world— first sketched by Jonas in talking to young Cecilia and then lived by him in fantastic reverie—all the ugly elements of reality are converted into a comforting fairy tale. Cecilia takes on the role of a princess; Ellen, her grandmother, who in reality had borne an illegitimate child by Jonas, reigns as a beautiful queen, her heart having been made cold and her love for her king having been temporarily put asunder. Jonas's real-life enemy, Alfred, has treacherously replaced him in Ellen's affections, but Jonas returns to cast him out, regain her love, and rule benevolently over his subjects.

Lagerkvist returns in *Midsummer Dream in the Workhouse* to his earlier esthetic, that which led him to his attack on Ibsenism (although oddly enough he has followed Ibsen's construction of plot in the method he uses to reveal piecemeal the reality of Jonas's life).[46] The beautiful and joyous fairy tale is used to counteract realism. Art for Lagerkvist serves as a substitute for faith; only in a dream, only by maintaining illusions, can people be happy. Jonas is aware that the fairy tale is a fairy tale. He recognizes that in life "things don't always turn out as one thought" (III, 66; 51).[47] For Cecilia, as well as for himself, Jonas has deliberately created a counterforce to reality, a world, as in his novella *Själarnas maskerad*, in which man can pretend an order to confront a chaotic real world. To combat the ugliness of existence, Lagerkvist turns to art, for through man's imagination alone there can be a "great—kingdom—of Joy . . . where it is always Midsummer" (III, 69; 53). In his return to his old lyrical style, Lagerkvist calls forth his earlier theme as well: life's effect on man; and here Lagerkvist, with his growing awareness of the importance of human relationships, shows how life's struggle can affect man's treatment of his fellows.[48]

De vises sten (*The Philosopher's Stone*, 1947) seems a lesser drama, with a more conventional plot that sets science and religion against each other and shows the effects of each when pushed unreasonably to its extreme. But even here the anti-realism remains. Lagerkvist deliberately casts contemporary comment and modern existentialist attitudes in a medieval or early Renaissance setting. His story of Albertus, a single-minded alchemist in pursuit of the philosopher's stone, and Simonides, a rabbi devoted to a mysterious God, has its meaning not in its historical setting, but rather in the forces that threaten modern life, the obsessional drive for absolutes that incapacitates man in his attempt to discover the significance of life, which, for Lagerkvist, is only to be found in the living of life itself.

Both Albertus and Simonides deny normal emotions and expectations, and their antilife force destroys their progeny and every prospect of happiness for human existence. Albertus ignores the human concerns of Catherine, his daughter. If he has not indeed made a pact with the devil, as his wife Maria charges, the effect of his obsession makes that point inconsequential, for through his conduct, he has driven his daughter into whoredom and eventually into dreadful tragedy. Simonides, too, by his willful denial of the realities of the world brings about the destruction of Jacob, his son, and leads his people from one ghetto to another. As a consequence of Simonides' conduct, Jacob dies by the executioner's blade, and because of Albertus's drive, Catherine ends her life in the exile of a convent. At the end, the two old men have nothing left but their obsessions, with which, apparently, they will spend their final days.

If in summary Lagerkvist's play seems no more than an allegorical debate, the truth is that Lagerkvist's dramatic techniques overcome its philosophically static qualities. The very Faustian character of its theme breathes life into its allegorical figures, not only into the powerful drives of Albertus and Simonides, but even into the less fully developed characters like Maria, who represents "conventional belief" and the evil prince, a symbol of "opportunism" as he takes advantage of Catherine's vulnerability.[49]

Much of Lagerkvist's dramatic power comes from his use of setting, the backdrop of historical corruption in the court life and the consequent poverty in the ghettoes. Here, too, Lagerkvist's technique is allegorical, for there can be no question that his concern is more contemporary than historical. What enables Lagerkvist to lift his setting from its allegorical simplicity is his use of his earlier expressionistic techniques to provide mood and to create atmosphere. At the same time, he has matured artistically, and the failures in his early use of expressionism have been almost eliminated. The dialogue is no longer chaotic or disjointed, and the action is no longer presented in emotional shorthand. Like the political dramas, *The Philosopher's Stone* combines the earlier techniques, now handled more skillfully, with Lagerkvist's overriding purpose as an artist, whether in poetry, drama or fiction.

Whatever the conventionalities of *The Philosopher's Stone*, in *Låt människan leva* (*Let Man Live*, 1949) nothing is conventional, as Lagerkvist's characters—each with a tale of martyrdom—step forth on a barren stage and recount their woes. Once more Lagerkvist's play taxes the critics' energies as they search for appropriate terms to describe it. If the technique suggests Thornton Wilder's in *Our Town*, the effect of Lagerkvist's treatment has nothing of Wilder's maudlin sentimentality. The moral comment is a savage attack on orthodox morality,[50] and its message is consistent with Lagerkvist's fundamentally existential attitude.

In Lagerkvist's unconventional setting, Socrates, Christ, Paolo and Francesca, and a host of other characters raise their voices in a kind of antiphonal poetry out of which Lagerkvist questions the meaning of life and the nature of good and evil. First it is Socrates who declares: "Men have judged me. And so the judgment is quite imperfect. Men themselves are imperfect, so it is not surprising if their judgments are imperfect too" (III, 211; 114). Then Christ with supreme charity declares to his oppressors:

I cannot accuse you, can I? . . . And I cannot accuse God, for of course He meant well when He sent me to you; He hoped that my coming would help you. If it has not helped, neither He nor I am responsible. We have both done our best.

The question is whether *you* too have done your best. . . . It is quite true that you have behaved dreadfully. . . . But what chances had you to avoid that, how could you fulfill your high destiny and be quite different? One must know that before one can rightly judge your actions. Nor must one forget how much you have done that was good and beautiful, how much that shows you to be not entirely evil but makes up to some extent for your evil deeds. . . . (III, 213; 116)

It is no either/or philosophy that Lagerkvist offers in the play, but rather one that shows an acute understanding of the human condition. In the presentation of historical characters telling stories of martyrdom, Lagerkvist strikes at conventional codes of morality that destroy the individual, that negate the very character of human existence. From its very title, *Let Man Live*

makes a plea for faith in man and his destiny. The words of
Paolo and Francesca accurately summarize the existential conclusions that may be drawn from his work. "Fall to the ground?"
asks Francesca; "Why should we? Do you think death has such
power? How could it? It is life that is mighty and not death.
It is life that is great and infinite—although men do their best to
deny it." And Paolo answers, "Yes, that is true. It is life that
is great and infinite. Come, dearest, let us live! Life forever!"
(III, 218; 120).

How much Lagerkvist's play suggests how far ahead of his
times he has been! How much of his technique and his philosophy have foreshadowed European existentialist drama and the
"Theater of the Absurd." And yet, how much Lagerkvist's
creative world is his own and a unified whole. Life and morality
in *Let Man Live* do not differ greatly from the way Lagerkvist
dealt with them in his first play, the unpublished *Life*, or again
in the later essay *The Conquered Life*. It is not an easy acceptance of life, but a concept of it as a struggle, something that
man must live with because he has no choice. Lagerkvist is
that odd combination of the classical writer, whose choice of a
lean, hard prose is an attempt to escape the romantic abyss
that he feels deep down in his own soul, in his emotions. The
tension between feeling and intellect that characterizes his
work is in itself one more example of the dualities that Lagerkvist sees in life and that he responds to with an art that is an
endless struggle after answers that he knows can never be final.

VI Barabbas *and the Dramatic Achievement*

In 1953, Lagerkvist successfully adapted his novel *Barabbas*
for the stage, and its popularity provides a reminder that his
plays appeal to the public as well as to the critics. *The Secret
of Heaven* has been adapted as an opera; his dramas have been
presented on Swedish radio; they have appeared in Stockholm's
Royal Dramatic Theater under the sophisticated direction of
such outstanding artists as Per Lindberg, Olof Molander, and Alf
Sjöberg. Whether performed in the provinces or in major cities,
whether seen in the theater or merely heard over radio, they have
gained widespread audience approval, making Lagerkvist's career
as a dramatist—as Buckman declares—one in which any playwright might take pride.[51]

Notes and References

Chapter One

1. For Lagerkvist's background, see Sven Linnér, *Pär Lagerkvists livstro* (Stockholm, 1961), pp. 9 ff. and Irene Scobbie's monograph, *Pär Lagerkvist: an Introduction* (Stockholm, 1963).
2. Sven Linnér, "Introduction" to *Scandinavica,* 10 (May, 1971), Supplement, 1.
3. See later discussion of *Aftonland* (1953), in which collection Lagerkvist uses these images.
4. Erik Blomberg, "Det besegrade livet: en studie i Pär Lagerkvists författarskap," *Ord och bild,* 42 (1933), 201-14, 267-78, 325-32 (reprinted in *Stadens fångar* [Stockholm, 1933]). Although Blomberg later revised somewhat his estimate of what he saw as these limitations on Lagerkvist's work ("Pär Lagerkvists tidssatirer" in *Mosaik* [1940]), the point seems quite accurate in itself without the question of whether it is detrimental to Lagerkvist's art.
5. Scobbie, *Pär Lagerkvist,* p. 46.
6. *Ordkonst och bildkonst* (Stockholm, 1913). For the influences on Lagerkvist's essay, see L. Åslund, "Pär Lagerkvists *Ordkonst och bildkonst* och det nya måleriet," *Ord och bild,* 64 (1955), 35-49.
7. Johannes Edfelt, "Pär Lagerkvist," *Norseman,* 10 (1952), 42.
8. Marie Gabrieli, "Pär Lagerkvist—the Lyrical Poet," *Scandinavica,* 10 (May, 1971), Supplement, 81.
9. See Gösta M. Bergman, *Pär Lagerkvists dramatik* (Stockholm, 1928), pp. 22 ff. I am also indebted here and elsewhere (particularly in my final two chapters) to Jöran Mjöberg, who has permitted me to use a manuscript revision of his book, *Livsproblemet hos Lagerkvist* (Stockholm, 1951).
10. Edfelt, "Modern Swedish Poetry," p. 397.
11. Arthur Flodstrom, "*Ångest* and Cubism," *Scandinavica,* 10 (May, 1971), p. 5.
12. Walter Gustafson, "The Patterns of Art of Pär Lagerkvist," *Edda,* 41 (1954), 348.
13. Walter Gustafson, "*Sibyllan* and the Patterns of Lagerkvist's Works," *Scandinavian Studies,* 30 (August, 1958), 133.
14. Alrik Gustafson, "Pär Lagerkvist and *Barabbas,*" *American-Swedish Monthly,* 45 (November, 1951), 11, 23.

15. Kai Henmark, *Främlingen Lagerkvist* (Stockholm, 1966), pp. 137-59.

16. H. O. Granlid, *Det medvetna barnet. Stil och innebörd i Pär Lagerkvists Gäst hos verkligheten* (Oslo, 1961), *passim*.

17. Alrik Gustafson, *A History of Swedish Literature* (Minneapolis, 1961), p. 403.

18. Otto Oberholzer, *Pär Lagerkvist: Studien zu seiner Prosa und Seiner Dramen* (Heidelberg, 1958), Chapters II-IV. For a full discussion of Lagerkvist's complex use of the word *life* in various stages of his career, see Linnér, *Pär Lagerkvists livstro* and Gunnel Malmström, *Menneskehjertets verden* (Oslo, 1970).

19. Richard B. Vowles, "Introduction," *The Eternal Smile and Other Stories* (New York, 1954), p. xix. References to "E." are to the translations from this volume.

20. *Ibid.*, p. xv.

21. A. Gustafson, *History of Swedish Literature*, p. 403.

22. "P." refers to Pär Lagerkvist, *Prosa* (Stockholm, 1955).

23. The title is mistranslated in *The Eternal Smile* as "The Waves of Osiris."

24. Vowles, "Introduction," *The Eternal Smile*, p. xix.

25. Mjöberg, *Livsproblemet hos Lagerkvist*, p. 98.

26. "S." refers to Pär Lagerkvist, *Skrifter* (Stockholm, 1932), 3 vols.

27. Vowles, "Introduction," *The Eternal Smile*, p. xviii.

28. Published in *BLM*, 20 (1951), 733-35, and in *Les prix Nobel en 1951* (Stockholm, 1952), pp. 55-58.

29. The translation is by Alan Blair, *Norseman*, 12 (1954), p. 196. Further references appear in text in parentheses after semicolon.

30. The reference in the original is to *Kämpande ande* (Stockholm, 1930), p. 33.

31. *Kämpande ande*, p. 70.

32. While both "Father and I" and *Guest of Reality* have biographical importance, Granlid's warning (f.n. 16 above) is important. See, however, G. Tideström, "Tankar kring Pär Lagerkvists *Sibyllan*," *Samlaren*, 80 (1959), 80-96.

33. See preceding note.

34. Scobbie, *Pär Lagerkvist*, pp. 7, 22-23.

35. Sven Linnér, "Pär Lagerkvists barndomsmiljö," *Samlaren*, 58 (1947), 53-90.

36. See Vowles, "Introduction," *Eternal Smile*, p. xvi; A. Gustafson, *History of Swedish Literature*, pp. 293 ff.; Mjöberg, *Livsproblemet hos Lagerkvist*, p. 61; Oberholzer, *Pär Lagerkvist*, pp. 9-17.

37. Linnér, *Pär Lagerkvists livstro*, pp. 79 ff.

38. Everett M. Ellestad, "Pär Lagerkvist and Cubism: A Study

of His Theory and Practice," *Scandinavian Studies,* 45 (Winter, 1973), 37-52.

39. Alone of these novellas, *Masquerade of Souls* was not published separately, but appeared in *Kämpande ande.* "Sm." refers to *Själarnas maskerad* (Stockholm, 1962).

40. The recent translation of the novella by David O'Gorman in *The Eternal Smile: Three Stories by Pär Lagerkvist* (New York, 1971) is entitled *The Executioner.* Although it is more appropriate to the work, I have retained the more generally known title. References to the title are marked "ER."

41. A. Gustafson, *History of Swedish Literature,* p. 354.

Chapter Two

1. For the relationship of *The Dwarf* to Lagerkvist's canon generally, see Oberholzer, *Pär Lagerkvist,* pp. 164 ff.

2. A. Gustafson, *History of Swedish Literature,* p. 404.

3. Scobbie, *Pär Lagerkvist,* p. 10. For the type of persona, see Jöran Mjöberg, "Clowner och frälsare," *Ord och bild,* 62 (1953), 85-91, which deals with symbolic figures of the clown and savior in Lagerkvist's work and compares them with those in Faulkner's novels and Rouault's paintings.

4. For many of the details here, I am indebted to Mjöberg, *Livsproblemet hos Lagerkvist,* pp. 166-78.

5. A. Gustafson, *History of Swedish Literature,* p. 405. His comment, however, overemphasizes the allegorical reading of the novel.

6. Scobbie, *Pär Lagerkvist,* p. 37. Although speaking of the Dwarf's effect on other characters, Miss Scobbie, in her recent article —"The Significance of Lagerkvist's *Dwarf,*" *Scandinavica,* 10 (May, 1971), Supplement, 35-44—still holds to an essentially allegorical reading of the novel.

7. Flodstrom, "*Ångest* and Cubism," p. 6.

8. Wayne C. Booth, *The Rhetoric of Fiction* (Chicago, 1961), pp. 211 ff.

9. "D." refers to Pär Lagerkvist, *Dvärgen* (Stockholm, 1944). The translation used is by Alexandra Dick (New York, 1945).

10. Ellestad, "Lagerkvist and Cubism," p. 45.

11. Roy Arthur Swanson, "Lagerkvist's *Dwarf* and the Redemption of Evil," *Discourse,* 13 (Spring, 1970), 192, 195, argues justifiably that the contrast between good and evil might logically be described as between "*love* and evil." It seems most appropriate to the Dwarf's relationship to Teodora and Angelica.

12. See Roy Arthur Swanson, "Evil and Love in Lagerkvist's Crucifixion Cycle," *Scandinavian Studies,* 38 (November, 1966), 305.

See my own earlier article, "Lagerkvist's Uses of Deformity," *Scandinavian Studies,* 33 (November, 1961), 215-16.

13. Henmark, *Främlingen Lagerkvist,* pp. 64-76, discusses Lagerkvist's use of the outsider in his fiction.

14. See Chapter 8.

Chapter Three

1. Adolph B. Benson, "Pär Lagerkvist: Nobel Laureate," *College English,* 13 (May, 1952), p. 417, notes that 60,000 copies were sold in Sweden during the first year, and the novel was translated immediately in eleven foreign countries.

2. Swanson, "Crucifixion Cycle," p. 307. Hjalmar Sundén, "Tobias's Pilgrimage," *Scandinavica,* 10 (May, 1971), Supplement, 69 ff., separates the trilogy of the Tobias novels from the two preceding them. Andreas Skartveit, *Gud skapt i menneskets bilete* (Oslo, 1966), sees *The Sibyl* as the point of departure.

3. For Lagerkvist's conception of God, see Henmark, *Främlingen Lagerkvist,* pp. 112 ff.

4. Ellestad, "Lagerkvist and Cubism," p. 45.

5. *Ibid.,* p. 50.

6. Neville Braybrooke, "Pär Lagerkvist," *Catholic World,* 176 (January, 1953), 266.

7. Swanson, "Crucifixion Cycle," p. 304, n. 5; Ellestad, "Lagerkvist and Cubism," p. 47.

8. Walter Gustafson, "The Patterns of Art of Pär Lagerkvist," p. 348, describes the structure "as a series of 15 dramatic scenes, drawn from, and elaborated on the Biblical story of Barabbas." The persistent sense of a narrator in *Barabbas* seems contrary to Gustafson's dramatic analogy, and his comparison with medieval morality plays requires a critic to note the distinction between Lagerkvist's theme and those of the dramas.

9. "B." refers to Pär Lagerkvist, *Barabbas* (Stockholm, 1964). Translations are from Alan Blair (New York, 1951).

10. André Gide, "Preface" to translation, p. xi.

11. See footnote 7.

12. Irene Scobbie, "Contrasting Characters in *Barabbas,*" *Scandinavian Studies,* 32 (November, 1960), 219.

13. *Ibid.,* p. 214.

14. See Scobbie, "Contrasting Characters," p. 212. G. Fredén, *Pär Lagerkvist. Från Gudstanken till Barabbas* (Stockholm, 1954), p. 10.

15. Gide, "Preface," to translation, p. xi.

16. Scobbie, *Pär Lagerkvist,* p. 40.

17. Scobbie, "Contrasting Characters," p. 213.

18. Mjöberg, *Livsproblemet hos Lagerkvist,* pp. 185 ff.
19. Gunnel Malmström, "The Hidden God," *Scandinavica,* 10 (May, 1971), Supplement, 62, sees the relationship of Barabbas and Christ as archetypes.
20. Scobbie, "Contrasting Characters," pp. 213, 217.
21. *Ibid.,* pp. 213, 200.
22. *Ibid.,* p. 213.
23. *Ibid.,* p. 215.
24. *Ibid.,* p. 215.
25. *Ibid.,* p. 216.
26. For a discussion of the relationship of Barabbas and Sahak, see Oberholzer, *Pär Lagerkvist,* pp. 193 ff.
27. See Scobbie, "Contrasting Characters," p. 218.
28. *Ibid.,* p. 218.
29. "Dover Beach."

Chapter Four

1. W. Gustafson, "*Sibyllan* and the Patterns of Lagerkvist's Works," p. 136.
2. *Ibid.,* p. 136. However, this view represents a change in W. Gustafson's earlier opinion about seeking a philosophy in Lagerkvist's work.
3. Scobbie, *Pär Lagerkvist,* p. 41, sees *The Sibyl* and later work generally sharing the attitudes in *The Clenched Fist,* but notes here "a new note of resignation." Gustafson, "*Sibyllan* and the Patterns of Lagerkvist's Works," p. 133, sees the novel as "much more complicated and mysterious" because it conveys "a modern world of religious doubt and questioning." Sven Linnér, "Pär Lagerkvist's *The Eternal Smile* and *The Sibyl,*" *Scandinavian Studies,* 37 (May, 1965), 163-65, discovers a "more bitter note" in the novel and describes the corresponding stylistic and philosophical changes.

W. Gustafson's suggestion, p. 134, that *The Sibyl* is "more directly concerned with theological speculation than is usual in Pär Lagerkvist's works" seems inaccurate particularly applied to *Barabbas,* but even to *The Dwarf* and *The Eternal Smile.* In the same way, Linnér's view (p. 160) that perhaps *The Sibyl* "should be read as an ironic refutation of the young author's all too easy acceptance of life, his 'belief in life' or his *livstro*" scarcely seems an accurate description of his earlier work.

For the recurring themes from *The Dwarf* through *The Sibyl,* see Oberholzer, *Pär Lagerkvist,* pp. 203 ff.
4. George Woodcock, *Mohandas Gandhi* (New York, 1971), p. 7.
5. W. Gustafson, "*Sibyllan* and the Patterns of Lagerkvist's Works," pp. 133-34.

6. E. Lagerroth, *Svensk berättarkonst* (Lund, 1968) argues that in *The Sibyl* Lagerkvist found a form in which he could place his ideas without yielding to earlier abstractions or theorizing. My discussion throughout this work indicates my disagreement with such a viewpoint.

7. W. Gustafson, "*Sibyllan* and the Patterns of Lagerkvist's Works," pp. 131-32.

8. *Ibid.*, pp. 131-32, details the autobiographical elements in the portrayal of the Sibyl's childhood and upbringing. See, too, Tideström, "Tankar kring Pär Lagerkvists *Sibyllan*," pp. 80-96.

9. "Si." refers to *Sibyllan* (Stockholm, 1963). The translation is by Naomi Walford (New York, 1958).

10. Malmström, "The Hidden God," *Scandinavica* (Supplement), May, 1971, p. 64, inaccurately asserts that it is only after meeting God that he "loses the ability to love."

11. Swanson, "Crucifixion Cycle," pp. 303-4.

12. Henmark, *Främlingen Lagerkvist*, pp. 112 ff., discusses the Freudian and religious aspects of *The Sibyl*.

13. W. Gustafson, "*Sibyllan* and the Patterns of Lagerkvist's Works," p. 132.

14. Swanson, "Crucifixion Cycle," p. 305. For Dostoevsky's influence on Lagerkvist, see Brita Wigforss, "Pär Lagerkvist och Dostojevsky," *Ord och bild*, 70 (1961), 169-77, and Linnér, *Pär Lagerkvists livstro*, pp. 282-312.

15. Linnér, "*Eternal Smile* and *The Sibyl*," p. 160.

16. W. Gustafson, "*Sibyllan* and the Patterns of Lagerkvist's Works," p. 132.

17. "Ode on a Grecian Urn."

18. Scobbie, *Pär Lagerkvist*, p. 41.

19. Malmström, "The Hidden God," p. 57.

Chapter Five

1. Winston Weathers, *Pär Lagerkvist: A Critical Essay* (Grand Rapids, Michigan, 1968), p. 19.

2. Swanson, "Crucifixion Cycle," p. 307; Weathers, *Pär Lagerkvist*, p. 19.

3. Ellestad, "Lagerkvist and Cubism," p. 47.

4. *Ibid.*, pp. 47-48.

5. The quotation is from the final page of *The Eternal Smile*.

6. Sundén, "Tobias's Pilgrimage," *Scandinavica* (Supplement), May, 1971, pp. 69-80, which applies Jungian psychology and the use of myths to the trilogy, separates it from the preceding two novels and emphasizes the search for self-knowledge in the trilogy.

7. Malmström, "The Hidden God," p. 65, notes the relationship between Diana's manner of death and "the central spear-thrower poem in *Aftonland.*"

8. "Ad." refers to *Ahasverus död* (Stockholm, 1967). The translation used is by Naomi Walford (New York, 1962). Italics have been added in this passage.

9. The comparison is made with *Barabbas* by Ellestad, "Lagerkvist and Cubism," pp. 47 ff.

10. Sundén, "Tobias's Pilgrimage," p. 72, sees "her love, her willingness to sacrifice her life for the one she loves" as her sole redeeming feature.

11. See Henmark, *Främlingen Lagerkvist,* pp. 77-100, for a discussion of the Christian themes in the novel.

12. Sundén, "Tobias's Pilgrimage," p. 73, notes the influence of Viktor Rydberg's "Prometheus och Ahasverus" on Lagerkvist's novel and of Rydberg's "Grubblaren" on the conclusion.

13. Weathers, *Pär Lagerkvist,* p. 19.

14. See Linnér, *"Eternal Smile* and *The Sibyl,"* p. 164.

15. See Malmström, "The Hidden God," p. 64.

16. Sundén, "Tobias's Pilgrimage," p. 73, sees Ahasuerus's death in a monastery as a kind of succumbing to Christ, but this quotation suggests otherwise. For this discussion of Ahasuerus's and Tobias's deaths, I owe much to Swanson, "Crucifixion Cycle," *passim.*

17. "Ph." refers to *Pilgrim på havet* (Stockholm [1962], 1968). The translation is by Naomi Walford (New York, 1964).

18. Sundén, "Tobias's Pilgrimage," p. 74, describes Ahasuerus and Giovanni as haters of God through whom Tobias comes to his God.

19. Some examples of the technique: "as if lulled by the sea," "He seemed to have been" (Ph. 6; 6); "as if hoping" (Ph. 7; 7); "which the other appeared not to notice" (Ph. 10; 10); "face no longer seemed" (Ph. 16; 16); "ship seemed to be handling herself," "seemed built for just such weather as this" (Ph. 17; 17), etc.

20. Swanson, "Crucifixion Cycle," p. 303.

21. Ph. 13-14; 14. See, too, Ph. 54, 110; 55, 112.

22. Swanson, "Crucifixion Cycle," p. 306.

23. "H." refers to *Det heliga landet* (Stockholm, 1964). The translation is by Naomi Walford (New York, 1966).

24. See, for example, the shift to the second-person point of view for Tobias, H. 72-73; 63-64.

25. Swanson, "Crucifixion Cycle," p. 312.

Chapter Six

1. Sundén, "Tobias's Pilgrimage," p. 79, cites the novel as evidence that Lagerkvist's personal conflict has remained unresolved.

2. "M." refers to *Mariamne* (Stockholm, 1967). The translation by Naomi Walford is *Herod and Mariamne* (New York, 1968).
3. Malmström, "The Hidden God," p. 67, notes the desert as "a recurring symbol in Lagerkvist's more recent work for a condition of separation from God."

Chapter Seven

1. For Lagerkvist's early poems in newspapers, see Harald Elovson, "Från Pär Lagerkvists läroår" in G. Tideström, ed., *Synpunkter på Pär Lagerkvist* (Stockholm, 1966), pp. 45-89.
2. Johannes Edfelt, "Modern Swedish Poetry," *Norseman*, 11 (1953), 397.
3. *Ibid.*, pp. 396-97.
4. C. W. Stork, "Contemporary Swedish Poetry," *American-Scandinavian Review*, 5 (1917), 343-44.
5. Bengt Larsson, "Pär Lagerkvists litterära kubism," *Samlaren*, 85 (1965), 66-95, discusses the effect of cubist theory on Lagerkvist's work.
6. A. Gustafson, *History of Swedish Literature*, p. 401.
7. See Linnér, *Pär Lagerkvists livstro*, p. 271. Lagerkvist's letter appears in T. Brunius, "Det kubistiska experimentet," *BLM*, 23 (1954), 812. Arthur Flodstrom, "*Ångest* and Cubism," *Scandinavica*, 10 (May, 1971), Supplement, 5-18, argues against Linnér's position.

Numbers in the text, following quotations from the poetry, refer to Pär Lagerkvist, *Dikter* (Stockholm, 1965). The following translations have been used in this chapter: *Twentieth-Century Scandinavian Poetry*, ed. by Martin S. Allwood (Marston Hill, Mullsjö, 1950); *Seven Swedish Poets*, ed. and trans. by Frederic Fleisher (Uddevalla, 1963); *American-Scandinavian Review*, 29 (1941), 25; 36 (1948), 46; 39 (1951), 135; 40 (1952), 306; *Norseman*, 10 (1952), 46-47; *Western Humanities Review*, X (1956), 118; *Hallmark Book of Poetry* (Garden City, N. Y., 1960), pp. 149-50; *Times Literary Supplement*, March 10, 1972, p. 273. I am also indebted to Leif Sjöberg and W. H. Auden for permitting me to use manuscript translations from *Aftonland* and to Jöran Mjöberg for translations in his manuscript revision of his book. The translation of "Torso" in Mjöberg's manuscript is by Richard Vowles.
8. Pär Lagerkvist, *Modern Theatre: Seven Plays and an Essay*, ed. and trans. by Thomas R. Buckman (Lincoln, 1966), p. xxi.
9. Flodstrom, "*Ångest* and Cubism," p. 6.
10. *Ibid.*, pp. 9-10.
11. *Ibid.*, p. 6.
12. See Erik Hörnström, *Pär Lagerkvist. Från den röda tiden till det eviga leendet* (Stockholm, 1946), pp. 100-101.

13. G. Fredén, *Pär Lagerkvist*, p. 10, describes these variations in Lagerkvist's treatment of a theme as alternating spiritual attitudes within the writer. For the development of Lagerkvist's philosophy of life from *Kaos* to *Det eviga leendet* and *Den Lyckliges väg,* see Linnér, *Pär Lagerkvists livstro.*

14. Edfelt, "Pär Lagerkvist," p. 43.

15. Scobbie, *Pär Lagerkvist,* p. 16.

16. Mjöberg, *Livsproblemet hos Lagerkvist,* p. 55.

17. See Mjöberg, *Livsproblemet hos Lagerkvist,* and "Det förnekade mörkret," *Samlaren,* 35 (1954), 78-112.

18. See, for example, Scobbie, *Pär Lagerkvist,* p. 18.

19. See Scobbie, *Pär Lagerkvist,* p. 23; Edfelt, "Pär Lagerkvist," p. 43; and Gunnel Malmström, *Menneskehjertets verden. Hovedmotiv i Pär Lagerkvists diktning* (Oslo, 1970). The following quotation in the text is from Jöran Mjöberg's review of Mrs. Malmström's book— *Scandinavica,* 10 (May, 1971), Supplement, 93.

20. Mjöberg, "Review of Malmström," p. 92.

21. Edfelt, "Pär Lagerkvist," p. 47.

22. The poem is an excellent example of Lagerkvist's view of the connection between suffering and ultimate harmony. See Gunnar Tideström, *Lyrisk tidsspegel* (Lund, 1956), p. 183.

23. For the significance of "stars" used as metaphors by Lagerkvist, see P. Hallberg, "Stjärnsymboliken i Pär Lagerkvists lyrik," *Göteborgsstudier i litteraturhistoria tillägnade Sverker Ek* (1954), pp. 313-42.

24. See Edfelt, "Pär Lagerkvist," p. 43, and Flodstrom, "*Ångest* and Cubism," p. 18.

25. See footnote 17.

26. Gunnel Malmström, "The Hidden God," *Scandinavica,* 10 (May, 1971), Supplement, 59.

27. *Ibid.,* p. 59.

28. *Ibid.,* p. 62.

29. Scobbie, *Pär Lagerkvist,* p. 41.

30. See Mjöberg, "Review of Malmström," p. 91; Irene Scobbie, "The Significance of Lagerkvist's *Dwarf,*" *Scandinavica,* 10 (May, 1971), Supplement, 35; A. Gustafson, *History of Swedish Literature,* p. 402.

31. Gabrieli, "Pär Lagerkvist—the Lyrical Poet," p. 84.

32. *Ibid.,* p. 85.

33. See footnote 4, Chapter One.

34. A. Gustafson, *History of Swedish Literature,* p. 393.

35. This information was provided to me by Henry Goddard Leach.

Chapter Eight

1. Prior to publication of his edition, Buckman published his translation of *Modern Teater, Den svåra stunden,* and his own essay, "Pär Lagerkvist and the Swedish Theatre," in *The Tulane Drama Review,* 6 (1961), 3-89.

2. For Lagerkvist's relationship to Bergman, see Agne Beijer, "Two Swedish Dramatists, Pär Lagerkvist and Hjalmar Bergman," *World Theatre,* 4 (1955), 14-24. For Lagerkvist's influence on Bergman, see Helmer Lång, "Marionetterna i 'Spelhuset,'" *Ord och bild,* 60 (1951), 220.

3. Buckman, "Lagerkvist and the Swedish Theatre," p. 67.

4. I am particularly indebted here to Mjöberg's manuscript. See, too, Bergman, *Lagerkvists dramatik, passim.*

5. For a description of *Livet,* see Elovson, "Från Pär Lagerkvists läroår." Robert Rovinsky, however, has informed me that the manuscript indicates Lagerkvist's early dependence on Ibsen (as, indeed, some comments in *Ordkonst och bildkonst* suggest in spite of Lagerkvist's disclaimer), while the play also demonstrates the thematic concerns that were to mark his later work.

6. See Buckman, "Lagerkvist and the Swedish Theatre," pp. 61, 67, 68.

7. For some of these influences on Lagerkvist, see Mjöberg, *Livsproblemet hos Lagerkvist,* pp. 129 ff.

8. Buckman, "Lagerkvist and the Swedish Theatre," p. 73, notes about forty reviews and articles on the drama and a few on new art books. See, too, Hörnström, *Pär Lagerkvist,* pp. 34 ff. For *Modern Theater* and Lagerkvist's plays, the text referred to by volume number and page is *Dramatik* (Stockholm, 1956), 3 vols. References after the semicolon and marked with "B." are to the translations by Buckman in his edition of *Modern Theatre.*

9. Buckman, "Lagerkvist and the Swedish Theatre," p. 73, and *Modern Theatre,* p. xv.

10. Buckman, "Lagerkvist and the Swedish Theatre," p. 67, notes that Lagerkvist's only other expository writing since 1919 has been his memorial addresses to the Swedish Academy. Buckman, "Stylistic and Textual Changes in *Modern teater,*" *Scandinavian Studies,* 33 (August, 1961), 138-39, 142-43, notes that Lagerkvist has never permitted the reprinting of *Ordkonst och bildkonst.* He also makes the important point of the essential consistency in all three works.

11. See footnote 8.

12. Buckman, "Lagerkvist and the Swedish Theatre," p. 68.

13. *Ibid.,* p. 81.

14. Buckman, *Modern Theatre,* pp. xii-xiii.

15. Bergman, *Lagerkvists dramatik* is still a reliable discussion

of Lagerkvist's early expressionism. I am indebted to his comments on *Sista mänskan* (pp. 39-75) and *Den svåra stunden* (pp. 76-109). Oberholzer, *Pär Lagerkvist*, presents a detailed discussion of the relationship between Lagerkvist's philosophy and plays.

16. Mjöberg, *Livsproblemet hos Lagerkvist*, pp. 122-23. The translation is from Mjöberg's manuscript.

17. Scobbie, *Pär Lagerkvist*, p. 13.

18. Buckman, "Lagerkvist and the Swedish Theatre," p. 82.

19. See my discussion of the play in "Lagerkvist's Dialogue of the Soul," *Scandinavian Studies: Essays Presented to Dr. Henry Goddard Leach*, ed. by Carl F. Bayerschmidt and Erik J. Friis (Seattle, 1965), p. 304.

20. Buckman, "Lagerkvist and the Swedish Theatre," p. 86, sees the third part of the trilogy as a forerunner of Sartre's *No Exit*.

21. *Ibid.*, p. 84.

22. Buckman, *Modern Theatre*, p. xvi.

23. *Ibid.*, pp. xvii-xviii.

24. Buckman, "Lagerkvist and the Swedish Theatre," pp. 79-80. The play was produced at the Intima Theatre to rather surprisingly receptive reviews.

25. Mjöberg, *Livsproblemet hos Lagerkvist*, pp. 166-78, describes its relationship to *The Dwarf*, but not, of course, to the later works.

26. Buckman, "Lagerkvist and the Swedish Theatre," p. 80.

27. See Scobbie, *Pär Lagerkvist*, p. 20; Mjöberg, *Livsproblemet hos Lagerkvist*, pp. 130 ff.; Bergman, *Lagerkvists dramatik*, pp. 133-56.

28. Scobbie, *Pär Lagerkvist*, p. 21.

29. Kay Nolte Smith, "Pär Lagerkvist: Playwright and Philosopher," *American-Swedish Monthly*, 54 (1960), 25.

30. Scobbie, *Pär Lagerkvist*, p. 25.

31. The translation used is by Walter Gustafson in *Five Modern Scandinavian Plays* (New York, 1971).

32. Scobbie, *Pär Lagerkvist*, p. 26, speaks of the double as an "alter ego" and notes the close resemblance to the beggar in Strindberg's *To Damascus*.

33. Mjöberg, *Livsproblemet hos Lagerkvist*, pp. 139-40. The translation is from his manuscript.

34. Benson, "Lagerkvist: Nobel Laureate," 420, notes a mellowing in Lagerkvist beginning with *The Man Who Lived His Life Over*, but the statement seems insupportable. Bengt Larsson, "Den röda tiden och den rena konsten. Pär Lagerkvists litterära utveckling fram till Ordkonst och bildkonst," *Samlaren*, 85 (1964), 19-39, discussing politics in Lagerkvist's art, notes the impossibility of restricting it to a particular period.

35. For a discussion of *The King* as a political play, see Maurice

Gravier, "*Konungen* (*Le Roi*) ou Le Drame de l'engagement," *Scandinavica*, 10 (May, 1971), Supplement, 19-34.

36. Buckman, *Modern Theatre*, p. xix.

37. Scobbie, *Pär Lagerkvist*, p. 27.

38. Buckman, "Lagerkvist and the Swedish Theatre," p. 80. See earlier discussion of the novella in Chapter One.

39. Mjöberg, *Livsproblemet hos Lagerkvist*, p. 158.

40. *Scandinavian Plays of the Twentieth Century, First Series*, ed. by Alrik Gustafson (Princeton, 1944), pp. 12-13. The translation cited for this play is by Helge Kökeritz in this volume.

41. *Ibid.*, p. 13.

42. Mjöberg, *Livsproblemet hos Lagerkvist*, p. 163; Scobbie, *Pär Lagerkvist*, pp. 32-34.

43. Mjöberg, *Livsproblemet hos Lagerkvist*, pp. 158 ff. I am also indebted here to Mjöberg's manuscript.

44. See earlier comment on *Modern teater*.

45. A. Gustafson, *History of Swedish Literature*, p. 399.

46. Mjöberg, *Livsproblemet*, p. 164.

47. The translation cited here is by Alan Blair, *Midsummer Dream in the Workhouse* (London, 1953).

48. Scobbie, *Pär Lagerkvist*, p. 34.

49. Buckman, *Modern Theatre*, pp. xx-xxi, and "Lagerkvist and the Swedish Theatre," p. 80.

50. *Scandinavian Plays of the Twentieth Century, Third Series*, ed. by Alrik Gustafson (Princeton, 1951), p. 10, describes the play as profoundly moral. The translation is by Henry Alexander and Llewellyn Jones.

51. Buckman, "Lagerkvist and the Swedish Theatre," p. 67.

Selected Bibliography

BIBLIOGRAPHIES

Ryberg, Anders. *Pär Lagerkvist in Translation: A Bibliography.*
Stockholm: Albert Bonniers, 1964.
Willers, Uno. *Pär Lagerkvists bibliografi på sextioårsdagen, 23 Maj
1951.* Stockholm: Albert Bonniers, 1951.
Yrlid, Rolf. *Pär Lagerkvists kritiker: En recensions-bibliografi.* Lund:
Studentlitteratur, 1970.

IMPORTANT COLLECTED WORKS

Prosa, I-V. Stockholm: Albert Bonniers, 1956.
Dramatik, I-III. Stockholm: Albert Bonniers, 1956.
Dikter. Stockholm: Albert Bonniers, 1965.

INDIVIDUAL WORKS

(Unless otherwise stated, published by Albert Bonniers
Förlag in Stockholm.)

Människor. Stockholm: Frams förlag, 1912.
Ordkonst och bildkonst. Stockholm: Frams förlag, 1913.
Två sagor om livet. Stockholm: Frams förlag, 1913.
Motiv. 1914.
Järn och människor. 1915.
Ångest. 1916.
Sista mänskan. 1917.
Teater. Den svåra stunden. 1918.
Kaos. 1919.
Det eviga leendet. 1920.
Den lyckliges väg. 1921.
Den osynlige. 1923.
Onda sagor. 1924.
Gäst hos verkligheten. 1925.
Hjärtats sånger. 1926.
Det besegrade livet. 1927.
Han som fick leva om sitt liv. 1928.
*Kämpande ande: Bröllopsfesten, Guds lille handelsresande, Själarnas
maskerad, Uppbrottet.* 1930.

187

Vid lägereld. 1932.
Konungen. 1932.
Bödeln. 1933.
Den knutna näven. 1934.
I den tiden. 1935.
Mannen utan själ. 1936.
Genius. 1937.
Den befriade människan. 1939.
Seger i mörker. 1939.
Sång och strid. 1940.
Midsommardröm i fattighuset. 1941.
Hemmet och stjärnan. 1942.
Dvärgen. 1944.
De vises sten. 1947.
Låt människan leva. 1949.
Barabbas. 1950.
Aftonland. 1953.
Sibyllan. 1956.
Ahasverus dö ˙. 1960.
Pilgrim på havet. 1962.
Det heliga landet. 1964.
Mariamne. 1967.

SELECTED ENGLISH TRANSLATIONS

The Man Without a Soul. Translated by Helge Kökeritz. *Scandinavian Plays of the Twentieth Century.* First Series. Princeton: Princeton University Press, 1944.

The Dwarf. Translated by Alexandra Dick. New York: Hill and Wang, 1945.

Twentieth-Century Scandinavian Poetry, ed. by Martin S. Allwood. Stockholm: Kooperativa förbundets bokförlag, 1950.

Barabbas. Translated by Alan Blair. New York: Random House, 1951.

Let Man Live. Translated by Henry Alexander and Llewellyn Jones. *Scandinavian Plays of the Twentieth Century.* Third Series. Princeton: Princeton University Press, 1951.

Midsummer Dream in the Workhouse. Translated by Alan Blair. London: W. Hodge, 1953.

The Eternal Smile and Other Stories. Translated by Alan Blair, Erik Mesterton, Denys W. Harding, Carl Eric Lindin. New York: Random House, 1954.

The Sibyl. Translated by Naomi Walford. New York: Random House, 1958.

The Death of Ahasuerus. Translated by Naomi Walford. New York: Random House, 1960.

Seven Swedish Poets, ed. by Frederic Fleisher. Malmö and Lund: Bo Cavefors, 1963.

Pilgrim at Sea. Translated by Naomi Walford. New York: Random House, 1964.

The Holy Land. Translated by Naomi Walford. New York: Random House, 1966.

Pär Lagerkvist: Modern Theatre: Seven Plays and an Essay. Translated by Thomas Buckman. Lincoln: University of Nebraska Press, 1966.

Herod and Mariamne. Translated by Naomi Walford. New York: Alfred A. Knopf, 1968.

The Man Who Lived His Life Over. Translated by Walter Gustafson. *Five Modern Scandinavian Plays.* New York: Twayne, 1971.

The Eternal Smile: Three Stories. Translated by Erik Mesterton, Denys W. Harding, David O'Gorman. New York: Hill and Wang, 1971.

SECONDARY WORKS

(An asterisk denotes an important foreign book or article for the study of Pär Lagerkvist.)

ÅSLUND, LEIF. "Pär Lagerkvists *Ordkonst och bildkonst* och det nya måleriet," *Ord och bild,* 64 (1955), 35-49.

BEIJER, AGNE. "Two Swedish Dramatists, Pär Lagerkvist and Hjalmar Bergman," *World Theatre,* 4 (1955), 14-24.

BENSON, ADOLPH B. "Pär Lagerkvist: Nobel Laureate," *College English,* 13 (May, 1952), 417-24.

*BERGMAN, GÖSTA M. *Pär Lagerkvists dramatik* (Stockholm: P. A. Norstedt and Sons, 1928).

BLOMBERG, ERIK. "Det besegrade livet: en studie i Pär Lagerkvists författarskap," *Ord och bild,* 42 (1933), 201-14, 267-78, 325-32.

————. "Pär Lagerkvists tidssatirer," *Mosaik,* 1940.

BRANDELL, GUNNAR. *Svensk litteratur 1900-1950* (Stockholm: Aldus edition, 1958).

BRAYBROOKE, N. "Pär Lagerkvist," *Catholic World,* 176 (January, 1953), 266.

BRUNIUS, TEDDY. "Det kubistika experimentet," *BLM,* 23 (1954), 805-14.

BUCKMAN, THOMAS. "Pär Lagerkvist and the Swedish Theatre," *Tulane Drama Review,* 6 (1961), 3-89.

————. "Stylistic and Textual Changes in *Modern teater,*" *Scandinavian Studies,* 33 (August, 1961), 137-49.

EDFELT, JOHANNES. "Modern Swedish Poetry," *Norseman,* 11 (1953), 396-402.

————. "Pär Lagerkvist," *Norseman,* 10 (1952), 42-48.

190   PÄR LAGERKVIST

ELLESTAD, EVERETT M. "Pär Lagerkvist and Cubism: A Study of His Theory and Practice," *Scandinavian Studies*, 45 (Winter, 1973), 37-52.

FEARNLEY, RAGNHILD. *Pär Lagerkvist* (Oslo: Gyldendal, 1950).

*FREDÉN, G. *Pär Lagerkvist: Från Gudstanken till Barabbas* (Stockholm: Bonnier, 1954).

*————. *Uppbrott till verkligheten* (Stockholm: Gummessons, 1963).

*GRANLID, H. O. *Det medvetna barnet. Stil och innebörd i Pär Lagerkvists Gäst hos verkligheten* (Oslo: Scandinavian University Books, 1961).

GUSTAFSON, ALRIK. *A History of Swedish Literature* (Minneapolis: University of Minnesota Press, 1961).

————. "Pär Lagerkvist and *Barabbas*," *American Swedish Monthly*, 45 (November, 1951), 11, 23, 25.

GUSTAFSON, WALTER. "The Patterns of Art of Pär Lagerkvist," *Edda*, 41 (1954), 346-50.

————. "*Sibyllan* and the Patterns of Lagerkvist's Works," *Scandinavian Studies*, 30 (August, 1958), 131-36.

HALLBERG, PETER. "Stjärnsymboliken i Pär Lagerkvists lyrik," *Göteborgsstudier i litteraturhistoria tillägnade Sverker Ek* (1954), 313-42 .

HEGGELUND, KJELL. *Fiksjon og virkelighet* (Oslo: Scandinavian University Books, 1966).

*HENMARK, KAI. *Främlingen Lagerkvist* (Stockholm: Rabén and Sjögren, 1966).

HÖRNSTRÖM, ERIK. "Klassikern Pär Lagerkvist," *Ord och bild*, 60 (1951), 516-20.

————. "Pär Lagerkvist och religionen," *Årsbok för kristen humanism*, 8 (1946), 40-56.

*————. *Pär Lagerkvist. Från den röda tiden till det eviga leendet* (Stockholm: Bonnier, 1946).

JACKSON, NAOMI. "The Fragmented Mirror: Lagerkvist's *The Dwarf*," *Discourse*, 8 (1965), 185-93.

JOHANNESSON, ERIC O. "Pär Lagerkvist and the Art of Rebellion," *Scandinavian Studies*, 30 (February, 1958), 19-29.

LAGERROTH, E. *Svensk berättarkonst* (Lund: Gleerup, 1968).

LARSSON, BENGT. "Den röda tiden och den rena konsten. Pär Lagerkvists litterära utveckling fram till *Ordkonst och bildkonst*," *Samlaren*, 85 (1964), 19-39.

————. "Pär Lagerkvists litterära kubism," *Samlaren*, 85 (1965), 66-95.

LINDBERG, PER. *Bakom masker* (Stockholm: Bonnier, 1949).

————. "Några synpunkter på Pär Lagerkvists dramatik," *Svensk litteraturtidskrift*, 3 (1940), 155-86.

*LINDER, ERIK HJALMAR. *Fem decennier av nitton-hundratalet* (Stockholm: Natur och Kultur, 1966), 2 vols.

*LINNÉR, SVEN. "Pär Lagerkvists barndomsmiljö," *Samlaren*, 58 (1947), 53-90.

————. "Pär Lagerkvist's *The Eternal Smile* and *The Sibyl*," *Scandinavian Studies*, 37 (May, 1965), 160-67.

*————. *Pär Lagerkvists livstro* (Stockholm: Bonnier, 1961).

————, ed. "Special Issue Devoted to the Work of Pär Lagerkvist," *Scandinavica*, 10 (May, 1971), Supplement.

LÅNG, HELMER. "Marionetterna i 'Spelhuset,' " *Ord och bild*, 60 (1951), 218-24.

*MALMSTRÖM, GUNNEL. *Menneskehjertets verden. Hovedmotiv i Pär Lagerkvists diktning* (Oslo: Gyldendal, 1970).

MJÖBERG, JÖRAN. "Clowner och frälsare," *Ord och bild*, 62 (1953), 85-91.

————. "Det förnekade mörkret," *Samlaren*, 35 (1954), 78-112.

*————. *Livsproblemet hos Lagerkvist* (Stockholm: Bonniers, 1951).

*OBERHOLZER, OTTO. *Pär Lagerkvist: Studien zu seiner Prosa und seiner Dramen* (Heidelberg: Carl Winter, 1958).

SCOBBIE, IRENE. "Contrasting Characters in *Barabbas*," *Scandinavian Studies*, 32 (November, 1960), 212-20.

————. *Pär Lagerkvist: An Introduction* (Stockholm: Swedish Institute [New ed.], 1963).

————. "Strindberg and Lagerkvist," *Modern Drama*, 7 (1964), 126-34.

SKARTVEIT, ANDREAS. *Gud skapt i menneskets bilete: Ein Lagerkvist studie* (Oslo: Norske samlaget, 1966).

SMITH, KAY NOLTE. "Pär Lagerkvist: Playwright and Philosopher," *American-Swedish Monthly*, 54 (1960), 24-26.

SPECTOR, ROBERT D. "Lagerkvist's Dialogue of the Soul," *Scandinavian Studies: Essays Presented to Dr. Henry Goddard Leach*, ed. by Carl F. Bayerschmidt and Erik J. Friis (Seattle: University of Washington, 1965).

————. "Lagerkvist and Existentialism," *Scandinavian Studies*, 32 (November, 1960), 203-11.

————. "Lagerkvist's Short Fiction," *American-Scandinavian Review*, 57 (1969), 260-65.

————. "Lagerkvist's Uses of Deformity," *Scandinavian Studies*, 33 (November, 1961), 209-17.

STENSTRÖM, THURE. *Berättartekniska studier* ... Stockholm, 1964.

STORK, C. W. "Contemporary Swedish Poetry," *American-Scandinavian Review*, 5 (1917), 343-47.

SVANBERG, VICTOR. "Heidenstam och Lagerkvist: en studie i diktens sociologi," *Tiden*, 33 (1941), 104-18.

Swanson, Roy A. "Evil and Love in Lagerkvist's Crucifixion Cycle," *Scandinavian Studies,* 38 (November, 1966), 302-17.

————. "Lagerkvist's *Dwarf* and the Redemption of Evil," *Discourse,* 13 (1970), 192-211.

Tideström, Gunnar. *Lyrisk tidsspegel* (Lund: Gleerup, 1956).

————. "Tankar kring Pär Lagerkvists *Sibyllan,*" *Samlaren,* 80 (1959), 80-96.

*————, ed. *Synpunkter på Pär Lagerkvist* (Stockholm: Bonniers, 1966).

Vowles, Richard B. "The Fiction of Pär Lagerkvist," *Western Humanities Review,* 8 (1954), 111-19.

Weathers, Winston. *Pär Lagerkvist: A Critical Essay* (Grand Rapids: William B. Eerdmans, 1968).

Wigforss, Brita. "Pär Lagerkvist och Dostojevski," *Ord och bild,* 70 (1961), 169-77.

Index

Acropolis, 146
"Adventure, The," 22
Aftonland, 18, 97, 137, 143, 150, 151
Ahasverus död, 17, 64, 89, 91, 100-112, 118, 123
Andersson, Dan, 138
Ångest, 18, 137-42, 147, 151
Anguish, 18, 137-42, 147, 151
"Anguish," 145, 149
Apollinaire, Guillaume, 17
"Araby," 32
Arnold, Matthew, 79
"At the Salvation Army," 139
Athens, 146
"Äventyret," 22
Avesta, the, 17

Barabbas, 64-81, 82, 99, 104, 112, 119, 123, 125, 174
Barabbas (a play), 174
"Basement, The," 31, 32
Baudelaire, Charles Pierre, 17
"Beauty Fills Us," 141
"Beauty Grows," 144
Beckett, Samuel, 161
Bergman, Bo, 138
Bergman, Hjalmar, 153, 154
Bible, the, 17, 22, 126
Blake, William, 165
Blomberg, Erik, 16, 17, 138, 152
Bödeln, 19, 20, 41-44, 164, 166, 167
Book of the Dead, 17, 22
Borgias, 45
Braque, Georges, 15
"Bröllopsfesten," 30
Brunius, August, 138
Buckman, Thomas, 153, 154, 158, 165, 174
By the Campfire, 145, 146

Camus, Albert, 78

Carlyle, Thomas, 20
Cézanne, Paul, 17
Chaos, 140, 141
"Children's Campaign, The," 27, 28, 29
Christianity, 67, 94, 108, 109, 114, 116, 124
Clenched Fist, The, 82, 99, 145, 146
Collected Poems, 137, 138
Commedia dell'arte, 154
Conquered Life, The, 143, 144, 174
Courbet, Gustave, 17
Cupid, 23

Da Vinci, Leonardo, 45
De vises sten, 149, 170-73
"De vördade benen," 27
Death of Ahasuerus, The, 17, 64, 89, 91, 100-112, 118, 123
Delphi, 86, 96
Delphic Oracle, 84, 90
"Demanding Guest, The," 26, 141
"Den fordringsfulla gästen," 26, 141
Den knutna näven, 145, 146
Den lyckliges väg, 142, 143
"Den onda ängeln," 23
Den osynliga, 156, 161, 162
Den svåra stunden, 156, 158, 159, 161
Denmark, 141
"Det är vackrast när det skymmer," 141
Det besegrade livet, 143, 144, 174
"Det blir vackert," 144
Det eviga leendet, 19, 21, 34, 37-39, 45, 82, 102, 142, 160
Det heliga landet, 17, 64, 82, 111, 118-26
"Det kom ett brev," 143
"Det lilla fälttåget," 27-29
"Det märkvärdiga landet," 27-29

"Det sörjande Norden," 148
Difficult Hour, The, 156, 158, 159,
    161
Dostoevski, Feodor, 95
Dream Play, A, 161
"Du stora, vreda Natur," 145
Dubliners, The, 32
Dvärgen, 33, 45-63, 148, 160
Dwarf, The, 33, 45-63, 148, 160

Ecclesiastes, 131
Eden, 21
Edfelt, Johannes, 17, 141, 147
Ekelund, Vilhelm, 138
"En hjältes död," 27
Endgame, 161
Eternal Smile, The, 19, 21, 34, 37-
    39, 45, 82, 102, 142, 160
Evening Land, 18, 97, 137, 143,
    150, 151
Everyman, 168
"Evil Angel, The," 23
Evil Tales, 19
"Experimental World, The," 22
"Experimentvärlden," 22

"Far och jag," 31, 32, 35
"Father and I," 31, 32, 35
"Fisherman's Burial, The," 149
"Fiskarbegravning," 149
Flodstrom, Arthur, 18, 139
"Folket på kyrkogården," 149
"Fragments, The," 24-26
"Frälsar-Johan," 29, 30
Frazer, Sir James, 164

Gabrieli, Marie, 152
Gandhi, Mohandas, 82
Gäst hos verkligheten, 19, 31, 34-38
Genesis, 23
Genius, 145-47
Germany, 28, 42
Ghost Sonata, The, 158
Gide, André, 68, 69
"God's Little Traveling Salesman,"
    30, 31
Goethe, Johann Wolfgang, 153
Golden Bough, The, 164
Golgotha, 66, 72, 105

Granlid, H. O., 20, 34
"Grieving North, The," 148
"Guds lille handelsresande," 30, 31
Guest of Reality, 19, 31, 34-38
Gullberg, Hjalmar, 143
Gustafson, Alrik, 21, 138, 168, 169
Gustafsson, Walter, 83, 94, 96

Hallberg, Elaine, 143
Han som fick leva om sitt liv, 162,
    169
Hangman, The, 19, 20, 41-44, 164,
    166, 167
Hardy, Thomas, 157
Heidenstam, Verner von, 138
Hemmet och stjärnan, 147, 149
Henmark, Kai, 20
Herod and Mariamne, 17, 33, 127-37
"Hero's Death, A," 27
Himlens hemlighet, 141, 156, 158,
    159, 161, 174
"Hissen som gick ner i helvete," 30
Hitler, Adolf, 28, 42
Hjärtats sånger, 143, 144
Holy Land, The, 17, 64, 82, 111,
    118-26
Holy Land, the, 81, 100, 102, 103,
    108, 110, 113, 114, 116, 118,
    119, 123, 125
Holy Sea, the, 118
Home and the Stars, The, 147, 149
Human Basement, The, 169

I den tiden, 19
I stället för tro, 141
Ibsen, Henrik, 153-55, 158, 171
"In Memoriam," 133
In That Time, 19
India, 82
Instead of Faith, 141
Invisible One, The, 156, 161, 162
Iron and Man, 15, 19, 24, 25
Italy, 28

Järn och människor, 15, 19, 24, 25
Jerusalem, 66-68, 72, 74
Johnson, Eyvind, 42
Joyce, James, 32

"Källervåningen," 31, 32
Kämpande ande, 19
Kaos, 140, 141
"Kärleken och döden," 23
Karlfeldt, Erik Axel, 143
Keats, John, 96
King, The, 164-67, 169
Konungen, 164-67, 169
Koran, The, 17
Krilon novels, 42

Last Man, The, 156, 157
Låt människan leva, 170, 173, 174
Let Man Live, 170, 173, 174
"Letter Came, A," 143
Life, 24, 154, 174
"Lift That Went Down into Hell, The," 30
"Lilla hand, som ej är min," 139
Lindberg, Per, 174
Lindegren, Erik, 143
Linnér, Sven, 34, 96, 138
"Little Hand, that Is not Mine," 139
Livet, 24, 154, 174
"Love and Death," 23
Lowell, Robert, 140
Löwenhjelm, Harriet, 138
Luke, 72

Maccabees, 128, 129
Madonna, the, 22, 48, 57
Maeterlinck, Maurice, 154
Malmberg, Bertil, 138
Malmström, Gunnel, 151
Man Who Lived His Life Over, The, 162, 169
Man Without a Soul, The, 164, 167
Mannen utan själ, 164, 167
Människokällaren, 169
Människor, 19
Mariamne, 17, 33, 127-36
Mark, 72
"Marriage Feast, The," 30
Mary, 95
Masquerade of Souls, 39-41, 171
"Mater dolorosa," 147
"Maurice Fleury," 24-26
Midsommardröm i fattighuset, 170, 171

Midsummer Dream in the Workhouse, 170, 171
"Mitt barn, mitt barn," 141
Mjöberg, Jöran, 22, 70, 141, 143, 146, 150, 163
Moberg, Vilhelm, 42
Modern teater, 152, 154-57, 159, 162, 170
Modern Theater, 152, 154-57, 159, 162, 170
Modern Theatre: Seven Plays and an Essay, 153
Molander, Olof, 174
Motifs, 15, 137, 138
Motiv, 15, 137, 138
Munch, Edvard, 19
Mussolini, Benito, 28
"My Child, My Child," 141
"Myten om människorna," 23, 24
"Myth of Mankind, The," 23, 24

Nazis, 166
Night Training, 42
Nobel Prize, 24, 64

Oberholzer, Otto, 20
"Oh Thou Great Wrathful Nature," 145
Onda sagor, 19
Ordkonst och bildkonst, 15, 17-20, 37, 45, 49, 83, 137, 138, 141, 152, 156
Osiris, 22
Österling, Anders, 138
"Our only Home Is Love," 143
Our Town, 173
"Ours Is Heaven," 150
"Ozymandias," 131

"På frälsningsarmén," 139
"På Osiris' våg," 22
Palestine, 146
"Paradise," 21
"Paradiset," 21
Paris, 40
People, 19
"People in the Churchyard, The," 149
Philosopher's Stone, The, 170-73

Picasso, Pablo, 15
Pilate, Pontius, 58
Pilgrim at Sea, 64, 112-18, 122
Pilgrim på havet, 64, 112-18, 122
Pilgrim, The, 99
Pilgrimen, 99
Poe, Edgar Allan, 17
"Princess and the Kingdom, The," 23
"Prinsessan och hela riket," 23

Renaissance, the, 60
Ride This Night!, 42
Rome, 67, 132

Sång och strid, 147, 149
Sartre, Jean Paul, 78
"Saviour John," 29, 30
"Scales of Osiris, The," 22
Scobbie, Irene, 17, 49, 57, 69, 70, 75, 97, 141, 151, 158
Secret of Heaven, The, 45, 57, 141, 156, 158, 159, 161, 174
Seger i mörker, 164, 169
Shakespeare, William, 153
Shelley, Percy Bysshe, 131
Sibyl, The, 22, 64, 82-100, 104, 112, 123
Sibyllan, 22, 64, 82-100, 104, 112, 123
Sista mänskan, 156, 157
Själarnas maskerad, 39-41, 171
Sjöberg, Alf, 162, 174
Sjöberg, Birger, 138
"Skärvorna," 24-26
Småland, 162
Smith, Kay Nolte, 162
Södergran, Edith, 138
Soldier's Return, The, 42
Solomon, 127, 132
Song and Battle, 147, 149
Songs of the Heart, 143, 144
Spanish Civil War, 167
"Star Time," 149

"Stjärntimman," 149
Stork, C. W., 138
"Strange Country, The," 27-29
Strindberg, August, 15, 153-59, 161
Struggling Spirit, 19
Svenska Dagbladet, 154
Swanson, Roy A., 95, 125
Swedish Academy, 16
Swift, Jonathan, 45

"Tanken har intet mål," 145
"Tanken som byggde en värld," 148
Tennyson, Alfred, 133
"Theater of the Absurd," 158, 174
"Thought Has Nowhere a Goal," 145
"Thought that Built a World, The," 148
To Damascus, 158, 161
Tolstoy, Leo, 154
"Torso," 145
Två sagor om livet, 19
Two Tales about Life, 19

Uppsala University, 15

"Vår är himmeln," 150
"Vårt enda hem är kärleken," 143
Växjö, 15, 16, 153
"Venerated Bones, The," 27
Victory in Darkness, 164, 169
Vid lägereld, 145, 146
Vowles, Richard B., 20-22, 24

Waiting for Godot, 161
Way of the Happy One, The, 142, 143
Wilder, Thornton, 173
Word Art and Picture Art, 15, 17-20, 37, 45, 49, 83, 137, 138, 141, 152, 156

Yeats, William Butler, 154

DATE DUE

GAYLORD   PRINTED IN U.S.A